Hellenic Studies 89

Greek Language, Italian Landscape

Recent Titles in the Hellenic Studies Series

GREEK LANGUAGE, ITALIAN LANDSCAPE

GRIKO AND THE RE-STORYING
OF A LINGUISTIC MINORITY

by
Manuela Pellegrino

CENTER FOR HELLENIC STUDIES
Trustees for Harvard University
Washington, DC
Distributed by Harvard University Press
Cambridge, Massachusetts, and London, England
2021

ISBN: 978-0-674-27132-6

Library of Congress Control Number (LCCN): 2021941957

Ja 'sena, tata Niceta,
ce jôle te' fonè ti' glossa grika, glicèe ce prikè

Dedicated to you, dad Niceta,
and to all the voices of the Griko language, sweet and bitter

Table of Contents

Acknowledgements

Many people accompanied me throughout 'my journey into Griko', others only along some of its paths. Too many of them left this world while I was 'traveling'. To my grandmother Lavretàna, the first 'Griko voice' I heard; to my uncle 'Melo, whose charming singing voice in Griko keeps echoing in my mind; and to my friend Uccio, whose life stories in and about Griko I will always carry with me. To 'Nzino, Tommasino, Carmelo, Tetta, Grazio, Donato, Uccia, and Splendora. This work is affectionately dedicated to all of them; they are deeply missed. And to my father Niceta, who did not live long enough to hold this book in his hands, but long enough to share his Griko with me; it became our special affective code and strengthened our bond during his last years.

My first and deepest expression of gratitude goes to Charles Stewart, for his yearslong dedication and guidance, and for providing me with invaluable inspiration. Not coincidentally, the story of Griko was a mutual passion, having brought him to the Griko-speaking villages during his undergraduate studies in Classics. I owe an immeasurable debt to him and I will continue to look up to his example as an academic and as a person. I am grateful to Michael Herzfeld for sharing his wealth of knowledge, for his support, and for encouraging me to trust my own arguments. Our conversations have helped me immensely. My gratitude goes also to Alexandra Geourgakopoulou and Ben Rampton, who welcomed me at Kings College prior to fieldwork, and who introduced me to and trained me in the fascinating world of sociolinguistics/linguistic anthropology theory and methodology. For her inspiring insights and encouragement I thank Eleana Yalouri of Panteio University; she allowed me to make the most of my stays in Greece, and has been to me not only an academic referent, but a friend. My gratitude goes as well to Spiros Moschonas, who invited me to follow his enlightening lectures at the National and Kapodistrian University of Athens, and for sharing his archive of Greek newspaper articles dealing with Griko. Many thanks also to my friend and gifted anthropologist, Nikola Kosmatopoulos, who first introduced me to the wonderful world of anthropology. Σε ευχαριστώ!

Acknowledgements

Portions of this research have been published in Italian by local editors. My gratitude goes also to all those who, through conversations and feedback, offered insights and advice on aspects or arguments of this book: Eleni Papagaroufali, Alexandra Georgakopoulou, Ruth Mandel, Stavroula Pipyrou, Maria Olimpia Squillaci, Janine Su, Rodney Reynolds, Christina Petropoulou, Jennika Baines, Daniel Knight, Naomi Leite, Eric Hirsch, Nicolas Argenti, Peggy Froer, Liana Chua, Maria Kastrinou, Naor Ben-Yehoyada. My warmest thanks to Giovanna Parmigiani for accompanying me emotionally and conceptually, and for being the first one to read this book from beginning to end.

It took me 'more time' than I had hoped before I managed to place the final period on this book. Different reasons—at times totally unpredictable—delayed the process. Yet, I never considered this book a step in my career path. The responsibility of 'presenting' this story stopped me along the way more than once. Or else, as Uncle Giò says, "Some things simply take time and need time." I thank personally all those who patiently waited, but also my mother Assunta—'Ntina—who more pragmatically keeps reminding me that this is 'just a book'.

Yet, if you are holding this book in your hands now it is only because I then encountered—in some instances re-encountered—people who believed in its value, and who helped me find my way back to it. I will therefore always be indebted to the Center for Hellenic Studies, Harvard University, for welcoming me warmly and stirring in me renewed enthusiasm in this project. My warmest thanks to Gregory Nagy for offering me the opportunity to awake and explore my own—long silenced—humanistic/artistic interests; this has added value to my research. I thank Leonard Muellner, who promptly embraced this project; Zoie Lafis for lending an attentive and intrigued ear to the topic of Griko and its current revival; Lanah Koelle, who was a constant reference throughout my stay at CHS in Washington, and who keeps providing guidance and support; and Jill Robbins and Noel Spencer for their patience through the editing process of this book.

My deepest gratitude goes to my elderly friends from Grecìa Salentina—Antimino, 'Ndata, Splendora, Uccio, Uccia, Grazio, Gaetano, Cosimino, Giglio, etc.—who not only taught me Griko, but let me wander freely in 'their story-worlds,' even when that brought to the surface not-so-nice memories. I cannot express the debt of eternal gratitude that I owe them. I thank also all the Griko activists and aficionados for sharing their ideas, hopes, and uncertainties about the future of Griko; I owe my gratitude particularly to Luigi and Sandra, with whom I embarked on endless conversations, and who never got tired of my continual checking and double checking that I was faithfully reporting their views. Many thanks to my friends in Salento—Monica, Antonio, Massimo, Annu, Miro, Flora, Helen, Daniele—who each in their own ways encouraged me to keep going. I also thank my new friends Kosma and Stefano for helping to manage my anxiety crisis right at the end of this journey.

I am very grateful to my Greek 'informants' for making me feel at home. Many thanks to my Greek extended family: Ms. and Mr. Kosmatopoulos (Vaso and Yannis) and Aspasia, my first Modern Greek teacher; and my Athenian friends, Thodoris, Marina, Panayiotis, and Vaso. I also have a sentimental debt to my Ikarian friends, with whom I spent some of the most intense months of my life. This did not help my writing, but it prolonged my field-work and showed me yet another face of Greece.

I would also like to thank for their support the friends and colleagues I met in the Department of Anthropology at University College of London at different stages of this endeavor, for sharing their ideas and sugges-tions and for keeping me company. I cannot possibly name all of them, but I must name Janine Su—who also rendered my English polished and clear—Galina Oustinova-Stjepanovic, Dimitra Kofti, Beata Świtek, Dimitris Dalakoglou, Viorel Anastasoaie, Yiannis Kyriakakis, Piero Di Giminiani, Nico Tassi, Matan Shapiro; and Alessandra Basso-Ortiz, with whom I started this journey, and who would be proud to know that I finally made it to my desti-nation. I am also grateful to my former students at Brunel, from whom I came to understand the strong link between research and teaching, and who made me feel I was contributing positively to their lives by helping them discover anthropology.

I wrote this book in different places, not only 'at home' in Salento; I also worked on it in Calabria, in Sicily, in Greece. Many thanks are therefore due to my friend Andrea, my friend and colleague Maria Olimpia, and Ms. and Mr. Cocuzza, who let me 'hide' at their places when I was overwhelmed by my family responsibilities, and by the guilt of not being able to recon-cile them with my writing. My warmest thanks to my sister Luciana, who patiently 'replaced' me in my role as a daughter during my absences, and also to my sisters Laura and Tonia, who are my biggest fans.

I am also thankful to an anonymous reader of the very first draft of this book, whose feedback caused me a sort of 'crisis'—both academic and personal—but which eventually has helped me make a better final product.

This research has been generously financed by several sponsors. Most of my fieldwork in Grecìa Salentina was funded by a grant from the Wenner-Gren Foundation, while the Central Research Fund of the University of London assisted with expenses for the initial phases of my research in

Acknowledgements

Italy. I would also like to acknowledge the financial support of the Greek State Scholarship Foundation (IKY) and the Ministry of Education and Religious Affairs, which facilitated my fieldwork in Greece, as well as the UCL Graduate School.

* * *

Unless otherwise stated, all translations from Italian are mine; as for the names I used to refer to my informants: some people preferred to be anonymized, while others asked expressly to be named. In both cases I respected their preferences.

Notes on Orthographic Conventions and Transcription of Griko

Griko lacks a standardized orthography. In this book I have respected the author's transcription when I quoted written texts. For the transcription of my ethnographic material I have tried as much as possible to follow the orthographic conventions adopted in the text book *Pos Màtome Griko* (2013). This choice produces some inconsistencies but captures the variation in conventions found in the social field:

ts	(pronounced as in "nuts")
ch	(equivalent to the Greek χ)
k	(as in "walk")
c	(as in "cheap")
ddh	(as in "finished")
sc/sci	(as in "sheep")
j	(as in "yes")

Tonic accent is used on every word, except two-syllable words whose accent does not fall on the last syllable: *Tela, Ivò*.

For the contraction of vowels the circumflex accent is used:

a + e = â (na erto = nârto)

u + e = ô (su erkete= sôrkete)

u + i = û (su ipa = sûpa)

The use of an apostrophe indicates the elision of a letter or a syllable of the word/verb:

Fonàsa' (= Fonàsane); *'en* (= den); *e'* (= ene); *'in* (= tin)

If the word which follows begins with a consonant, the pronunciation is doubled:
Pame sti' tàlassa becomes *Pame sti' ttàlassa*

I also draw attention to the main phonetic variation with respect to the pronunciation of the Greek consonant clusters ψ /ps/ and ξ /ks/, which at present interests the villages of Zollino, Castrignano and Martano:

> *sciomì* (Zollino and Castrignano), *ssomì* (Martano) and *tsomì* elsewhere
> Standard Modern Greek = *psomì*, ψωμί (bread)

> *scero* (Zollino and Castrignano), *ssero* (Martano) and *tsero* elsewhere
> Standard Modern Greek = *ksero*, ξέρω (I know)

Next to the text in Griko I have indicated the home village of the speaker:

> Zollino
>
> Sternatia
>
> Corigliano d'Otranto
>
> Calimera
>
> Martano

Wherever possible, I have consulted with Griko scholars regarding doubts about transcription; any remaining mistakes, of course, are mine.

Image Credits

Introduction

Figure 1.	'Ndata and I	Photo by Daniele Coricciati
Figure 2.	Map of the extant administrative area of Grecìa Salentina	Map by Jill Curry Robbins, after http://www. agriturismosalento.com/ ricettivita.shtml?area=grecia
Figure 3.	Map tracing the progression of the Salentine-Greek -speaking area	Map by Jill Curry Robbins, after Spano 1965, as reproduced in Rohlfs 1980:50
Figure 4.	The village of Calimera	Photo by Daniele Coricciati
Figure 5.	The village of Zollino	Photo by Daniele Coricciati
Figure 6.	The village of Sternatia	Photo by Daniele Coricciati
Figure 7.	The village of Martano	Photo by Daniele Coricciati
Figure 8.	The village of Corigliano	Photo by Daniele Coricciati

Chapter One

Figure 9.	The remains of the Monastery of San Nicola di Casole	Photo by Manuela Pellegrino
Figure 10.	The church of Santa Sofia and Stefano (exterior)	Photo by Daniele Coricciati
Figure 11.	The church of Santa Sofia and Stefano (interior)	Photo by Daniele Coricciati

Image Credits

Chapter Two

Figure 12.	Antimino and I	Photo by Daniele Coricciati
Figure 13.	Uccio carving	Photo courtesy of Monica Costa
Figure 14.	Uccia	Photo by Theodoros Kargas

Chapter Three

Figure 15.	The Attic marble stone, Calimera	Photo by Daniele Coricciati
Figure 16.	The performance of *I passiùna tu Christù*	Photo by Daniele Coricciati
Figure 17.	Festa di San Rocco, Torre Paduli, one *ronda*	Photo by Theodoros Kargas

Chapter Four

Figure 18.	*Martedì Lu Puzzu*, 2008	Photo by Theodoros Kargas
Figure 19.	The welcoming sign at the entrance of each village	Photo by Daniele Coricciati.
Figure 20.	La notte della Taranta, touring festival 2008, Zollino	Photo by Theodoros Kargas
Figure 21.	The dancing audience, Zollino	Photo by Theodoros Kargas

Chapter Five

Figure 22.	Teaching material	Photo courtesy of Sandra Abbate
Figure 23.	The Journal *Spitta*	Reprinted courtesy of *Spitta*
Figure 24.	The sign of a bakery shop, Martano	Photo by Theodoros Kargas

Chapter Six

Figure 25.	Giglio and I, Sternatia	Photo by Theodoros Kargas
Figure 26.	Attraversando il Griko, Maria and Sandra performing, Calimera	Photo by Manuela Pellegrino
Figure 27.	Attraversando il Griko, the crowd following the event, Calimera	Photo by Manuela Pellegrino

Chapter Seven

Figure 28.	The leaflet of the trip to Grecìa Salentina	Photo by Manuela Pellegrino
Figure 29.	The poster of the event: "Greeks meet Greeks," Athens	Photo by Manuela Pellegrino, reproduced by permission of the organizers.
Figure 30.	The entrance of the association Chora-Ma, Sternatia	Photo by Theodoros Kargas

Introduction

THE first Griko voice I ever heard still echoes in my mind, that of my grandmother Lavretàna asking me, "*Teli spirì nerò?*" (Griko)—"Do you want some water?" I was very little and, after she handed me the glass and I drank my water, I recall thinking that those sounds were 'her' way of speaking, that it was 'her' language. Griko was indeed her language; it was, however, not *just* hers. It was also my grandfather's and my eldest uncles' and aunties' language. Why was it not mine too? Would I have to wait for my hair to turn white and my clothes black to speak it, I wondered?

I grew up hearing these almost mysterious sounds being used by elderly relatives and, from time to time, by my parents too. They were a very discrete but reassuringly constant presence. My parents would usually speak Salentine (the local Italo-Romance variety) to one another; more often than not, that was the language they used to address me too. By contrast, my eldest sister, eighteen years older, would glare at me and insist, "*Parla bene!*" (Italian)—"Speak well!"—by which she meant "Speak Italian." I ended up studying and learning languages, but Griko was not among them. Since it was considered 'a dying language'—one that belonged to the domain of the elderly—it remained inaccessible to me until I finally set myself the goal of making sense of it.

Over two decades later, 'Ndata—now a smiley lady in her nineties—became not only my best friend but also one of my teachers. My parents' house and hers are just a few meters away from one another, and I am privileged to have learned Griko by spending so much time with her (see Figure 1). Sometimes she still finds puzzling this late interest of mine and now of others: "All these people who want to learn about Griko now and even learn it! Let them go and learn the 'Griko' of Greece! Now we are told we are important! Like monuments. Of what? Of ourselves by now!" And she laughs. She sings in the chorus of Zollino's center for the elderly (she is tone deaf, but don't tell her), which also performs for visiting Greek tourists, and 'Ndata is amused to see their astonishment when they hear her say "*Tèlete glicèa?*"—"Do you want some sweets?" And then she drops her guard for a moment and asks me to take her to Greece, "Just to see what all this fuss is about. I'm curious," she adds.

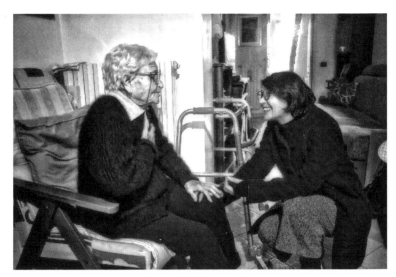

Figure 1. 'Ndata and I

This book is about Salentine Greek—or simply Griko—a language of Greek origins transmitted orally from generation to generation in Salento, in the Apulian province of Lecce, the 'heel' of the boot of Italy.[1] Its pool of speakers started shrinking after the contact that had once existed with Greece receded in the fifteenth century; interestingly, ever since the Italian linguist Giuseppe Morosi encountered Griko in the middle of the nineteenth century, the language has been considered to be on the verge of disappearing. Unexpectedly, however, it survived such prophecy. Locals continued speaking it in a few villages until WWII, but stopped transmitting it as a mother tongue; and, under the 'symbolic power' of the national language—to use the wording of Bourdieu (1991)—Griko was deemed to be a 'language of the backward past.' Together with Calabrian Greek—or simply Greko—which is spoken in Calabria in the 'toe' of Italy,[2] Griko belongs to the Southern Italian Greek dialect enclaves. In 1999, National Law 482 recognized Griko and Greko together in one category among the twelve

---

[1] *Griko* is the Griko word for 'Greek.' The traditional label in Italian is *Greco Salentino* (Salentine Greek), although Griko has prevailed in common use; in this book I will use both interchangeably. When referring to the community as a whole and to its individual speakers, I will use the terms Griko-speaking and Griko speakers.

[2] It is also known as Grecanico; more recently Greko (literally 'Greek') has prevailed. In Modern Greek common parlance, the Griko- and Greko-speaking villages are generally defined as *ta ellinofona choriá,* literally, 'Greek-speaking villages' (both for Apulia and Calabria); these linguistic enclaves were re-discovered by the German philologist Karl Witte in 1821. In Greek literature Griko and Greko are referred to as varieties or dialects, and in common use, they generally fall together under the label *katoitaliká,* literally 'Southern Italian.' I conceptualize Griko as a language, as locals do.

'historical linguistic minorities' on Italian soil, in conformity with the European Charter for Regional or Minority Languages (1992).

I am sure that my grandmother, 'Ndata, or any other elderly Griko speaker could not have foreseen the more recent developments in the story of Griko, whose already rather paradoxical plot as 'the ever-dying language' was about to be complicated further. The current revival of Griko—with everything that entails—originated in the late 1990s, when political tuning and intuition at the local level, coupled with the availability of legal instruments and financial resources at the national and European levels, prompted the positive response of local politicians who historically had been insensitive to Griko and the local cultural heritage. Now sensing not only their cultural but also the economic potential, the mayors of the Griko-speaking villages have collaborated to create the Union of the Municipalities of Grecìa Salentina. Griko and folk music (*pizzica*) have become "an essential instrument to give sense and meaning to a potential growth and development of our territory," said Sergio Blasi, then mayor of Melpignano.[3] In the process of that revival, a broader reevaluation of the local cultural repertoire has been enacted in the name of Griko, a reevaluation that incorporates cultural expressions of the larger Salentine individuality and extends to the spheres of music, gastronomy, art, and landscape. The region's overall popularity has increased, attracting growing numbers of tourists and rendering Salento one of the top tourist destinations in Italy: what was until recently Italy's *finis terrae*, or land's end, is now in the spotlight.

This is particularly telling considering that attempts to raise awareness about Griko and its heritage are all but new; already at the turn of the nineteenth century local philhellenic intellectuals had been engaged in restoring prestige to the language—what I call 'the first revival of Griko' (Chapter 1). When, by the mid-1970s, the number of Griko mother-tongue speakers had dramatically decreased, politically sensitive cultural activists began promoting what I label 'the middle revival.'[4] The revival was this time not restricted to the language, but included a reevaluation of those indexes of the past that locals had internalized as signs of their own inferiority, including music and local traditions in Griko, but also—and this is crucial—in the local Italo-Romance variety of Salentine (Chapter 3). Yet these efforts lacked a legal framework that would articulate and legitimize their claims; the 1990s were instead a time in which language rights specifically were the focus of international attention. Indeed, the adoption by

---

[3] From the introduction to *La tela infinita* (Mina and Torsello 2005).

[4] According to the official surveys dating back to 1901, 1911, and 1921, the percentage of Griko speakers was 89.3%, 87.8%, and 66.3%, respectively, within a total population that increased from 22,519 inhabitants in 1901 to 24,172 in 1921. According to a study by Spano (1965:162) in the mid-1960s, at the time there were about 20,000 Griko speakers.

the Italian government of Law 482 for the protection of its minority languages (fifty-one years after the Italian Constitution was written!) points to the interplay of transnational and national policies, and ideologies regarding language. The ethnographic account of the situated case of Griko in this crucial moment of transition and opportunity shows the transformative effects of these policies on the ground.

This book therefore recounts the story of Griko, the multiple ways in which locals viewed and used it in the past, and the ways in which they view and use it today. It traces Griko speakers' multiple ideologies about the language. The lens of language ideologies brings into focus the relationship between language, politics, and identity; Paul Kroskrity defines language ideologies as "beliefs, feelings and conceptions about language structure and use" (2010:192). The term 'ideology' should not mislead the reader into thinking we are dealing with 'ideas' in contraposition to 'facts,' or that some ideologies are 'true' and others 'false,' as Deborah Cameron stresses (2003); language ideologies are social contracts which are not abstract but rather "enact ties of language to identity, to aesthetics, to morality, and to epistemology" (Woolard 1998:3).

As cultural frames and historical products, ideologies about 'language' continuously transcend it and emerge out of various domains of social life; at the same time they act upon them by affecting the very setting in which they originate. Thus, Griko speakers have shifted away from Griko and back to it again by interpreting and reacting to situated social changes, which then recursively affected their ideas about themselves, about their language and its use. Particularly since the end of World War II, Griko speakers had internalized it as a 'language of shame.' *"Mas èkanne vergogna,"*—"We felt shame," Uccio (born in 1933) from Zollino told me, as do many of his generation. This shift in language ideologies meant that the generation born during the socioeconomic boom of the postwar years was not taught Griko as their mother tongue (Chapter 2). This is the generation that "grew up with one foot in the old world and one in the new world," as Mario (born in 1961) from Sternatia told me, his words characteristic of what I label the 'in-between generation,' suspended between different worldviews associated with Griko and, respectively, Salentine and Italian.

This story's plot is, in fact, further thickened by the presence of this third linguistic code. What, building on Appadurai (1996), I call the *languagescape* is constituted not only by Griko and more recently by Italian, but also by Salentine, which derives from Latin, and which locals refer to simply as *dialetto* (dialect). Together with Sicilian and Southern Calabrian, Salentine belongs to the subgroup of 'extreme Southern dialects' of Italian; however, what distinguishes them is the 'Greek flavor' of their grammar, the result of the previous presence of the Greek language in these territories. Salentine and Griko have indeed long coexisted in the area, in historical symbiosis, each entangled in the other's corpus. As my friend Adriana from Corigliano summarizes, "*Lu grecu è mbiscatu cu lu dialettu. Ca poi ete lu dialettu ca se mbisca cu lu grecu*" (Salentine)— "Griko is mixed with Salentine. And then again, Salentine is mixed with Griko." Because of its hybridity, Griko was long internalized as a "bastard dialect"—"*nu dialettu bastardu*" (Salentine).

By languagescape I mean, in fact, not only Griko as a spoken language in the context of other locally spoken languages, but also the metadiscursive landscape surrounding them. However, this is more broadly an Italian phenomenon. The *questione della lingua* (language question) reflects the history of Italy's linguistic diversity, which is considered unique in Europe; indeed, in Italy today there are several 'dialects' spoken in everyday life, the result of centuries of cultural and political diversity before the unification of the country.[5] The local languagescape today has been influenced by the language ideology promoted by Italian governing forces ever since Italy emerged as a nation-state. The diachronic approach I take in this book in fact captures the varying sociocultural and political landscapes and ideological structures that have mediated the language shift away from Griko and those supporting the various phases of its revival; in addition, the heteroglossic local languagescape I present shows how locals have experienced, over time, blended linguistic realities.

This book does not embark on yet another tired exercise of defining the identity of speakers—at least not in the strict sense of that term. Nor does it contribute to the longstanding philological debate about the origins of Griko, which remains a fascinating puzzle to which I will return in order to highlight its ideological underpinnings (Chapter 1). This is neither a "salvage ethnography" nor "salvage linguistics"—to use the wording of James Collins (1998:259); I do not predict the demise of Griko, nor do I prescribe therapies to 'heal' it. Here instead I narrate how a variety of social actors (speakers, local intellectuals, language connoisseurs and aficionados, cultural activists, and more recently politicians) have engaged with Griko over time, including shifting claims, aims, and modalities. I highlight how they have built on specific language ideologies

---

[5]   See De Mauro and Lodi 1979; Telmon 1993; Tosi 2004. From the fall of the Western Roman Empire to the Unification of Italy the territory was divided into various states and cities; through the 'Romanization' of the peninsula, Latin spread as a *written* language, but it was spoken differently because it was influenced by the 'substrata' of languages spoken before Romanization. In reality, the so-called 'Italian dialects' are themselves unofficial languages that are not varieties of Italian, but distinct Italo-Romance varieties; these developed from Latin at the same time as Florentine, which was selected as the national language at the time of the unification of Italy. I use the terms Salentine, (Italo-)Romance variety, and dialect interchangeably to reflect locals' usage.

to do so, and how such ideologies have simultaneously acted upon the social, political, and economic domains (in Chapters 3 and 4).

Among such social actors figure Greek aficionados of Griko, who have intensified their collaborations with local cultural associations since the 1990s. I therefore investigate the popular but also institutional engagement of Greece in the reproduction and circulation at the local level of a language ideology celebrating Griko as *"ena zondanó mnimeío tou Ellinismoú"*—"a living monument of Hellenism." This way the 'linguistic kinship' between Greek and Griko (*beyond* Griko's hybrid nature) is selectively highlighted by Greek aficionados of Griko, who indeed feel an emotional, almost visceral, attachment to the language and to its speakers, as well as to the very place where, according to Dimitri, "the heart of Greece beats"—*"chtypáei i kardiá tis Elládas"* (Modern Greek). In addition, in 1994 the Greek Ministry of Education began sending Greek teachers to the area to teach Modern Greek in public schools and cultural associations. Understandably, this policy has affected the local languagescape (Chapters 6 and 7).

In short, this book is based on an anthropological study, and in it I provide a purposeful linguistic analysis in order to recount the 'story' of Griko through written sources, and through the narratives I have collected both from those who speak it and from those who have engaged/engage with it in different ways. What you are about to read is ultimately *my story* of their stories, in which I trace how the multiple language ideologies of Griko were and are negotiated locally, in a dialogical relationship with language practices and policies promoted by the European Union, Italy, and Greece. I recount how locals have been generating social relationships, fueling moral feelings and political interests in the process, ultimately transforming the language and its predicament.

Defining My Place, Contextualizing Salento

Grecìa Salentina[6] is located at the center of Salento. The Salentine peninsula—often called 'the heel of the Italian boot'—is the southeastern extremity of the Apulia region and the eastern extremity of the Italian Republic. It comprises Brindisi, Lecce, and Taranto provinces. The province of Lecce has a very flat landscape; it is a fertile plain granting an all-encompassing gaze upon the

---

[6] Greeks tend to translate it as *Elláda tou Saléntou* or *Salentiní Elláda* (Salentine Greece). To be sure, in Italian 'Greece' is *Grecia*, without the accent mark. The term *Grecìa* is an artifact—one that has acquired a widespread currency since the latest revival; crucially, the accent put on *Grecìa* serves to distinguish it from Greece as nation-state. The first written reference I identified dates to 1929 in the title *Da Soleto e la Grecìa Salentina* by Giuseppe Palumbo, cited in Aprile (1972:26).

horizon, which appears ever widening. If you raise your eyes, you will find few obstacles—and never higher than two-hundred meters above sea level. You will then see the sea; you are surrounded by two-hundred kilometers of coastline, sandy and rocky. The administrative borders of what today goes by the name Union of the Municipalities of Grecìa Salentina (Unione dei comuni della Grecìa Salentina), constituted in 2001, includes eleven villages (see Figure 2). Griko is still spoken in seven of them: Calimera, Castrignano dei Greci, Corigliano d'Otranto, Zollino, Sternatia, Martano, and Martignano. Melpignano and Soleto counted Griko-speakers mainly until the beginning of the twentieth century. In the villages of Carpignano and Cutrofiano, Griko was spoken until the beginning of the nineteenth century and the end of the eighteenth century, respectively. These same two villages were annexed to the Union of the Municipalities of Grecìa Salentina in 2005 and 2007, respectively.

Figure 2. Map of the extant administrative area of Grecìa Salentina

The locals, however, used to refer to the Griko-speaking villages with the expression *ta dekatrìa chorìa*, referring to a past (the nineteenth century) during which Salentine Greek was spoken in 'thirteen villages.' Located contiguously, with the greatest distance between villages being ten kilometers, these villages create a sort of island within Lecce province, representing what is left of a much larger area that gradually receded: in the sixteenth century this territory comprised twenty-four villages; toward the end of the eighteenth century, fifteen villages; thirteen villages in the nineteenth century; then nine in the twentieth century; and seven today (see Figure 3). The Griko-speaking area can be visualized as a 'puddle' that has dried up progressively; its outskirts are by definition in contact with non-Griko-speaking villages, and its borders have progressively contracted.

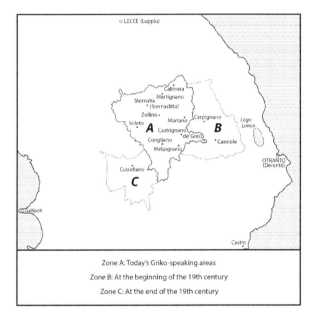

Figure 3. Map tracing the progression of the Salentine-Greek-speaking area

Yet Salento is known not only for Griko. As early as in the 1950s, it had been the subject of anthropological studies thanks to the research of Ernesto de Martino, the father of Italian anthropology. He investigated the phenomenon of *tarantismo*, the ritual in which the music of *pizzica tarantata* was used therapeutically to cure those women (*tarantate*) who claimed to have been bitten by the tarantula (*taranta*). In his 1961 book, *La Terra del Rimorso*, de Martino linked this phenomenon to female existential and social suffering, and understood it as a manifestation of class and gender inequality. Giovanni Pizza (1999, 2004) has stressed the legacy of de Martino's pivotal work, which was 'rediscovered' by Italian anthropologists in the mid-1990s (three decades after his death). Studies have proliferated in recent years around what is now known as neo-tarantism—a contemporary re-appropriation of tarantism—further rendering Salento the "topos of Italian ethnology" (Bevilacqua 2005:74).

By writing about a language that has not been the subject of an anthropological study,[7] my aim is to shift the focus from the much more popular topics of tarantism and neo-tarantism. Yet it would be misleading to refer to the repercussions of Griko's current revival in isolation from its Salentine surroundings; it would be equally impossible to appreciate fully its dynamics without also considering the revival of folk music, as the two are in a metonymic relationship. The folk music festival of La Notte della Taranta, now known internationally, effectively inserted the whole of Salento into the circuit of cultural tourism. Indeed, what de Martino defined at the time as 'the land of remorse' has now been turned, I argue, into 'the land of resource': Griko and pizzica have gone from signifying backwardness to cultural richness, and become the symbol of the local identity, as well as the trademark of Salento; this has further implications.

This book is therefore not only or narrowly about Griko. Instead, in it I use language as a lens through which to gaze into the past, the present, and the future of this land and its people.

Beyond Endangerment: Language Ideological Debates

Griko and Greko are recognized by Unesco as "severely endangered"; in her analysis of the case of Calabrian Greek, Stavroula Pipyrou (2016:14) suggests that the approach of national and transnational organizations such as Unesco is motivated by the fact that the "Grecanico language is distinctive and rich yet 'in danger of extinction.'" Justified through the claim that preserving a language means preserving a unique worldview that would otherwise be lost, the idiom of 'diversity' seems to have bypassed the other long-used catchword 'identity,' yet without transcending it entirely. The European Charter, with which Italy's National Law 482 complied, is in fact embedded in a discourse that celebrates the notion of unity in diversity. Moreover, in order to avoid the specter of Western European cultural nationalism—one language, one people, one country—the Charter follows an 'ecological' approach that positions regional or minority languages as a threatened aspect of Europe's cultural heritage. This European and global type of diversity discourse prompts us therefore to expand

---

[7] The existing literature about Griko is mainly linguistic in nature. This is in contrast to Calabrian Greek, which has been the focus of anthropological studies as early as the '80s (see Petropoulou 1995, 1997; and more recently Pipyrou 2016). For sociolinguistically oriented research, see Profili (1996); Romano, Manco and Saracino (2002); Romano (2016, 2018); Sobrero and Miglietta (2009, 2010), among others.

on previous investigations of linguistic/ethnic revivals, where language was often used to assert a minority identity and not necessarily for the benefit of the minority groups. This is true regardless of the shift from the discourse of identity to the current one of diversity.

A language ideological approach, importantly, allows us to reposition the speakers at the center of our analysis, and to recognize their agency—their ability "to interpret and morally evaluate their situation," to borrow the words of Sherry Ortner (1995:185). If these insights shed new light on situations of language shift, 'obsolescence,' 'endangerment,' 'suicide,' 'death,' and 'extinction,' the widespread discourse on 'language endangerment' transcends the academic realm and appeals to a vast audience; it also engenders a 'moral panic' about the fate of languages.[8] Biological and ecological metaphors applied to language (death, extinction) are indeed powerful, but they may also carry dangerous reductions; viewing languages as organisms that are born and die leaves unanswered the question of *when* one can truly say that a language has died: Is it when the last speaker of such a language dies, or when it stops being used as a medium of regular communication? Linguistic anthropologists have highlighted how such metaphors are therefore essentializing (Cameron 2007; Jaffe 2007) and potentially dangerous, as they reproduce the nineteenth-century view of an unquestioned link between language and ethnicity/culture. An emphasis on 'natural' processes, moreover, may end up reinforcing the view that language loss and/or death is equally 'natural,' thus deflecting attention away from the role played by sociopolitical factors (Pennycook 2004:216).[9]

In the case of Griko, the moral panic around its impending death has a long history. In fact, in the spring of 1867, the Italian philologist Morosi wrote, "Perhaps in less than two generations from now, scholars will only be able to infer that—a century earlier—Greek colonies existed here" (Morosi 1870:182). In spring 2008, Paolo Di Mitri from the village of Martano reflected on the death of Griko in an article for the local newspaper *Spitta: "O Grikomma pesane? Refrisko n'achi. Ce mì pu grafome grika, imesta pesammeni? Esi ka mas meletate pesanato?*

---

[8]   A moral panic is a "condition, episode, person or group of persons [that] emerges to become defined as a threat to societal values and interests" (Cohen 1972: 9). Cameron (1995: 83) draws from Cohen, and argues that "a moral panic can be said to occur when some social phenomenon or problem is suddenly foregrounded in public discourse and discussed in an obsessive, moralistic and alarmist manner, as if it betokened some imminent catastrophe."

[9]   Scholars have increasingly warned against the commodification of a discourse of 'moral panic' surrounding so-called language endangerment, both in academic and lay discourses (see Duchêne and Heller 2007; Hill 2002; and Silverstein 1998, among others). Such discourse is then further articulated through the notion of rights, those of the speakers to preserve their language and/or of minority languages themselves to be preserved against dominant ones and the specter of globalization (see Coluzzi 2007; May 2001; O'Reilly 2001; Skutnabb-Kangas and Phillipson 1995).

(Has Griko died? May it rest in peace. Are we who write Griko dead then? Are you who are reading it dead then?)[10]

My grandmother Lavretàna died in March 2008, at the age of 104. Griko is still the language of other women and men with white hair and sometimes black clothes. What I found is that, over a century and a half after Morosi's wistful pondering, locals still deal daily with this pending prophecy: the pool of mother-tongue speakers keeps shrinking, while linguistic competence, if any, varies widely across generations. As James Clifford (1986) argued, proclaiming the extinction of people and languages as soon as they are discovered by outsiders/scholars is indeed part of the Western rhetorical ideology to which ethnography has complied. Yet what may still strike the reader about the apparent paradox of Griko as perpetually dying is that locals' attempts 'to keep it alive' have not been aimed specifically at fostering new speakers—which is typically understood as the aim of language revival and revitalization efforts. Crucially, whether to actively participate in such efforts or to challenge them is ultimately linked to locals' own language ideologies and their situated interpretations of the revival processes.[11]

An immediate causal relationship between language ideologies and practice is indeed not a foregone conclusion. If for Griko speakers the ideologies of Griko as the 'language of shame' had completely won over those of Griko as the 'language of resource,' there would be no Griko speakers at all by now, linguistic competence aside. Nothing new or surprising here for anthropologists, who often record inconsistencies between discourse and practice. Likewise, if the ideology of Griko as the 'language of pride' had prevailed over its current lack of imperative communicative currency, the pool of speakers would be larger—or at the very least you would expect language activists to be Griko speakers, or to strive to become Griko speakers. This is often not the case either. In fact, inconsistencies between ideologies and practices emerge sharply, and the challenge has been to reveal what these inconsistencies hide.

Certainly locals are not silent. In various contexts, I have heard them offer reflexive comments about the current situation of Griko, at times lamenting that today "we talk more *about* Griko than *in* Griko." Indeed, Griko keeps on generating what sociolinguist Jan Blommaert (1999) defines as "language ideological debates"—that is, contentions about language ideologies and not

---

[10]   Excerpt from an article by Paolo Di Mitri published in the local newspaper *Spitta* (April 2008). Paolo, who writes in Griko today, belongs to the 'in-between generation.'

[11]   Language revival and revitalization efforts may prove to be elusive; this happens at times because educational programs conflict with community goals (Meek 2007) or pedagogical approaches (Nevins 2004), and this may lead speakers to develop strategies to resist language policies based on the acceptance of/challenge to dominant language ideologies (Jaffe 1999).

language per se. Old ideological debates persist today about the origins of the language (Chapter 1), or about the varying degrees of agency and the responsibility of speakers in the process of language shift (Chapter 2), while new debates emerge and take center stage. By debating, for instance, how to transcribe it and whether to rely on Italian, the local Romance variety, or Standard Modern Greek (MG) to integrate its limited vocabulary, speakers, activists, and local *cultori del griko* (Griko scholars) and locals at large reveal their understandings and projections about the role of Griko in the past-present-future (Chapter 5).

It should come as no surprise that Griko means, meant, or is meant to mean, different things to different people of different ages or backgrounds; anthropological studies have attested time and time again to the multiplicity of language ideologies that have been linked to gender, social position, and generation, to mention just a few. Expecting, however, to find a 'homogeneous' language ideology within a single social formation would be equally misleading. A crucial tool for this research has, therefore, been to attend not only to locals' explicit language ideologies but also to their metalinguistic comments—that is, those reflexive and often implicit comments about Griko that, in a performative way, keep shaping the story of this language. This approach has helped me to disentangle the multiple language ideologies present in the community, and to realize how they are often emotionally charged and may be interest-laden. The basic premise here is that language itself is multifunctional, and that its referential function is one of many.[12]

Language is not simply a tool to describe the world, but rather a tool that allows us to connect with it. One of the semiotic processes through which language ideologies are instantiated is indexicality, a term introduced by the semiotician Charles Peirce that builds on the notion of index and captures the ability of language to go beyond the semantic meaning of words: through linguistic indexes such as pronunciation, accents, and/or genres, a language reestablishes a connection with places, contexts, groups of people, and moments in time.[13] Crucially, in the case at hand, the language itself functions as an index, as a sort of imaginary arrow, and the object it points to is the past. As one would expect, the past is multifaceted; foremost, it is not simply a temporal category but a critical ideological terrain of self-representation.

---

[12]   Malinowski (1923) long ago talked about the "phatic function" of language as performing a social task as opposed to conveying information. This notion was further developed by Jakobson (1960), who extended the range of metalinguistic functions to include the referential, poetic, metalingual, conative, and emotive.

[13]   For early treatments of indexicality see Silverstein (1992), who builds on the work of Peirce. See also Ochs 1992.

Textures of Time

Modern Greek classes: "Back then things were not like today"

It was a rainy evening and the little alley leading to the cultural association Chora-Ma (Griko: My Village) in Sternatia, was particularly quiet. *"Pame stin ekklisìa"* (MG)—"We go to church"—I heard Eleni say when I entered Palazzo Granafei, the eighteenth-century baroque building that houses the association. The class had started! In 1994, the Greek Ministry of Education began sending Greek teachers to the area to teach MG in public schools and cultural associations; Eleni was the appointed MG teacher at the time. The hour passed as usual: Gaetano and Cosimino, two retired Griko mother-tongue speakers from Sternatia, exchanged notes and views comparing MG and Griko, whispering to avoid being scolded by Eleni. *"Imi ittù leme itu: aklisìa. To stesso pramma, torì?"* (Griko)—"Here we say *aklisìa*. The same thing, you see?" Gaetano noted, noting with satisfaction the similarity with the MG word *ekklisìa*.

After the class, as Gaetano and I were walking to my car, I stepped in a puddle and complained that the shoes I was wearing were not suitable for the rain. He intervened, *"Scarpe lei isù ... tis iche scarpe toa?"*—"You talk about shoes ... Back then who wore shoes?" That was to be the beginning of yet another conversation about the past, a past whose language of expression was Griko. Gaetano (born in 1947) from Sternatia—who earned his living as a prison guard as an adult—had been a shepherd when he was a child; he started recalling how hard life had been back then, how shoes were only worn on Sundays, that he used to go to work in the fields barefoot, to run on thorns and stones, and how he could not even feel them because the soles of his feet had become so tough. Gaetano here, as many others do, was referring to his own experiential past and his sensorial memories. We reached my car, but he went on talking about the past. *"Toa 'en ìane kundu àrtena"*—"Back then things were not like today," he concluded. It had started raining again.

Griko classes: "Our language is not a bastard, the one who says it is, is the bastard!"

Daniele (born in 1952) was sitting in front of us, hunched over a piece of paper, checking the spelling of poems written by the class. At the time, every Thursday afternoon, he taught an intermediate Griko class organized by the cultural association Kaliglossa (Good Language) based in Calimera. He is a retired computer programmer with a degree in astrophysics, but with an early background in and vivid passion for classical studies. Once the lesson was over, Daniele and I continued to talk about some issues that had arisen during the lesson.

For instance, if you write *lio nerò*—'a bit of water'—you pronounce it as it is, but *lio* comes from *oligon*, and since there is an elision, you have to pronounce the consonant of the following word as double—*lio nnerò*—but how to spell it then? It is ugly to start with a double consonant. With all due respect it would look like an African language; it could wake up old prejudices ... our language is not a bastard, the one who says it is, is the bastard! Some used to say Griko was a barbaric language ... calling it barbaric when we ... when our ancestors invented the word ... it would be an absurd historical anamnesis, for Griko contains traces of Hellenism!

Daniele here is vehement about disassociating Griko from its longstanding negative perception as a 'bastard language'; hidden behind philological and orthographic issues, he indeed makes a clear claim to a distant but 'glorious Hellenic past' also influenced by the romantic ideology of Hellenism. Gaetano, in contrast, refers to his own experiential memory of the hardship of a relatively recent past immersed in the subalternity of the South of Italy. They ultimately make different references and claims about the past that Griko points to. Given the small gap in their ages, this difference is more attributable to their differing backgrounds and life experiences. Daniele's knowledge about Greek history and view of Greek as the language of culture were, for many years, unusual outside of the intellectual world. Moreover, there are no popular accounts of the origins of ancestors or the language (of the kind that Tsitsipis [1998] found among the Arvanites of Greece); so, for generations, the majority of Griko speakers commonly ignored the cultural wealth of Greek (Parlangeli 1960); elderly speakers may still do so today.

Through the current revival, however, Griko speakers and locals at large have now been informed—reminded, as it were—about the noble origins of the language. Among them is Gaetano himself, who has been attending MG classes for years, and who is a main resource for Greek tourists and aficionados who visit Sternatia; he understandably enjoys his popularity now. The formulaic expression *"Toa 'en ìane kundu àrtena"*—"Back then things were not like today"—that Gaetano used, and that the elderly use time and again, captures how the past and present keep being dialogically compared and contrasted; yet what now prevails is a discursive reevaluation of Griko, which is not perceived anymore as a 'language of peasants' or indicative of a backward past. Through this ideological shift, locals reevaluate the past associated with speaking Griko, together with all indexes, which become forms of 'cultural capital.' This increased prestige happens not only *despite* the level of language endangerment; I would also argue that the increase in cultural capital occurs in part *by virtue* of the level of endangerment. Hence, the Griko community largely conforms to what Netta Rose Avineri has defined as a "metalinguistic community"; that is, one "of positioned social actors engaged primarily in discourse about language and cultural symbols tied to language" (2014:19). As in the case of the Yiddish she describes, it is through speaking *about* Griko, rather than speaking it, that linguistic identities emerge. In the case of Griko, furthermore, it is by engaging with and evoking the multiple pasts of Griko that locals provide community self-representations.

Rather than a 'revival of Griko' per se, I consider this a 'language ideological revival,' as what has been revived or revitalized is not the language itself, but instead ideas, feelings, and emotions about the role of Griko in the past. In the process, locals now blend autobiographical references and experiential realities with historiography and global discourses about cultural diversity. The people I introduce in the pages that follow—speakers, cultural activists, language connoisseurs, politicians, and locals more broadly—are not only the protagonists and the tellers of this story, they are also its very writers; they 'rewrite' the story of Griko, as it were, by recounting its multiple pasts. In the process, however, this generates tensions. As the vignettes indicate, the past remains a highly contested terrain: the questions of which chapter of Griko's past locals recall and build on to reconstruct its story, and which chapter of Griko's past from the multiple repertoires available best represents Griko and is best represented by it, become discursive struggles for community self-representation. The discursive practice of evoking the past indeed links locals to a network of earlier experiences and/or discourses, anchoring Griko to a specific time-space framework—to what Mikhail Bakhtin (1980) referred to as a chronotope—and enabling them to identify and represent themselves. To restore the past means equally to re-story it; this way, Griko becomes a metalanguage for talking about the past in order to position oneself in the present.

I therefore introduce the concept of the cultural temporality of language, which aims to capture the multiple relationships locals entertain with the language through its past, and with the past through language. While temporality has been understood as either a cultural relationship with time or as a phenomenological sense of time, I use the term here to emphasize how language stimulates temporal thought and talk, and how these are generated by cultural models and accounts of past-present-future; that is, by multiple historicities in the sense given to this term by Eric Hirsch and Charles Stewart (2005:262). In cases of minority languages involved in processes of so-called endangerment and revival, the ways in which members of the community experience and/or construct the past become central. In the case of Griko, locals do not challenge linear representations of temporality as such; rather, they engage systematically in 'evoking the past'—Griko's multiple pasts—and the very textures of that past: its glory, its hardship, its opportunities, and its failures.

This is why I integrate the cultural, in order to stress how language is itself anchored in time and space as a material presence. By evoking the recent past locals in fact evoke its textures together with their morally and emotionally loaded aesthetic values, which in turn affect language ideology and practice in the present and future. In this sense I am in intellectual dialogue with the theoretical strand of language materiality that has recently emerged, and that specifically proposes "to view language as a material presence with physical and metaphysical properties and as embedded within political economic structures," to use the words of Jillian Cavanaugh and Shalini Shankar (2017:1). Through the materiality of language, its sounds and form, language ideologies are therefore linked to locals' lived experiences and memories of language use, as is often the case with minority languages gone into disuse.

Being socially distributed, however, such ideologies may equally rest on projections of a temporally distant but glorious past, a past which connects Southern Italy and Greece, and which in turn also influences language choices and 'tastes.' This phenomenon highlights how language ideologies linked to a specific historicity may reinforce cultural ties between contemporary Italy and Greece, connecting communities across national borders as the ongoing contact with Greek aficionados of Griko attest. Since the 1990s, the intensification of contact with Greece, the availability of MG courses provided by the Greek Ministry of Education, and the interest shown by Greek aficionados of Griko who visit the area have been adding new layers to the unfolding Griko 'story.' In the midst of economic, demographic, and sociopolitical changes affecting southern Europe, the ideological alignment to the Hellenic cultural heritage as an idiom of global belonging and as "a preordained category of relatedness" (Pipyrou 2016:10) takes on broader sociopolitical meanings. In fact, depending on which past is evoked, Griko becomes a symbolic resource from which to write a different future.

Traces of Language

The journey from Soleto to Calimera is a short one. As I often do, I chose to drive through the villages of Sternatia and Martignano in order to enjoy the embrace of the landscape, its countryside, and the forest of olive trees swaying gently. That afternoon in late fall, the warm sunshine was still assured. Luigi from Calimera (born in 1963) wanted to update me on the progress of his album of songs written in Griko; he defines himself as an *operatore culturale* (literally, a 'cultural operator,' a term that bridges into activism), and although he has spent more than half of his life teaching in Bologna, he is one of the most passionate people about Griko that you will ever meet. His mother, Gilda, was a Griko mother-tongue speaker, but he learned Griko growing up in Via Atene, with his grandmother and her neighbors—mainly war widows and *zitelle* (Salentine: 'unmarried women'), he says. He belongs to the 'in-between generation,' that was not taught Griko as their mother tongue, and whose linguistic competence is often only partial (see Figure 4).

Figure 4. The village of Calimera

Luigi speaks MG and continues to improve his Griko; he talks about his project in very humble terms and describes the lyrics as simple, with his goal being for "the language to resound in its simplicity." Yet he is also very proud of his achievement. His songs are indeed full of references to love, to memories of the past, and to the language itself; they are the result of a musical adaptation, as they were conceived as poems. Luigi defines Griko as "*e glossa ti' kardìa, e glossa pu milì i kardìa*"—"the language of the heart, the language that the heart speaks." Experiential echoes of the language fuel this affective attachment to it as "the language that the heart speaks." That is, the emotional textures Griko evokes are linked to the speaker's memory, and are ultimately fueled by the affective attachments that locals feel toward the people they associate with Griko.[14]

---

[14]　See Cavanaugh 2004 on the case of Bergamasco, a vernacular spoken in the Italian region of Lombardia; her concept of "social aesthetics of language" captures precisely the "interweaving of culturally shaped and emotionally felt dimensions of language" (2004:11).

Luigi is equally vehement in stressing how important it was for him to learn about the noble past, as it were, of Griko; this sparked his intellectual interest rather early in life, and drove his subsequent efforts to valorize it. His account in fact shows how affect engenders a sense of moral responsibility toward both the people and the predicament of Griko itself. He continues:

> We often play with memory, with nostalgia, and some emotions help us more than others. But sometimes we direct our gaze from the past, which we believe we know, to the unknown future. So, what counts the most is our desire and hope to be part of it, to carve the language and ourselves into somebody else's memory forever. Yet this is not only a need but also a duty.

The cultural temporality of language is indeed produced by the intersection of affect and morality, which then impacts language ideology and practice. As one might expect, what is considered to be 'right' or 'wrong' for Griko is contingent, perspectival, and highly contested—and this points again to the multiplicity of social actors engaged in the story of Griko, and to their clashing claims about the past and thus the future of Griko (see Chapter 5). Luigi, for instance, has fulfilled his duty, as it were, by leaving evidence of the language in the form of songs and poems. Throughout time locals have indeed left such 'traces of language.' In this respect the category of local *cultori del griko* ('scholars of Griko') acquires an even stronger relevance with regard to the management of the Griko cause, since they have dedicated themselves to documenting the language. At the same time, as the etymology of the word *cultore* itself (from Latin 'cultivate,' 'worship') suggests, they have ceaselessly 'nourished' Griko over the years, further filling its materiality. The collection of oral popular culture compiled in the past, as well as their own production of new poems, songs, and other writings over the course of time, represent a material legacy through which locals keep building connections between language and people, times, and place *in the present* (Pellegrino 2016a).

Used as a form of cultural capital, the symbolic value Griko has acquired transcends its use as a medium of daily communication. The overall pool of Griko speakers shows in fact varying degrees of competence; age remains one of the decisive factors, a temporal marker of the distance since the shift away from Griko. This is often the case when a language shift takes more than one generation, and takes place through a restriction in the language communicative functions. In particular, this means that those who belong to the younger generation are bilingual in Italian/Salentine, and in fact cannot be defined as Griko speakers in prescriptive terms. If they have any, their competence in Griko varies considerably and depends on their degree of exposure to the language, which in turn is strictly related to the time spent with their grandparents and the elderly in general. In such a language ideological revival, however, those who have actively engaged or engage in either improving their competence or in acquiring it represent 'a minority within a minority.'[15]

In this book I therefore demonstrate the semiotic relevance of all 'traces of language,' highlighting the multiple ways in which locals engage with Griko, and the creative ways in which those who belong to the in-between and younger generations may resort to it (Chapter 6). Inspired by the work of sociolinguist Ben Rampton, I call these instances 'generational crossing,' with "crossing" referring to "the use of a language which is not generally thought to 'belong' to the speaker" (Rampton 2009:287).[16] In the case at hand, Griko is perceived as the language of the elderly and of their experiential world, a world that the younger generation has not inhabited, and that the 'in-between generation' has only experienced in passing. However, the younger and in-between generations resourcefully decontextualize and recontextualize the limited linguistic resources available to them, and by crossing the generational distance between the elderly and themselves, they perform an act of symbolic identification with them, and with the cultural repertoire.

In this book I therefore deconstruct the notion of 'language death' by emphasizing the functions of language that transcend its referential and indexical meanings, demonstrating how multiple forms of language practice become socially and culturally meaningful for the locals as ways to re-present themselves beyond the use of Griko for mere communicative purposes, and despite its selected and limited use.[17] No one can deny that Griko has remained a linguistic resource for a minority of the locals, but I contend that it never stopped being perceived as a resource; it was a resource even when it was perceived as a

---

[15] The very terminology used in the study of language shifts and death to define linguistic competence is telling. Dorian (1982:26) was the first to introduce the term 'semi-speaker' now widely used to define "individuals who have failed to develop full fluency and normal adult proficiency [in East Sutherland Gaelic], as measured by their deviation from the fluent-speaker norms within the community." 'Semi-speakers' seems to me to 'amputate' speakers in comparison to a full-bodied abstract ideal speaker. Tsitsipis's proposed label of 'terminal speaker,' which defines his Arvanitika speakers of a young age, has not proliferated—fortunately, I add. This is why I, in contrast, highlight the heteroglossic local languagescape by avoiding a competency-based taxonomy and employing one related to age ranges.

[16] Rampton specifically refers to white, Asian, and Caribbean British adolescents who borrow and mix codes as a way of crossing ethnic boundaries.

[17] Scholars have highlighted how, even when locals show little interest in revival efforts, languages may become emblems of identity and local culture, and acquire a symbolic value despite their limited use in interactions. See Coupland 2003 for Welsh; Paulston 1994 for Irish; and Fellin 2001 and Cavanaugh 2009 for Italian dialects.

language of shame (Chapter 2). I therefore move to deflect attention from the moral panic about the endangerment and extinction of Griko, and highlight instead its mobilization as a cultural resource that has become productive of personal values and social relations—but also, and crucially, a catalyst for the articulation of multiple claims.

The power game of minority politics

As I show in this book by tracing the various phases of the revival of Griko, the very social actors who promoted them shifted over time, as did their claims and aims; the educated middle class philhellenists of the first revival pursued 'recognition' of the value of Griko, while the politically engaged 'generation in between' of the middle revival aimed at the 'redemption' of the Southern Italian past and its indexes. The management of Griko and cultural heritage at large has more recently been adopted by local politicians, engendering tensions and conflicts within the community. Similarly, Pipyrou (2016:11), with reference to Calabrian Greek, has highlighted how questions of owner-ship emerge, as well as conflict and contestation as to who has the right to represent whom through language. She captures the plurality of actors involved in the management of the Calabrian Greek language and culture by deploying the concept of fearless governance—meaning here how they have developed the means to participate actively in the power games of minority politics. Significantly, they have done so by appropriating the available polit-ical and bureaucratic channels of governance rather than being subject to them; she argues that they have successfully promoted self-governance and inverted hegemonic culture (2016:6).

In the case at hand, a variety of social actors reclaim a space in the manage-ment of Griko and the right to participate in it. It is indeed highly disputed not only who retains authority over the language (its speakers, language connois-seurs and experts, cultural activists, or politicians) but also what defines it (whether linguistic competence, philological expertise, active engagement, or political entrepreneurship). Since in terms of linguistic competence, few people 'master' the language, this minority enhances its cultural capital, but the phenomenon also produces debates and conflicts over linguistic and cultural ownership, often also provoking frictions and estrangements among them (Chapter 5) and extending to the management of cultural heritage more broadly (Chapter 4). Moreover, as Pizza (2004, 2005) claims regarding the phenomenon of tarantism, conflicts framed over linguistic/cultural ownership may also be metacomments about the division of labor, and disputes over access to the symbolic and financial resources provided by the revival.

In what follows, I reveal a picture of Grecìa Salentina—and hence Salento—that is far from the homogenized one portrayed on global stages and often reproduced rhetorically locally. The case of Griko shows how the dynamics of the current revival have progressively led to a sense of discursive pride in the rediscovered value given to the language, its past, and to cultural heritage, which may be generic and superficial, as well as deeply felt or strategically articulated. Yet this scattered feeling of empowerment not only generates debates about the role of Griko in the future, but hides locals' fears of losing control over cultural ownership and what this may entail. Crucially, in a place such as Salento that has long been the subject of the anthropological gaze, and where cultural politics and the politics of culture have been dominant, issues of authenticity and authority turn into a struggle for representation.

Methods and relationships: Anthropology and home

This book is the product of multi-sited research and ethnographic evidence collected in Grecìa Salentina and in Greece.[18] Yet my interest in Griko goes way back, as I originally come from Zollino, the home of my father (1932–2014), and my home until my early twenties; this makes me a native anthropologist.[19] My own positionality therefore merits some discussion. Increasingly scholars are expected to recognize the inevitable ideological dimension inherent in their work; in this vein, I highlight from the start that I used anthropology as a tool to scrutinize my own reality and give meaning to the story of Griko. My father, a proud man from 'the old world,' never quite understood my need to put on paper what, he claimed, was already written on his skin. Before his death he acquiesced, but added a proviso: *"Enna to grasci? Teli daveru na to grasci? Ma, enna to grasci kalà, kui?"* (Griko)—"Well, if you really have to ... if you want to, then don't make any mistakes, OK?" Keeping my word to him in writing this book has been a years-long effort, an emotional challenge as much as an intellectual endeavor.

---

[18]   I began to conduct fieldwork in Grecìa Salentina in 2008 and in Greece in 2009 as part of my PhD research (2013). While writing my doctoral thesis I was involved in a European project that addressed the lack of teaching material for Griko as the author of the first of four levels of Griko textbooks (*Pos Màtome Griko*, "How We Learn Griko"). This experience, together with ten hours of teaching Griko in Zollino primary schools, demanded further reflexive interrogation, and further shaped my analysis of the data.

[19]   The pros and cons of conducting ethnography at home were extensively commented upon and debated when the topic was in vogue in the late 1980s and through the '90s. Since there is no view from nowhere, my personal experience indicates that the very grounds on which the distinction between anthropology and anthropology-at-home is based are shaky ones, and ultimately the perceived pros and cons of both endeavors neutralize the dichotomy.

Introduction

When I first started my fieldwork in Italy, I spent four months in Zollino and ten months in the village of Soleto, five kilometers away. In Zollino, acquaintances, neighbors, family friends, relatives, and my own parents—my mother is from Martano—were my resources. In the nearby villages, my interlocutors and I engaged constantly in a mapping exercise, which would end only once the relative/friend/acquaintance we had in common was identified; this usually granted me a warm welcome to their homes and unconditional access to their story worlds and their pasts: it made of me one of them. Common languages (Italian/Salentine and then Griko) and shared social norms (cf. Gefou-Madianou 1993) certainly rendered my role as a researcher easier.

The physical proximity of the villages, combined with the relatively small number of people involved, made conducting qualitative research manageable. I engaged in two main kinds of investigation: first, I attended to everyday linguistic practices and embedded ideologies, and moved away from the prescriptive/descriptive linguistics tradition, focusing instead on the study of language in context, on what speakers do with language, and on the cultural rules they follow. But I was equally interested in investigating the politics of the revival; to that end, I identified the main social actors involved in the middle and the current revivals. Because I already knew those from Zollino, it was easy to identify those in the nearby villages, which again facilitated my work. On the other hand, at times being 'one of them' made my questions sound weird and redundant, as my interlocutors expected me to "know the answer," or to have heard it before—which indeed I often did and had. In those cases, I had to reassure them that I was interested in their personal views, not just the common understanding. This also made me feel frustrated, for I imagined that if I had been a foreign researcher, someone not known to them, any question would have been plausible.

Figure 5. The village of Zollino

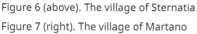

Figure 6 (above). The village of Sternatia
Figure 7 (right). The village of Martano

Part of my ethnography consisted of collecting and recording elderly Griko-speakers' life histories in Griko and/or Salentine, the two languages between which they often alternate. The speakers mainly come from the villages of Sternatia, Zollino, Martano, and Corigliano (see Figures 5–8), and I employed a narrative analysis approach to dissect their stories. Even when I explicitly asked them to recount their memories of the progressive shift away from Griko, my elderly friends constantly compared and contrasted past and present. As you might expect, they were not only talking about themselves and their own lives, they were also indexing collective experiences.

Figure 8. The village of Corigliano

In these encounters with elderly Griko mother-tongue speakers, it became particularly apparent how being/not being one of them was a constantly shifting and negotiable concept, for me as much as for my interlocutors. In other words, I had indeed to learn quickly that "the grounds of familiarity and distance are shifting ones," as Marilyn Strathern put it (1987:16). What put distance between us was my age. Countless times they told me, "*Toa en' ìane kundu àrtena*"—"Back then things were not like today." Indeed, I did not inhabit the experiential reality of the past, hardships included, as they did. Yet there was more to it than that. My elderly friends not only had lived a past of which I had no experience, they also lived in a world they recall and narrate in a language they feel is theirs, and that is not my mother tongue. Although over the course of time, they welcomed and encouraged my attempts to learn and speak Griko, my friends initially told me that speaking Griko to me did not come naturally to them (*'E' m'orkete na kuntèscio Grika 's esèna*). This should come as no surprise since Griko is perceived as a language that belongs to the elderly. Indeed, when I began the fieldwork, my Griko consisted of a limited stock of words, sentences, and formulaic expressions; learning Griko meant spending time every day with elderly villagers, mainly from Zollino and Sternatia. That, in turn, meant visiting them in their homes—learning to make pasta with Maria, drinking coffee with 'Ndata, accompanying Antimino when he went to water his orchard, etc. I quite simply followed them around on their daily activities and reminded them that I wanted to learn Griko. It was a slow process, one in which they made fun of my mistakes, taking revenge, as it were, against the "young" people who often make fun of their mistakes in Italian. This process of negotiation that is at play in any ethnographic encounter here acquired a further dimension, and over time it allowed us to bridge the generational/experiential gap and communicate in Griko. Antimino, more recently, took all the credit in front of other villagers and proudly announced, "*Ivò ti' màttesa to Griko*"—"I taught her Griko."

In reality my fascination with this language started early in life. So I was not surprised when I stumbled upon an old notebook of Griko from my secondary school years, in which I had jotted down every sentence my grandmother would say while living in my parents' house. I had started learning French at school at the time and, modeling my French textbook, I scribbled in this notebook some Griko 'rules.' This was the product of my tortured and no doubt tiresome attempts to decipher them during long winter nights sitting by the fireplace with my father, who patiently tried to answer my questions. This fireside scene shows not only my personal and emotional involvement with the topic, but crucially the role of memory—and not just mine—in retrieving images of the past as they are linked to the language and its use.

Ethnography in Grecìa Salentina

The ethnographic study of Griko cultural associations (*associazionismo*) consti-tuted a large part of my fieldwork. I conducted semi-structured interviews with the leaders and members of the most active cultural associations engaged in the Griko cause; as one might expect, the initial interview would often end up being only one of many long conversations; I continued meeting with some fairly regularly. I worked with a variety of people, not always those who were part of a specific association. Each in his or her own way shared a commitment to the language and to the place; among them were *cultori del griko* (scholars of Griko), authors of Griko grammar books, authors of poems and songs in Griko, amateur linguists, *appassionati di Griko* (Griko aficionados/enthusiasts), *operatori culturali* (cultural operators/activists), local intellectuals, and artists, singers, and musicians. Clearly, at times these categories overlapped. I participated in and observed a variety of local cultural activities, such as music festivals, semi-nars, a poetry competition, public debates, etc. I enjoyed local food at the two 'historical' taverns in Sternatia—Mocambo and Lu Puzzu—where people who were engaged in the revival typically met, and where live pizzica music was performed.

For my investigation of the application of language policy (Law 482) with regard to education,[20] I undertook participant observation of weekly Griko classes in primary schools, rotating through the villages of Grecìa Salentina (GS) over a two-month period. I conducted semi-structured inter-views with schoolteachers and *esperti di Griko* (Griko experts; that is, teachers specifically trained to teach Griko) and collected samples of teaching mate-rial when permitted. I also conducted semi-structured interviews with the mayors of each village of GS in order to assess how they were applying Law 482 in other activities.

I collected any type of material I could find regarding Griko, including CDs, newspapers, reports, and publications produced by cultural associations. I also conducted diachronic research using past newspaper articles on the topic of Griko and Grecìa Salentina, and by going through the archive provided by the Museum of Griko Culture and Peasant Society (Museo della civiltà contadina e della cultura grika) in Calimera. In addition to this, I conducted online ethnog-raphy of various forums and Facebook pages about and in Griko, locating meta-linguistic discourse and, when applicable, individual language preferences. I read the official website of Grecìa Salentina and the websites of the various villages, registering popular topics and metadiscourses.

---

[20] National Law 482, which recognizes twelve historical linguistic minorities on Italian soil, dates to 1999, but Griko was introduced in local schools in 2002.

Introduction

Ethnography in Greece

Investigating the production/reproduction and circulation of language ideologies of Griko led me to follow the network of collaborations between Greece and Grecìa Salentina. "Empirically following the thread of cultural process itself" (Marcus 1995:97) indeed impels multi-sited ethnography. This was therefore a choice dictated by the very nature of the subject of inquiry.

When I began my fieldwork in Greece in 2009–2010, I was based in Athens, where I initially attended language classes. Being based in the capital also allowed me to investigate the engagement of Greece in the Griko cause at the institutional level. In order to follow the network of collaborations between Griko and Greek associations, I traveled widely within Greece (Salonika, Ioannina, Patra, Corinth, and Corfu) and interviewed the social actors involved. It is important to stress here that before arriving in Greece, I had already made a list of people to interview. During my fieldwork in Grecìa Salentina, I systematically asked each of my interlocutors for the names of their contacts in Greece, those with whom they have collaborated or still collaborate. This web of contacts took me even further afield, and the list of people grew over the course of the research.

Not surprisingly, research among different segments of the population continually overlapped. I had the pleasure of meeting various Greek scholars who engaged with the Griko case, or on related issues; I also collected newspaper reports on the topic, and participated in musical events that included Griko speakers. I was exposed to a variety of contexts, which enormously benefitted my learning and observation, and I was attentive to both unconscious and metalinguistic observations about Griko and Grecìa Salentina (as well as about MG and Greece). Observations deriving from my stays in Athens over the years, as well as on the island of Ikaria, are equally part of the data from which I draw my analysis.

Structure of the book

The book has seven chapters plus a conclusion; the first three chapters look at the 'past of Griko,' while the remaining four chapters are devoted to ethnographic study of the present. It could have started from the last chapter; indeed, you may start reading this book from its end and then work backward through its previous chapters. I could have developed each chapter into a book –I am sure many authors could/would claim the same. Of course I could have structured it differently, I could have organized it by theme instead of following a chronological path. I have been saying for years as a sort of mantra that I became an anthropologist because I wanted and needed to explain the story of Griko to myself before anyone else. And I could not find any better way to trace the path leading to the current state of affairs of Griko than to start 'from the beginning.'

My other conviction, which was at the same time a stumbling block, has long been that 'capturing the present' is in a sense a delusive endeavor—no moment in time can be stopped, hence fully captured, so the 'present' of any anthropological work is itself 'history.' However, this is also just half the job anthropologists are called upon to perform. It is somehow ironic—or just obvious?—that in the process I had to deal with my own conceptualizations of how time unfolds, and to face its limitations. Yet the diachronic approach I adopted not only reflects and responds to my personal beliefs as well as anxieties, but it is what holds this book together.

With these methodological and conceptual considerations in mind, what follows is the story of Griko.

1

In the Land Between the Seas

We are Salentine, citizens of the world
deeply rooted in the Messapians
with the Greeks and Byzantines.
If you don't forget where you come from
you better value your own culture[1]

THIS is the refrain of the song *Le Radici ca tieni* (The Roots You Have), by the local Salentine band SudSoundSystem. It mentions the Messapians, as well as the Greeks and Byzantines, prompting the listener to engage with the past in order to grasp and give "value to your own culture," as they sing. Indeed, because of its strategic location, Salento has always been a territory of passage, a land in between the seas. Archaeological data confirm the Messapian presence between the seventh and the third centuries BCE, while the foundation of the polis of Taranto—which dates to 706 BCE—was part of the colonization of Southern Italy, an area known collectively as Magna Graecia. After two centuries, the Greeks were ousted by the Romans, and with the fall of the Western Roman Empire seven centuries later, Salento was conquered by Germanic tribes and the Saracens. Whether the Greek language endured during this time is a pivotal question that has long interested philologists and historians, and that has been answered only provisionally rather than conclusively. In the sixth century CE, the Byzantines established their presence in the area, aiming to recover the provinces of the former Western Roman Empire. They renamed the territory Terra d'Otranto, and for the most part it remained under Byzantine rule until the Norman Conquest in 1071 CE—other migrations were caused by Arab attacks in the ninth century. The Normans were followed by Swabians (in the twelfth century), Angevins (in the thirteenth), and Aragonese (in the fifteenth century).

---

[1]   All translations are mine unless otherwise indicated.

Despite the Norman Conquest, Greek culture continued to flourish, surviving through the centuries. With the probable aim of gaining local support and preventing revolts, in 1099 the Normans re-founded the monastery of San Nicola di Casole, located near Otranto, the easternmost Italian city. The monastery was populated by monks who patiently reproduced precious ancient Latin and Greek manuscripts and Holy Scriptures. During the Norman era, migrations from Greece continued, bringing priests and entire populations to the westernmost province of the Empire. At the height of its splendor, San Nicola di Casole was considered the most important monastery of southern Italy and played a pivotal cultural role (see Figure 9); its school was indeed open to whoever wanted to acquire greater knowledge of Greek and Latin literature. The creations of the poetic circle of Casole—founded by the priest Nettario, and to which Giovanni Grasso, Nicola d'Otranto, and Giorgio di Gallipoli belonged—synthesized sacred and profane themes. Even though this circle's creative output is not considered particularly innovative, it played a very important role in the preservation of the Greek language. Most importantly, for centuries the rich library of the monastery was a bridge between the West and the East that guaranteed the diffusion of Greek culture in the West and Latin culture in the East.

The fall of Constantinople to the Ottomans in 1453, however, broke the link with the East, and Otranto lost its status as the gateway between East and West par excellence. Not long afterward, in 1480, the Ottomans invaded Otranto, which belonged to the Kingdom of Naples at the time; this further contributed to the decline of Greek culture and language in the area. The monastery of Casole was destroyed together with its library, but some of the manuscripts survived and can now be found in a few European libraries (including Turin, Florence, Naples, Venice, Vatican City, Paris, London, and Berlin). The preservation of manuscripts is believed to be linked mainly to Sergio Stiso from Zollino, and to the activity of his scriptorium (Giovanni Bessarione, the patriarch of Constantinople, also contributed to the survival of certain manuscripts simply because he often borrowed them without ever returning them to the monastery). Among Stiso's disciples was Matteo Tafuri from Soleto, a philosopher, astrologer, and magician. Stiso and Tafuri are the most illustrious representatives of 'the Italo-Byzantine Humanism of Terra d'Otranto' epitomized by the Monastery of Casole itself. Moreover, several scriptoria located in the area of Nardò-Soleto-Gallipoli-Maglie in fact enabled the perpetuation of Byzantine culture until the beginning of the seventeenth century.[2]

---

[2] People from Zollino still remember the remains of Stiso's house, which was demolished in the late 1960s. The two inscriptions on the architraves of the windows of his house are reproduced as the work of Francesco Lo Parco (1919). One inscription was in Latin: "CHAOS NON CAPIT

Figure 9. The remains of the Monastery
of San Nicola di Casole

If the Normans had promoted Latin-rite Catholicism but opted for religious tolerance, the Council of Trento (1563), for its part, replaced Greek priests and liturgical books with Latin ones. This change had a profound effect on the religious as well as the linguistic configuration of the area: religious ceremonies, prayers, and the entire liturgy were to be administered in Latin; this struck another serious blow to the roots of the *grecità* (Italian: Greekness) of the area, favoring a shift away from the use of Greek. Surprisingly or not, however, the Byzantine rite did not disappear.[3] Rather, it survived by cohabiting with the Latin rite even after the Council. As attested upon the apostolic visit of the Archbishop of Otranto, Lucio De Morra (1606–1623), the Byzantine rite was still to be found in thirteen villages, as were a total of eighty Greek priests; it survived the longest in my home village of Zollino, where it was present until 1688; in Corigliano until 1683; in Sternatia until 1664; and in Castrignano until 1663. Transition to the Latin rite deprived locals of an important communicative environment. From this time onward, the Greek linguistic and cultural heritage was transmitted orally.

From the early eighteenth century, Southern Italy was ruled by the Bourbons until the Unification of Italy in 1861. By that time, contact with the East had long been severed, and the language that survived increasingly became associated with the peasant world; knowledge of Greek history and Greek as the language of culture was restricted to educated locals, while the majority

---

LUCEM" (Darkness does not exclude light), and the other was in Greek: "ΕΥΛΟΓΙΣΩ ΤΟΝ ΚΥΡΙΟΝ ΕΝ ΠΑΝΤΙ ΚΑΙΡΩ ΑΜΕΝ" (I will bless God in every moment).

[3]   In the Italian literature and common parlance it is often referred to as *rito Greco* (Greek rite). See for instance Cassoni (2000) *Il tramonto del rito greco in Terra d'Otranto* (The End of the Greek Rite in the Land of Otranto).

of Griko speakers typically lacked such historical consciousness. By the twentieth century, the Greek-speaking area had shrunk to a compact district south of Lecce made up of the villages of Calimera, Martignano, Sternatia, Soleto, Zollino, Martano, Castrignano dei Greci, Corigliano, and Melpignano.

"The Past Will Haunt Us Until We Acknowledge All of It!"

The streets of the historical center of Soleto are rather narrow, and the glow of amber lights at night gives it a mysterious atmosphere. And that is appropriate, for after all mystery and magic linger in this village, which is home to the astrologer Matteo Tafuri, popularly known simply as *il mago* (the magician). Indeed, so strong is this sense of magic that Soleto is referred to as *il paese delle macare* (the village of the witches). I enjoy wandering through the historical center of town, and I never tire of admiring the Guglia, the spire tower of the Chiesa di Maria Santissima Assunta, which, according to legend, Tafuri himself erected—with the help of seven little demons—rather remarkably, a century before he was born.[4]

Francesco and I had agreed to meet that evening in the building that hosts the cultural association Nuova Messapia (New Messapia), just a few meters away not only from the humble birthplace of Tafuri, but also from my own house. The walls of the room were plastered with copies of newspapers published by the association. The association was founded in 1995 by Francesco, and a few of his friends, when he was not even eighteen years old. He is now in his early forties and an expert in local history. Among other things, he works as a tourist guide and sings in a folk music group. I had never before explicitly asked him about the choice of that name for the association.

"We chose it because Soleto is a village of Messapian origin, because we are passionate about the history of Soleto, and because we have been researching it for years. It is the village's vocation in a way. For Soleto has a long tradition of local historians," he paused before continuing, "Nuova Messapia does not focus only on Griko," he emphasized, "but also on environmental issues, on art, on the territory at large, *e senò ce facimu?* (Salentine)—"Otherwise, what is the point?" As was our custom, we switched freely between Italian and Salentine in our discussions. Francesco started learning Griko as an adult; his mother from Corigliano understands it but is not a confident speaker, but her own father was.

He noticed I was looking around at the copies of the *Nuova Messapia* newspaper: "Have a look at the Soleto map! It is an extraordinary find," he said,

---

4   The Church was in reality commissioned by Raimondello Orsini, Prince of Taranto and Duke of Soleto, in 1397.

showing me the article they published. Francesco was referring to the discovery of a fragment of a black-glazed terracotta vase (5 cm by 2.8 cm), which is believed to represent southern Salento. It lists the names of twelve Messapian cities (including Otranto, Ugento, and Leuca) and the name of Taranto. He continued, "Here there were Messapians. They were most likely of Illyrian origins, but they had absorbed the Greek influence to the point that they used the Greek alphabet. But they spoke another language … You see, there is so little information about these people, we still do not know their cultural contribution."[5]

Francesco always speaks rather quickly and very confidently; from time to time he demands the listener's attention, interjecting an emphatic "*Attenzione*" (Italian: Listen up!) at the beginning of an important point he wants to make, or a rhetorical "OK?" at the end of a point he has just made. He continued, "Official historiography is a joke! History is not taught well, and Byzantine history is unfortunately not taught at all at school … I taught Griko for five years in local schools, but I didn't teach the language. I only taught children about local history and traditions. I did that on purpose, OK? You see, all this talk about Grecìa Salentina, Griko and the rest of it, there has been a lot of focus on language, but not on history." The cultural wealth of the Byzantine period highlights a specific temporal texture of Griko, as it were—which is recurrently referred to by cultural activists in order to vehemently reject the discourse of Griko as a "language of backward peasants."

Francesco went on to talk about how important the Byzantine chorion of Soleto once was, and how there had been a flourishing Italo-Greek community. He explained that Nuova Messapia intends to create a center of Byzantine culture in Soleto, and to recover Byzantine manuscripts copied in Salento and now dispersed throughout Europe. He went on to argue that the official late Byzantine historiography, which goes from the Norman Conquest of Salento in the eleventh century to the end of the Byzantine rite in the Terra d'Otranto in the second half of the eighteenth century, perpetuates some major "historical mistakes."[6]

---

[5]   The Messapi were familiar with literacy, and adapted the Ionic/Tarentine Greek alphabet as shown in the fifty inscriptions found in the area. Despite the use of Greek characters, their language is only partially decipherable. The map Francesco refers to here was found in 2003 during a dig carried out in Soleto by Belgian archaeologist Thierry van Compernolle of Montpellier University. It is now kept in the Archaeological National Museum of Taranto. Its authenticity has been—and still is—debated, but if confirmed, the Soleto Map would represent the oldest map of anywhere in the Western world, dating from about 500 BCE (see Lombardo 2011, 2014, among others).

[6]   To address them he recently published an article (Manni 2017) in which he questions that migrations from Greece were due to the iconoclastic wars as per the official historiography— such wars followed Pope Leon III's order (in 727) to suppress and destroy all holy images and icons. To escape from the massacres, thousands of monks would have left the eastern provinces

"Greek tourists, for instance, are convinced we were Orthodox and I will never stop repeating it: We have never been Orthodox! *Attenzione*, many people mistakenly believe and keep saying this; but it was a mixture of the two traditions, from the Norman Conquest onwards we were Catholics who followed the Byzantine rite, while that lasted ... And I always stress it when tourists come to visit La Chiesa di Santa Sofia e Stefano." I have indeed seen him spending hours explaining in great detail the frescoes of the church, painted in the mid-fourteenth century (see Figures 10 and 11).[7] "There must be a reason if we call ourselves Salentine Greeks, right? Salento has always been a bridge between the East and the West, and that's our beauty. People do not ... [and here he sighs] We do not know our own history well, Manu." At that point I knew another "Listen up!" was coming: "*Attenzione*: the past will haunt us until we acknowledge all of it!"

Figure 10. The church of Santa Sofia and Stefano (exterior)

---

of the Empire and moved to the Southern regions of Italy, in particular to Salento, where they established various monasteries. Manni suggests that what brought priests and entire populations to the westernmost province of the Empire was the threat of the Ottomans and the fact that in Southern Italy they found the same political administration, religion, and culture.

[7]   In the same article Manni argues that the church apse basin depicts the Latin version of the Filioque—the most important theological controversy between Orthodox and Catholics He also argues that, since the schism between the Orthodox Eastern and Latin Western Churches occurred in 1054, and until then there had been a formal union between the two religious confessions, the Greek churches of Southern Italy could not have been Orthodox. The council of Melfi in 1098 imposed on Greek churches to recognize the Roman Pope as religious authority and not the Patriarch of Constantinople, as had been the case for the previous five centuries (Manni 2017). It is only fair to assume that over the centuries and until the end of the Byzantine rite, a highly local and syncretic religiosity developed.

The historical sketch I presented at the beginning of the chapter may seem clear and comprehensive, but the sources available have not thus far provided all the factual evidence expected by historicism—and knowledgeable locals such as Francesco, as we have just seen. The origins of the Messapians are still debated—according to Herodotus they descended from Cretans who had been driven ashore on their voyage homewards from Sicily, to which they had traveled to avenge the death of Minos; it remains uncertain whether they were of Cretan-Mycenaean or Cretan-Illyrian origins, and whether they were Hellenized thanks to contact with Taranto or Greece. It is also debated whether today's Griko-speaking villages were even an integral part of the Magna Grecia Empire. Local history is indeed still immersed in mystery. Such lack of 'factual/historical data' may at times lead to confusion, at times specu-lation, Francesco argued; he is emphatic that "the past haunts us," and he is very clear about the need to search for it, to get to know it. He defines himself as a local historian and relies on the power of historiography to reveal to us the past of Griko and the past of the place.[8]

Figure 11. The church of Santa Sofia and Stefano (interior)

As you would expect, not everyone looks for the evidence Francesco is after. For others 'evidence' may lose its centrality, and may become less important if the past is based on a belief, or on the interpretation of historical facts. At times it is exactly this lack of factuality, whether real or perceived—these being uncer-tainties about the past and of the language itself—that keep locals engaged in it and/or in speculating about it. What I indeed witnessed in the field was locals' recurrent practice of 'evoking the past', and how they might select a specific

[8] Another episode of local history 'rectified' by locals, as it were, refers to the so-called martyrs of Otranto—eight-hundred men executed on the Hill of Minerva (reportedly because they refused to give up their Christian faith)—who were canonized by Pope Francis in 2013. Daniele Palma recently published a book with the evocative title *The Authentic History of Otranto in the War Against the Turks* (2013). In it, by decoding diplomatic letters that he found in the state archive of Modena, he demonstrates that the '*martiri di Otranto*' were men who were killed because their families lacked the financial means to save them from becoming slaves—as per the Ottomans' practice in the area.

chapter of the history of Griko and establish a cultural but also affective relationship with *that* particular past. For Francesco, for instance, it is particularly important to correct the 'historical mistakes' of the Byzantine period, which constitutes a central component of his discursive act of evoking the past.

If historicism fails to provide 'factuality,' as it were, so does philology, to which I turn next. Both of these approaches leave room for the persuasive power of ideologies about language, and for cultural perceptions of the past to emerge. This becomes apparent when considering the ideological debate about the origins of Griko and its first ideological revival promoted by local admirers of Ancient Greece—the philhellenists from Calimera.

The language debate

Ti ene e glòssama? Pedàimmu! ...	What is our language? My child!
'En i' lloja tze chartì, ...	It is not words on paper
E glòssama e' ffonì manechò. ...	Our language is voice only ...
Me rotà pos entzìgnase, pos èttase 's emà,	You ask me how it began, how it reached us,
is tin èfer' etturtea, is tin èmase pronò.	who brought it here, who learned it first.
Is to tzeri, pedàimmu!	Who knows, my child!
E' ssu ndiàzzete n'o tzeri.	It does not matter.
E' ffonì pu vizzàsamo atti' mmana ...	It is the voice we sucked from our mother's breast,
fonì pu mas èmase a traùdia,	that taught us songs,
ce a pràmata teù, ce in agapi,	prayers, love
ce o kkosmo (Tommasi 1996).	and the world.

> We do not know anything about the origins of the Greek villages[;] no authoritative document, no chronicle, no local or popular tradition allows us to establish ... even approximately the epoch to which these villages date. The same mystery blurs the origins of the Greek minorities that still exist today ... in Calabria.
>
> Rohlfs 1980:53

The origins of these villages is a mystery that has engaged historians, historical linguists, and dialectologists ever since they were 'rediscovered' in the nineteenth century by the German philologist Karl Witte. In the absence of authoritative and uncontested historical sources dating the origins of the Southern-Italian Greek dialect enclaves, the question became philological as scholars have tried to establish them, looking for linguistic proof to relate them either to the Magna Graecia colonies or to Byzantine times. Yet they have failed to resolve what we could call 'the Griko and Greko language question'; the origins remain immersed in a mysterious aura, as it were.[9] My aim here is not to contribute to this issue in linguistic terms but to point to the climate of Romanticism and nationalist bias in which the debate was long articulated; indeed, establishing when these areas were first Hellenized and whether the Greek language survived the seven centuries of Roman occupation was never simply a philological or historical question.

The German philologist Gerhard Rohlfs first visited these areas in the early 1920s, and provides the richest study on this topic. The retention of some Doric traits (the long /a/; the geminate consonants; and the infinitive after verbs of volition, seeing, and hearing, which have completely disappeared in MG) led him to argue for the Magna Graecia hypothesis. He also pointed to a long cohabitation in a situation of bilingual symbiosis between the Greeks and the Latins since early times, and to the influence of the Greek substratum on the local Italo-Romance varieties—in which following Greek the infinitive is replaced by the use of finite structures, for instance. The topic soon attracted the interest and attention of Greek scholars, who considered Griko and Calabrian Greek to be a continuation of the Hellenism of Magna Graecia. Non-Greek and non-Italian scholars instead consider them as continuations of the Hellenistic Koine, and therefore as participating until the late Middle Ages in the same linguistic evolution as the rest of the Greek language. However, the presence in their structure and vocabulary of a few archaic traits points to the survival of Doric elements, and to an uninterrupted Greek presence in Italy since ancient times.[10]

Yet the Magna Graecia thesis was met with strong opposition by Italian linguists—among them the local linguist Oronzo Parlangeli. They supported instead the Byzantine origin of Griko, which was first argued by the Italian linguist Morosi (1870) on the basis of its similarity to MG.[11] Among more recent

---

[9] Byzantine historiography mentions only three massive migrations to Southern Italy, and this contributes to the 'Ancient' argument. There are, on the other hand, few inscriptions in the Greek language from late Antiquity, which is taken to contribute to the 'Byzantine' argument (Manolessou 2005).

[10] Among Greek scholars supporting the 'ancient' origins of Griko and Greko, see Caratzas 1958, Kapsomenos 1977, and Tsopanakis 1968. Among non-Greek and non-Italian scholars who consider them as continuations of the Hellenistic Koine, see Browning 1983, Horrocks 1997, and Sanguin 1993. For a discussion of the arguments supporting the 'ancient' origins, see Manolessou 2005. According to her, the infinitive usage shows only that communication with the rest of the Greek-speaking world was interrupted in the Middle Ages. She calls for an in-depth reevaluation of the debate, taking into account the extant scholarly knowledge of bilingualism and the language shift of Medieval Greek and Italian. See also Ralli 2006.

[11] Among Italian scholars supporting the Byzantine thesis, see Battisti 1959, Spano 1965. More recently, Karanastasis (1992) suggested merging Morosi's and Rohlfs's theories by arguing that

contributions, the Italian scholar Franco Fanciullo defines the controversy between Rohlfs and Italian linguists as mainly ideological, and the debate as a "false problem," arguing that it was constructed on the premise of a strict Greek/Latin antithesis (2001:69). Instead, Fanciullo suggests an extensive symbiosis and millennia of linguistic exchange (the fact that there was Greek does not mean that Latin had not reached Southern Italy) and talks of a historical Greek/Italo-Romance bilingualism in the South of Italy since Byzantine times (proven by documents that refer to mixed marriages). Bilingualism indeed may have been the tool through which the Greek language managed to resist over time (Montinaro 1994:28).

The debate over the origins of the language, together with all its intricacies, ultimately hides more than it reveals. Indeed, Rohlfs's proposal came during the Fascist period, at a time in which, from the Italian standpoint, his argument put in danger the very 'Italianness' of its speakers (Fanciullo 2001:70). To accept the possibility that entire Italian regions (Sicily, Calabria, and Salento in Apulia) may have resisted a 'complete' Latinization, and that they continued speaking Greek for centuries after the end of the Roman Empire, would have been in opposition to this nationalist ideology, which regarded the Italian nation as the 'daughter' of the Roman conquest. Likewise, the tendency of Greek scholars to support the Magna Graecia origins reflects Romantic Hellenism, which supported the very emergence of Greece as a nation-state. It crucially points to the legacy of the discipline of classical philology that had been instrumental in constructing a continuous past that would link Modern to Ancient Greece; the presence of a unique language from Homer to the present time, despite its evolution, was to become proof of such continuity. The legacy of this historically produced language ideology therefore also manifested itself in the way that Greek philologists continued to treat the debate about the origins of Griko and Calabrian Greek.

The story of Griko I recount here is somehow still connected with what represents the first 'language ideological debate' (Blommaert 1999)—in which linguistic facts were adduced only to confirm the underlying ideologies. Not incidentally, Italian scholars have tended to support the Byzantine thesis, whereas Greek scholars, influenced by a Romantic Hellenism, have argued for the Magna Graecia thesis. The debate over the origins of these Greek varieties ultimately shows how contested language ideologies are appropriated differently, at different historical times, and by different people with different aims.

---

some Greek-language communities could have survived the end of the Magna Graecia period and later formed hellenophonic areas during Medieval times. Local intellectuals have also participated in this debate, supporting one or the other hypothesis over time, although they have mainly focused on its folkloristic aspects through the collection of songs and poems.

Yet the sociocultural effects of the different positions are ongoing, regardless of the fact that the philological debate per se seems to have moved further to the margins lately, as the scholarly attention given to these languages has fostered the circulation of specific language ideologies. With reference to the Calabrian case, Christina Petropoulou (1997) comments that speakers at large started to appropriate the discourse about the ancient origins of the language in the 1960s, when a Greek Orthodox priest told them that they spoke "like Homer." What I witnessed in Grecìa Salentina is that alternative and at times opposing language ideologies are reproduced locally, and their multifaceted effects persist in many of the current ideological debates about Griko.

A Diachronic Sketch: Historical Bilingualism

Today it has become accepted fact that premodern European countries were essentially multilingual, and that national languages are not a given; they are instead the result of historical processes of linguistic unification and standardization, and this is particularly true of Italy. Moreover, Standard Italian derives from Florentine, which became a model for a pan-Italian literary language thanks to Dante's *Divina Commedia*; in other words, it was not the language of a community but of a cultural tradition dating to the early fourteenth century that was selected as the 'national language' when Italy emerged as a modern nation-state in 1861, five-and-a-half centuries later. At that time, only 2.5 percent of the total population could speak 'Italian,' while 97.5 percent of the population—peasants and aristocrats alike—spoke other regional languages, and Italian was a foreign language to them (De Mauro 1970). After the political unification, national statesman Massimo d'Azeglio notably said, "We have made Italy, now we have to make Italians."[12]

The Italian philologist Morosi visited the Griko-speaking villages of Salento in 1867, and his work provides a picture of the local languagescape immediately after the Unification of Italy. The story of Griko I recount in this book starts with his prediction of 'Griko's death foretold'; Morosi indeed referred to the process of forced linguistic unification and to the destructive power of Italian, which informed his prediction that Griko would disappear within the following two generations. He even commented at the time that it was difficult to find monoglot Griko speakers, and observed that particularly men, because of their trading activities, "know and use both Greek and Italian ... and are, therefore, called

---

[12] While regional characterization of the national language is frequent in major European languages, Italy's linguistic diversity is considered unique also because 'national languages' had generally been more widespread socially and geographically for centuries before the emergence of their respective nation-states (De Mauro and Lodi 1979:9; see also Telmon 1993).

'uomini di due lingue'" (Morosi 1870:182). His reference to "Italian" is, however, misleading: these 'people with two languages' spoke Griko and Salentine—the local Italo-Romance variety used around the Griko-speaking area of Salento. The centuries-long contact between Griko and the surrounding Salentine-speaking environment intensified in the nineteenth century, when communications with nearby villages improved and when, due to commerce and trade, Griko speakers were brought to learn and increasingly use Salentine; this led to varying degrees of bilingualism, and to further language 'interference.'

The contact zone had definitely been shifting for centuries. Indeed, in the Middle Ages, the Griko-speaking area included the entire Salentine peninsula to the Taranto-Brindisi line, even though it remains uncertain whether it was inhabited by a Griko/Italo-Romance mixed population (Rohlfs 1980:76). The shifting boundaries of the Griko-speaking area therefore shed light on the issue of the identity, as it were, of the Griko-speaking community. Rohlfs himself had in fact argued that Griko speakers were not 'foreign bodies'—cultural outsiders who shared nothing with the nearby villagers; this was in contrast to, for example, the Albanian community of Taranto province and the Franco-Provençal people of Foggia province, both of whom had a strong ethnic and cultural identity separate from the majority. This fact points to a much longer period of coexistence, and to the exemplary integration of cultures and languages. Ultimately it shows how Griko speakers held and are holding onto their language, but also how they always shared and share much of their culture with speakers of Salentine. As far back as our information goes, they in fact did not consider themselves to be ethnically different (in the modern sense of the term) from Salentine speakers.

When I say that Greek and Salentine coexisted in symbiosis, I do not mean to infer that all locals were bilingual, nor that the penetration of bilingualism was either uniform or simultaneous across the villages; neither do I imply that it was internally equally distributed. Bilingualism here should not be taken to mean a widespread and undifferentiated use of both languages, but refers instead to the historical co-presence of Griko and Salentine in the area; in short, it is a case of "historical bilingualism" (Fanciullo 2001). Parlangeli (1952) argued that in the villages of Martano and Zollino, for instance, this co-presence is attested since the sixteenth century, while the villagers of Sternatia and Soleto were still monolinguals. This highlights the heterogeneity of this phenomenon within the very Griko-speaking area, with bilingual villages adjacent to Griko monolingual villages. Bilingualism, moreover, is often characterized by varying degrees of competence in the two languages—including passive competence— and depends on a number of variables, including occupation and gender. The educated bourgeoisie would have been closer to bilingualism, whereas peasants and the 'lower' strata of the populations would have been Griko monolinguals, or would have used the two languages in different contexts (Griko within the family and Salentine in more formal situations—what is known as *diglossia*).[13] Morosi's reference to 'people with two languages' therefore needs to be read in light of these observations.

The influence of Salentine on Griko is a common outcome of language contact, where languages influence each other to varying degrees; on the one hand, the Greek 'character' of South Italian 'dialects' is due to the influence/interference of the Greek substrata on them; on the other, the Romance 'character' of Griko is the result of vocabulary and structural borrowings from Salentine. Recall Adriana's comment in the previous chapter that Griko and Salentine are mixed. Indeed, this process gives rise to many 'mixed forms' such as *pensèo* (first-person singular); this is an adaptation of the Salentine/Italian infinitive *pensare* (to think), and such forms were already attested toward the end of the nineteenth century.[14]

Because of its mixed character, Griko started being referred to as a 'bastard language'—its very speakers had internalized this (mis)belief. Although when this label started being used cannot be established with certainty, it is fair to assume that it dates back to the nineteenth century, for this is when the progressive influence of Salentine on Griko reached an extensive phase. Not coincidentally, I found its first written reference in the writings of local intellectuals from Calimera in the early twenty-first century; locals continued to refer to Griko as a 'bastard language' throughout this time, and it is only recently that this pejorative label has lost its currency. In discussion of plants and animals, the term 'bastard' indicates mixed species; when extended from flora and fauna to people, it means 'illegitimate.' Likewise, a bastard language is the outcome of the mixture of two languages—a 'hybrid,' in neutral terms; the negative connotation of the term 'bastard' is, in turn, based on a belief in a presupposed

---

[13] This term was introduced by Ferguson (1959) and developed by Fishman (1965) to refer to a specific type of societal bilingualism that involves two varieties of the same language; these are hierarchically ranked into a High language (H) associated with certain high-status and formal domains of social activity, and a Low language (L) associated with low-status domains, such as family life and solidarity functions (a typical example being the distinction in Greek between *katharévousa* and demotic). Griko and Salentine are not varieties of the same language, but in this phase they were connected to mutually exclusive domains of use and value, as the notion of diglossia entails.

[14] Sobrero (1979) builds on Morosi's study, and argues for an extensive phase of grammatical interference at all levels (lexical, morpho-syntactic, phonological) toward the end of the nineteenth century. When speakers combine two languages by grafting the grammar of one onto the vocabulary of another, this gives rise to a particular type of language contact, called 'language mixing or intertwining' (Sebba 1997:16, cited in Garrett 2004:62). Needless to say, it is not straightforward where to draw the line between borrowing, interference, and other processes of language contact. See Garrett 2004; Woolard 2004.

purity of the two forms if isolated; a bastard language like a bastard animal or person therefore lacks 'purity.' Symbolically, Griko would therefore appear to be polluted.

The debate over the 'purity' and, by contrast, the 'pollution' of Griko emerges in the writings of local philhellenic intellectuals from Calimera, who set out to prove the noble origins of Griko and so strived to give it the same symbolic capital as Greek. As argued by Il Gruppo di Lecce (hereafter the Lecce Group), this ideological approach developed at the end of the nineteenth and beginning of the twentieth century in response to the social changes in post-Unification Italy, which broke a perceived sense of continuity. Yet these local intellectuals were not simply concerned with the 'purity' of the language. The unification of Italy had caused a rift between the high and the low strata of Italian society in general, which the intellectuals perceived as endangering their social role; to them, the past seemed 'pure' and in contrast to the changing social environment. Moreover, Palumbo and the philhellenists from Calimera were educated in the most active centers of the Italian culture of the end of the nineteenth century; they represented the link between the periphery and the center of the national culture, and participated in the Italian classical and humanistic tradition (The Lecce Group 1979).[15]

In what follows, I take The Lecce Group's argument a step further, showing how the underlying ideological orientation of the circle of Calimera was also informed by what was happening at the same time in Greece. The moral panic about the disappearance of Griko led to the 'first ideological revival of Griko'; this also represents the first instance of the interplay between the local, national, and transnational language ideologies of Griko.

Vito Domenico Palumbo and the First Ideological Revival of Griko

Vito Domenico Palumbo (1854–1918) of Calimera is considered the most illustrious Hellenist. Palumbo was a major local scholar and the father of the circle of local intellectuals that emerged toward the end of the nineteenth century. Gathering around him, they followed his attempt to give Griko a renewed prestige and prove its nobility and purity. Palumbo was an eclectic personality—a journalist, philologist, folklorist, and Griko poet. He was born into an affluent family; he studied Social Sciences in Florence, and then law and literature in

---

[15] The Lecce Group was constituted by six professors from the University of Lecce who published an article in 1979 analyzing the workings of the circle of Calimera. Sobrero had previously argued that the failure of their attempts was due to the "intellectualistic nature, which dramatically contrasted with the linguistic behavior of the social classes" (Sobrero 1974:77).

Naples (although he largely remained an autodidact). Among his many activities, Palumbo translated into Griko works by Dante, Goethe, Shelley, Poe, and Carducci, along with works from MG by Paparrigopulos, Bernardakis, and Drosinis, to mention but a few. Although he never completed his degree in Literature, he taught at various middle schools in Sicily and Apulia.[16]

A specific episode of Palumbo's life was to have a great impact not only on his personal story, but on the 'story of Griko' that was to follow. Because Palumbo had distinguished himself in medieval studies, the Italian Ministry of Public Education granted him a scholarship to improve his knowledge of MG in Greece. He spent one year in Athens (1882–1883), and there he got in contact with various Greek poets (such as Baby Anninos and Demetrios Bikelas) and intellectuals, with whom he subsequently maintained regular communication. His stay in Athens was, indeed, to have long-lasting effects: that year he was nominated as a correspondent member of the Parnassòs Literary Society (established in 1865), and managed to gain the esteem and admiration of Hellenists beyond Greece, including in Istanbul and Alexandria. His work on local folklore was also well-known among foreign philologists (such as Dawkins, director of the archeological Institute of Athens, and Pernot at the University of Paris) who respected him, and with whom he remained in regular contact. Some even visited him in Calimera.[17]

The contacts that Palumbo maintained with Greek intellectuals and Hellenists affected him profoundly. Yet, equally crucial for his formation must have been his friendship with Nikolaos Politis, the father of Modern Greek folklore studies, who was "the dearest of his Greek friends for the long and reciprocal esteem and brotherly affection" (Stomeo 1958). They shared a common interest in and commitment to folklore studies through the collection of popular songs and poems, and their mutual correspondence shows their intellectual affinities. Palumbo dedicated himself wholeheartedly to the collection of love and religious songs, lullabies, proverbs, and *morolòja*, which until then had only been transmitted orally, and which he transcribed into his 'notebooks.' It seems that part of his collection was lost after his death, for only fourteen of these many notebooks have survived.[18] It is not surprising, therefore,

---

[16] Palumbo was also the founder and editor of magazines such as *KAΛHMEPA* (Good Morning), *Cultura Salentina* (Salentine Culture), and *Helios*; he also collaborated with the quarterly magazine *Apulia*, where he published articles about Griko.

[17] For Palumbo's merits, King George of Greece conferred upon him a knightly order.

[18] The material collected by Palumbo in his notebooks has been published relatively recently by the Cultural Association Ghetonìa, Calimera, and curated by local *cultori del griko*. According to Silvano Palamà, current president of the cultural association Ghetonìa, these three works (edited in four volumes) constitute the most important and comprehensive collection of the popular literature of a linguistic minority in Italy.

that Palumbo—but also what I call 'the philhellenic circle of Calimera'—was also influenced both by the nation-building process in which Greek folklorists such as Politis participated, and by the national logos of sovereignty and nation-building that was developing in Greece at the time thanks to influential scholars.

On the other shore of the sea, Greece had recently emerged as a nation-state, thanks to the support of Western European philhellenism. A strong admiration of the Greek classical aesthetic and philosophy had developed in France, Germany, and England in the nineteenth century, providing Greece with the ideological foundations of its raison d'être, as it were. Together with philology, historiography, and archaeology, Greek folklore contributed to constructing a linear and continuous timeline linking Modern to Ancient Greece, which would in turn prove the continuity of the 'Greek identity' in all its manifestations and expressions (see Herzfeld 1986). Language was soon elevated as the purest 'substance' of Greek identity, and a central concern of Greek folklore studies was the collection of 'monuments of the word' (MG: *mnimía logou*). Thanks to Politis, these came to mean traditional narrations, songs, proverbs, and customs, which "are transmitted only [by] word of mouth from parent to child, from old to young" (Politis 1871:vix, cited in Herzfeld 1986:100); crucially they were to prove, as it were, a "partial but unbroken continuation of an earlier life" (Politis 1909:6, cited in Herzfeld 1986:104).[19]

Not coincidentally, Palumbo defined his ambitious project as the collection of "Literary and popular Salentine-Greek monuments."[20] This reference highlights how he shared the romantic vision that fascinated philhellenists. Palumbo followed in the modus operandi of Greek folklorists, collecting folklore and 'monuments of the word' with the intention of building a body of evidence that would prove Griko's prestige. He similarly engaged in reestablishing a written tradition, having internalized the belief that for a language to be recognized as 'real' it needed to be written down: folklore and language were thus turned into proof of the link with Greece. The philhellenists' gaze upon Greece, however, also guided Palumbo in following Greek folklorists' aims. To prove Griko's noble origins and to give it more prestige, he tried to link it to a remote and glorious past. Evidence of this emerges in the lecture that Palumbo gave to the Parnassòs Literary Society in Athens in 1896. In his talk, entitled *Le colonie Greco-salentine* (The Salentine-

---

[19]   See Herzfeld 1986 for an analysis of the establishment and history of Modern Greek folklore; see also his reference to 'ethnoarcheology' and 'verbal archeology.' The inscribed orality of the peasantry was conceptualized as a nonmaterial artifact, which in turn points to the archaeological nature of folklore studies (Herzfeld 1986:100).

[20]   "Monumenti greco-salentini letterari e popolari," from the preface to *Canti Grecanici di Corigliano d'Otranto*, edited by the local Griko scholar, Salvatore Sicuro (1978). The phrase 'the monument of the word' is attributed to the German philosopher Johann Gottfried von Herder (see Herzfeld 1986:10–11).

Greek Colonies), he refers to the origins of the language and its people, arguing for the presence in Southern Italy of "traces of Italic Hellenism, or of Byzantium; in some places one can find both together and in abundance" (in Stomeo 1958:59). He mentions a number of Byzantine migrations from various places occurring at different times, and suggests that they might have found in Salento the remains of Magna Graecia populations. He then proudly refers to Salentine-Greek as "the living monument of the ancient Hellenism of Southern Italy."

Palumbo's words attempt to defend the noble origins of Griko, tracing them back to Hellenism. Accordingly, Griko not only was not a 'bastard language' but ideologically became about the "extreme survival of the Greek/classical civilization, rendering the myth of Hellenism alive and eternal" (The Lecce Group, 1979:358). He concluded his talk by asking "mother Greece" to help him establish a school in Calimera in order to keep Griko alive. He also reassured the audience that Italy would not have any objections, as the Salentine Greek colony would render "mother Italy" even more beautiful (in Stomeo 1958:84).[21] Italy had recently emerged as a nation-state, and certainly the Italian language—as well as the social—question was in its early stages. Palumbo's double reference to mothers Greece and Italy also demonstrates how he skillfully moved between a Greek and Italian folklore modus operandi. Italian folklorists, in fact, emphasized Italy's local and regional character, whereas Greek folklorists engaged in incorporating local differences in the discourse of national homogeneity (Herzfeld 2003:287). At the same time, Palumbo deliberately sees Greece as the 'agent of recognition' of Griko's deserved prestige, and equally as an agent of support to avoid the danger that the language would ultimately be abandoned through the Italian post-unification process.

Yet in his ideological representation, Palumbo selectively ignores the linguistic complexities that had historically affected Griko, as well as the social complexities—past and present—affecting the community. He makes no mention of Griko's hybrid character—of the already widespread influence of Salentine on Griko. What is at play here is the semiotic process of 'erasure':

> the process in which ideology, in simplifying the field of linguistic practices, renders some persons or activities or sociolinguistic phenomena invisible ... elements that do not fit its interpretive structure—that cannot be seen to fit—must either be ignored or be transformed.
>
> Irvine and Gal 1995:974

---

[21] When Palumbo approached the Greek Ministry of Foreign Affairs in 1896 to find support for his Greek school of Calimera his aim was to receive 'help' from Greece to preserve the variety of Greek spoken in Salento. He saw the school institution as the only locus which could give life to the languishing Hellenism of Terra d'Otranto (Stomeo 1958).

This semiotic and equally ideological process becomes even more evident when one closely examines one of his notebooks, the 'Collection of Salentine-Greek Poems of Corigliano d'Otranto' (*Raccolta di poesie greche di Corigliano d'Otranto*). In reality these were not directly collected by Palumbo; as he clarifies in a footnote, he copied them from a notebook by someone identified simply as Mr. Fiorentino, a notebook that N. Marti gave Palumbo. This collection includes eight religious poems, forty love poems, and twenty-two funerary songs. Salvatore Sicuro (1922–2014), another distinguished Griko scholar from Martano, edited this notebook, which was published relatively recently (1978); in his introduction, he explains his editorial decision to "bring back the text to the local form commonly understood by Griko-speakers" (Sicuro 1978:12). He writes,

> Palumbo, being concerned by the idea to embellish the text, had purified it from phonetic characteristics specific of Corigliano in order to render it an ideal Salentine Greek, valid for the entire Grecìa, and he had introduced, or transcribed from the manuscript he received by Mr. Fiorentino, some variants which are not attested in Corigliano, nor in any other Griko-speaking village of Salento.
>
> Sicuro 1978:11

What Sicuro says here refers to the introduction of MG words into Griko. He also notes that only the section of the collection dedicated to love poems represents an oral heritage, one shared by the rest of the villages of GS. He argues that, in light of their linguistic and stylistic characteristics, the first and particularly the third section, dedicated to "funerary songs," should be ascribed to the same author and, crucially, to someone familiar with classical studies. In particular, funerary songs included in this collection distinguish themselves "for a great purity of the language. The assimilation of terms foreign to Griko appears to be almost intentionally avoided" (Sicuro 1978:18). This intentional 'erasure' of the linguistic influence of Salentine on Griko—a practice that other *cultori del griko* were also to follow—resembles what had recently happened in Greece; there *katharévousa* was crafted as the national language, and, in response to philhellenic ideals, the morphology of ancient Greek was adopted, and it was purified of foreign loanwords (mainly Turkish, but also of Italian, Slavic, and Albanian origin). This was ideology in action.[22]

---

[22]   The notebook of 484 pages is entitled "Collection of Salentine-Greek and Latin Popular Songs of the Salentine-Greek Colony Compiled by VDP" (*Raccolta di canti popolari greco-salentini e latini della colonia greco-salentina fatta da VDP*). Sicuro (1978) writes, "The presence of common characteristics in this section of the collections of songs from Corigliano, the limited infiltration of

This linguistic type of erasure is by its very nature also an erasure of the historical and social 'hybridity' of Griko and its community. The extensive Greek-Italo-Romance symbiosis and linguistic exchanges also meant that Griko cultural identity could not/cannot be compartmentalized and totally differentiated from the surrounding Salentine-speaking area, much as the Greek linguistic and cultural 'flavor' cannot be denied to the surrounding areas, even if over time they did not retain Griko. We see how, on the one hand, Hellenism is selectively highlighted from the available temporal repertoire; on the other hand, the linguistic, social, and cultural specificities of Griko that do not fit into this language ideology are selectively 'ignored or transformed.' The legacy of Palumbo was to live with the philhellenic circle of Calimera.

The Legacy of Palumbo: The Philhellenic Circle of Calimera

Various intellectuals from Calimera gathered around Palumbo to continue his mission. As was true of Palumbo, they were from Calimera, but were not 'local' scholars. They were educated in the most active centers of Italian culture at the end of the nineteenth century, centers such as Florence, Rome, and Naples. The most well-known among them are Giuseppe Gabrieli (1872–1942), brothers Pasquale (d. 1925) and Antonio Lefons (1882–1952), and Brizio de Sanctis (1863–1951).

Giuseppe Gabrieli attended the seminary of Lecce and Otranto; he then moved to Naples to study Oriental languages and civilizations, and then to Florence, where he graduated. He moved to Rome in 1902, where he worked first as librarian of the Royal Academy of the Lincei, and from 1915 at the University of Rome, teaching Arabic language and literature. He published several articles about Palumbo and Grecìa Salentina, mainly in scholarly journals dedicated to Byzantine and Oriental studies. Brizio de Sanctis contributed a biography of Gabrieli in which he stressed that Gabrieli "illustrated the traditions, customs, voices and soul of the past, and by now poor and small but still singing, Greek intellectual heritage" (cited in Aprile 1972:378). Brizio de Sanctis attended the seminary of Otranto and Lecce; he graduated in philosophy and letters from the University of Naples in 1888, and subsequently worked as a teacher and schoolmaster in Lecce.

Of the 'philhellenic circle of Calimera,' only Antonio and his brother Pasquale Lefons came from a humble family; however, thanks to their generous and educated uncle, Don Vito Lefons, a priest, they managed to get a formal

---

terms from the romance dialect, the presence of terms not used by the people (such as "vìvlio," "luturghìa," "anàstiema," "dromos," etc.)[,] the use of specific constructs (such as, for instance, the genitive appearing before the nominative) leads me to attribute these songs to the same author and to someone familiar with classic studies" (Sicuro 1978:19).

education. Antonio studied in Florence, where he spent his life working as a lawyer of the Florence Forum; an author of poems in Griko, he returned to Calimera in the last years of his life. His brother Pasquale, by contrast, studied philology in Florence under the guidance of Hellenists such as Domenico Comparetti. He was a poet, polyglot, and translator; he continued to collect linguistic data and traditions of Calimera, as well as of its contacts with Athens, where in 1912 he gave a talk about Griko at an Orientalist congress.[23]

The intellectuals of the 'philhellenic circle of Calimera' inspired by Palumbo both engaged in the collection of folklore and contributed to the literary repertoire in Griko with their own productions as poets. Following his path, they faithfully reproduced his ideological orientation, the same tropes and references to Hellenism, and a sort of idealization of the relationship to Greece. Their writings are, indeed, permeated by a romantic connection to Greece—ancient and modern—which becomes a spiritual connection. We hear it in their writing; referring to Palumbo, Stomeo—another philhellenist from Martano—writes, "He felt himself spiritually reunited with *our noble ancestors* and felt recalled with invincible impetus toward the soil of neighboring Greece, from a deep nostalgic feeling of brotherhood" (Stomeo 1971:xxi, my emphasis). Palumbo and his disciples perceived and depicted Greece as a second motherland. This language ideology led to them promoting the Magna Graecia origins of the language—although, as paradoxical as it may seem, the same authors elsewhere historically sustain the language's Byzantine origins (The Lecce Group 1979:358).

While I was looking for more information about them in order to analyze their own contribution, I noticed not only how they kept affectionately citing each other, but also how they abundantly produced linguistic, philological, and literary contributions about Griko. I repeatedly encountered sentences like, "In the name of the old master, local Hellenists engaged in battles, published magazines, held demonstrations, gathered anthologies" (G. De Santis 1960, cited in Aprile 1972:73). In other words, they represented what one might call the first metalinguistic Griko community, and did so consciously. Responding to the 'moral panic' about Griko's imminent death, as it were, and following Palumbo, their aim was "to save, divulge, impart scientific and artistic dignity to the Salentine-Greek heritage of language, poetry and folklore already in the process of rapid decline" (F. Gabrieli 1957, cited in Aprile 1972:77).[24]

---

[23]   The genealogy of philhellenic intellectuals from Calimera can be traced even further back to Don Vito Lefons (born 1834), a priest who had guided Palumbo himself, and Brizio de Sanctis and the Lefons brothers.

[24]   From *Calimera e i suoi Traudia*, an anthology edited by Giannino Aprile and published in 1972. These are the words of Gino De Santis and of Francesco Gabrieli, respectively the sons of Brizio

Through this ideological orientation and their very activities, the 'philhellenic circle of Calimera' enacted 'a performative contradiction' (see Tsitsipis 1998, who follows Eagleton 1991): their scholarly arguments and proposals explicitly contradicted the daily lives of Griko speakers at large. These intellectuals belonged to the well-educated class; most of them spoke Italian and MG—at least—and participated in the thriving national and transnational intellectual philhellenic community. The issue, however, is not only that they did not live in Calimera, that they did not use Griko daily, or that they wrote more *about* Griko than *in* Griko, as we have seen. Rather, the issue is that what they said contradicted the very genre through which they said it; they did so through philological and linguistic contributions while urging the bearers of the language—who still used the language, and who belonged to a lower social class—"to keep jealously these historical-linguistic monuments" (Giuseppe Gabrieli, cited in Stomeo 1972:xix). Thus, they also enacted a performative contradiction through their rhetoric, which strived to carve out a space for Griko in the glorious Hellenic past. Their rhetoric contrasted strongly with their experience: it had no currency for the majority of them, nor did it imply any moral or material reward. It is indeed not coincidental that the reevaluation of Griko originated mainly from the educated strata of the population, who 'upgraded' the language as a form of cultural capital, while the language's real bearers would instead discard it to climb the social ladder. Interestingly, their writings not only celebrate the glorious Hellenic past, but are also permeated by an idyllic representation of the local past. These intellectuals' own fear of the destabilizing effects that the post-unification process would cause to the social order in fact led them to project a romanticized image of a 'pure' local past in contrast with what they perceived as a 'hybrid' present. This image, which permeates their writings, equally ignored the social complexities (both past and contemporary) in the environment, as well as the real preoccupations of Griko speakers. The failure of the 'revival,' I argue, lies in this 'exclusionary' logic in essentializing blended subjectivities. Through this ideological but also interest-laden orientation, the intellectuals of the 'philhellenic circle of Calimera' simplified the past and ignored the then present of the Griko speakers themselves.

The first ideological revival did not reach the 'people,' ultimately because it was not directed to them. It therefore could not affect their linguistic practice and, indeed, it did not prevent the subsequent shift to Salentine and Italian. What delayed the shift was the isolation in which the majority of the 'bearers of the language' kept living, and this was linked to the underdevelopment of

---

and Giuseppe (introduced above). Digging into their own biographies, I also noticed that this philhellenic tradition was continued by a second generation related to the first, offering a kind of 'genealogy' of local philhellenism.

agriculture that persisted until the agrarian reforms of 1950–1951. Until then, by and large peasant 'sharecroppers' (*contadini*), 'tenant farmers' (*coloni*), and 'shepherds' (*pastori*), they continued to live a virtually self-sufficient existence in a semi-feudalistic regime, growing the 'huge properties' (*masserie*) of the 'landlord' (*massaro*) scattered around the territory, or his *fazzoletti di terra* (handkerchiefs of land), situated closer to inhabited centers.

The distance between this intellectual discourse and the preoccupation of the lower strata of the population continued indeed to grow in the twenty-first century, as Griko speakers were more directly affected by the changing social environment, and were faced with uncertainties and struggles. This is what I call 'language displacement'—an existential displacement that led them to stop transmitting Griko to their own children. I turn to discuss this in the next chapter.

2

"The World Changed"

The Language Shift Away from Griko

WHEN I began to research the process of language shift in my home village of Zollino and asked my elderly friends to recount what led them to shift away from Griko, with few variations they responded, "*O kosmo kàngesce!*"—"The world changed." Antimino (born in 1927) more reflexively preceded his "*O kosmo kàngesce*" with "*Pos enna po?*"—"How shall I say?" My friend and life teacher Splendora (1922–2015) prefaced her "*O kosmo kàngesce*" more inquisitively with "*Ti teli na sceri?*"—"What do you want to know?" My parents' neighbor 'Ndata (born in 1927) added her usual term of endearment—"my child"—to sweeten her tone: "*O kosmo kàngesce, kiaterèddhamu.*" Not surprisingly, my elderly friends from Sternatia, whom I had met more recently, and with whom I had built a personal relationship over time, almost apologetically stumbled over themselves in replying, "*Kàngetse o cerò, kàngetse o kosmo ce tikanè*" (Griko, Sternatia)—"The times changed, the world and everything with it." My Griko mother-tongue friends used these formulaic expressions as if they were self-explanatory and not much else needed to be added. But of course they had a lot to add, and gradually they did, glad to have found in me an attentive ear.

In the previous chapter we saw how the first ideological revival of Griko promoted by what I describe as the 'philhellenic circle of Calimera' did not reach Griko speakers at large. The social transformations of the post-unification process that these intellectuals feared in fact had little impact on the lived reality of the 'bearers of the language.' who lived in closed communities immersed in a rural society. It is precisely this reality and their therefore limited, albeit steadily growing, contacts with the surrounding Salentine-speaking environment that is considered a major reason for the preservation of Griko ... at least until "the world changed."[1] Elderly people do refer to 'change' in a rather systematic way when recollecting their past, and describe it as sudden, notwithstanding

---

[1] See Profili 1996. For the case of Calabrian Greek, see Petropoulou 1995; Profili 1996; Katsoyannou 1995. They argue that the isolation of the Grecanico-speaking villages was pivotal in the

it involved a progressive abandonment of agriculture and access to wage labor, often supplemented by farming. Change can be dressed up and be referred to as 'progress'; it almost takes on an anthropomorphic dimension, in expressions such as 'when progress arrived,' or 'when progress started accelerating.'[2]

The post-WWII period was indeed a time of profound socioeconomic changes, which affected Italy and the Italian linguistic landscape more broadly; until then, Italians at large continued to speak their local vernaculars, and languages as the rhetoric and policies of the Fascist period that aimed to eradicate 'dialects' and minority languages had failed to provide incentives to use Italian in daily life.[3] Language shift away from Griko is certainly embedded in this broader national transformation, but the story of Griko is not a 'typical case' of language contact/domination/shift to the national language. To fully appreciate this process, I necessarily pay attention to the multiform ways in which dynamics at the national level interacted with, and played out within, the local languagescape, which includes Salentine.

Until fairly recently, approaches to language shifts tended to attribute the phenomenon to macrosociological factors linked to modernization, such as economic development, urbanization, migration, etc., but it would be reductionist to consider them as mechanically *determining* the shift. Language shift is moreover a process that is not tidily periodized, nor can I explain it by simply narrowly identifying its causes, for there are many of them. So, drawing on personal accounts of the history of language use that I collected from my elderly friends in Zollino and Sternatia, I focus instead on their own interpretations of these processes—of the 'changing world'—and analyze how these recursively affected their language ideologies and use, leading them to stop transmitting Griko to the next generation.[4] As Don Kulick (1992:9) argues, "the study of language shift becomes the study of a people's conceptions of themselves in relation to one another and to their changing social world, and of how these conceptions are encoded by and mediated through language."

---

preservation of the language. Likewise, natural disasters caused the depopulation of these villages and the dispersion of Greko speakers, contributing to the rapid decline of the language.

[2] Until fairly recently the economy of the province of Lecce depended more or less directly on the size of the harvest of olives, tobacco, tomatoes, etc. Moreover, the existence of numerous huge landed estates (*masserie*) was one of the main reasons for the underdevelopment of agriculture that persisted into the 1960s.

[3] According to an approximate estimate (De Mauro 1970), at the end of WWII, 69 percent of Italians were in a state of diglossia, alternating between using their local Romance variety and the national language for diverse purposes and with different people: 13 percent were monolingual in the Romance variety, and 18 percent were monolingual in Italian.

[4] For studies that apply a language ideology approach to language shift see Gal 1978; Jaffe 1999; Kulick 1992; and Woolard 1989, among others. I also collected elderly people's accounts of their history of language use in Martano and Corigliano, but those accounts are not included here.

Talking About the Past

Identifying elderly Griko speakers in Sternatia who could help me with my research was a rather straightforward task. As my friend Gianni De Santis (1957–2015) bluntly told me, "You just need to go to the main square and you will find them sitting and chatting in Griko." I was aware of this; it is common knowledge locally that Sternatia has the largest number of Griko speakers. This was the last village to shift away from Griko, and there is general agreement that the 'turning point' could be located exactly in 1950: children born after that date were taught Salentine and not Griko at home.[5] "Why don't you go to Chora-Ma on Monday nights? You will find the most talkative of them attending Modern Greek classes," Gianni added. I followed his advice, and I particularly bonded with three of them: Cosimino (born in 1946), Gaetano (born in 1947)—whom you met in Chapter 1—and Uccio (born in 1942), three retired Griko mother-tongue speakers who indeed were eager to talk to me. Their life paths are rather similar to each other, and they all share crucial life experiences, such as working in the fields at an early age, migrating, and then moving back to Sternatia once they found a 'stable job,' after which they got married. What they ultimately share is the memory of *that* past whose language of expression was Griko.

One Monday I had asked them to meet at Chora-Ma before the MG class; the following "talk about the past"—as they themselves put it—highlights the multistranded processes embedded in the shift away from Griko. In the following segment, Uccio offers his own perspective on the process that led to the language shift.

Uccio:

Ivò leo ka o Griko atti' chora, attin Grecìa ichàti motti èstase i televisiùna jatì iche kane tseno, cioè armammènu ka echi artommèni si' chora, sia jinèke sia antròpi. Èrkotte merkanti, per esempio, ka pulùne ce 'e'sozzi milìsi pleo' is Grika kundu mia' forà. Cino 'e' se kapièi, o addho manku se kapièi. Poi su fènete fiakko motte ena 'e' to tseri na milìsi is Grika, jatì lei tuo 'e' me kapièi arà "ti tèlune na pune atse mena? Lei kakà atse mena, lei kakò," ce allora ... Ti tsero? O motte pai so merkato, so panìri leme itu, sa panìria, cino ka pulì 'e' milì is Grika! Cino apù de koste 'e' milì is Grika. Jatì mia forà, motte èrkotto cini ku pulùane rucha, o pulùane fruttu, motte stàzzane si' chora lèane: "Maledetti! Stu paese cu doi lingue!"

---

5   Within the general tendency to abandon Griko, there is indeed a variation internal to the Griko-speaking villages, although it is not critical. Between the villages of Zollino and Sternatia—located merely one kilometer away from each other—there is indeed about a ten-year disparity in the general trend to stop transmitting Griko to children as their mother tongue.

Cosimino:

"Jeno me diu glosse" (Griko)

Uccio:

Cu doi lingue (Salentine) lèane perché no no, 'e' lèane "me diu glosse". Lèane per esempiu: "Vàle-tu pleon alìo, vàle-tu pleon alìo"; allora cino ìkue "Vàle-tu pleon alìo, vàle-tu pleon alìo" ce 'e' kàpiegge però intùegge, èkane tin intu- iziùna ce ele "Tèlune na me piàkune ja fessa?"

Su fènete puru fiakko motte ena 'e' se kapièi na milìsi griko, ka pistèane ti lei, isù macari 'e' lei tìpoti atse kakò.

Uccio:

I'd say that Griko from Sternatia, from Grecìa, disappeared when the TV appeared because some foreigners married and moved to Sternatia, both men and women. Many tradespeople would come, for instance, who would sell, and it wasn't plausible to speak Griko anymore as it had been once. That person doesn't understand it, neither does the other. It seems bad to speak Griko when someone doesn't speak it. Because he would think, "What are they saying about me? They are saying some- thing bad about me," and so ... Or, for example, when you go to the market and the seller doesn't speak Griko! Neither does the seller next to him, because once upon a time when those who sold clothes or fruits came to Sternatia, they would say, "Damn them: this village with two languages!"

Cosimino:

"People with two languages" (Griko)

Uccio:

"*Cu doi lingue*" [Salentine] they'd say, no, no, they wouldn't say "*me diu glosse*". They [Griko speakers] would say "Give him less, give him less," so he would hear [in Griko] "*vàle-tu pleon allo vàle-tu pleon alìo,*" and he wouldn't understand, but he could guess and think, "Do they want to fool me?" It seems bad to speak Griko when someone doesn't understand you because they'd doubt, and maybe you are not saying anything bad.

Uccio begins his account by referring to broader macro-changes experienced through time, such as the advent of television. This was indeed more effective in spreading Italian than any language planning, but it only became truly accessible to locals in the 1960s. Crucially, he also refers to the dynamics of the local languagescape and mentions that Griko 'disappeared' (literally, 'went lost') in Sternatia and the rest of the villages because of intermarriage and the presence of *tseni*—both men and women coming from non–Griko-speaking villages. Indeed, by this point Salentine had slowly and with varying degrees of competence come to be part of the linguistic repertoire of the majority of Griko speakers. Increased mobility further favored trade and intermarriage between villages; thus, occasions to speak Salentine continued to increase, as did expectations of linguistic adaptation to it. Uccio in fact refers to the generalized impossibility of speaking Griko as they did "in the old days"—"*kundu mia forà*"—as merchants from neighboring monolingual Salentine-speaking villages would arrive in the village to sell their products. This is when Cosimino intervenes, commenting in Griko that Griko speakers were called "people with two languages." Uccio, equally promptly, repeats the expression, but in Salentine—"*gente cu doi lingue*"—insisting that it was in fact uttered by non-Griko speakers. The expression clearly describes the emerging power struggle enacted between Griko/Salentine bilinguals and Salentine speakers that started to play out in these instances. In a situation in which bilingualism is unidirectional—that is, when only one group is competent in the other's language—bilinguals have access to an additional code.

Their bilingualism thus lent them a degree of control: Uccio goes on to explain that in the typical process of market negotiation, in which Griko speakers were the sellers, in some cases they would use the language to agree among themselves and 'trick' the non–Griko-speaking buyer into paying the amount agreed, but for a smaller quantity of fruit, for example. Here we see the violation of the expected practice of speaking Salentine—the unmarked code—with unknown and known outsiders. In the market situation that Uccio describes, what we see at play is the practice of 'cryptolalia'—from the Ancient Greek κρυπτός (hidden, secret)—and from the Greek λαλέω (to talk, to utter words). Cryptolalia refers to the use of a language as a 'secret code' when speakers do not want to be understood; this function is indeed common in many situations of language shift, and in the case of Griko it intensified in the post-WWII period. Speaking Griko as a 'secret language' not only was an expression of social cohesion, but also an 'interested' practice at the expense of who did not.[6]

---

[6]   See Petropoulou 1995 for the case of Grecanico; Mertz 1989 for Scottish Gaelic speakers; Jaffe 1999 for Corsican; Dorian 1986 for East Sutherland Gaelic; Shandler 2006 for Yiddish, to mention only a few.

However, Uccio adds that it felt wrong, impolite ("*Su fènete fiakko*", fiakko curiously being a borrowing from Salentine) to speak Griko in these instances; he comments that this might have led non-Griko speakers to believe that something negative was being said about them—even when that was not the case—eventually leading them to distrust Griko/Salentine bilinguals. Crucially, Uccio's use of constructed dialogue (*Ti tèlune na pune atse mena? Lei kakà atse mena, lei kakò*) reveals how considerations about the 'politeness' or 'rudeness' of language use were in fact largely circulated and, to varying degrees, internalized by Griko speakers. As Bakhtin argued, "Every word tastes of the contexts in which it has lived its socially-charged life" (1981:293). Uccio indeed blends his own voice with the voice of monolingual Salentine speakers; this points to issues of perceived responsibility and agency in mediating language shift. Interestingly, elderly speakers still diffuse and negotiate their own personal and group responsibility.

Figure 12. Antimino and I

The level of circulation and internalization of this moral imperative to speak Salentine is further illustrated by considering the following example offered by Antimo (born in 1923) from Zollino in an informal interview. Antimino, as everyone knows him, is a sweet man of gentle manners and a polite smile, best known as the singer of *I Passiùna tu Christù* (The Passion of the Christ), a traditional Easter performance. Following in the footsteps of his father and grandfather, he used to be the sacristan of the main church of the village. At the same time, he worked as a photographer; virtually every middle-aged man and woman in the village had in their homes the portraits he had taken of them as children, with his characteristic choice of background and posture. More often than not when entering his little *avlì* (courtyard) the door to his back garden is open, which means he is watering or taking care of his plants. I go to visit him as often as I can—never enough, he complains—and we chat in Griko, all the while sipping limoncello, regardless of the time of day (see Figure 12, above).

Atsìkkose o progresso na pai pano eccetera	Progress started and so on
ikùane 's emèna ka kùntone grika me sena, ce lèane	they would hear me talking to you in Griko and they would say
"Oh ce 'e 'kuntèi sekùndu s'èkame i mana-su?" per dire	"oh and [why] don't you speak like your mother made you," so to say
"na anoìsune i kristianì?" Anzi ndirittura ma' lèane	So that people can understand? On top of that, they would even tell us
"E' skostumatezza! mottâchi addhu ka en'anoùne na kuntèscete grika!"	"It is rude for you to speak Griko when there are people who don't understand it!"
Ce 'llora ivò kunta iu per dire mia forà ce kunta diu	And so I would speak like this [dialect] one time once and twice
e allora cerkèamu cerkèane o cerkèsciamo pos enna po?	and so we would try, they would try or we tried, how can I say?
Passos ena kunte dialetto sekùndu ìscere 'nsomma' ecco!	Each of us would speak dialect to the extent he was able
Ecco pos ene ka atsìkkose o griko na min kuntescettì pleo' ce afìsti.	So this is how Griko started not to be spoken anymore and was abandoned.
Ce arte 'nvece e' pregiao!	And now on the contrary it is precious
Pane in cerca nô mattèsune, pos enna po?	They go and try to learn it, how shall I say?

Antimino chronologically situates the shift in the period of the area's economic development. Interestingly, like Uccio above, he too uses constructed dialogue, introducing it through the quotative verb *lèane* ("they would say," past continuous third person plural) and an undefined agent 'they'; this is the key to this account, the voice that represents a particular interested position. He refers here to situations in which Salentine monolinguals would tell off Griko speakers for using Griko in front of them, as they could not understand it. When 'they' would hear Antimino speaking in Griko, 'they' would tell him to "talk like your mother made you." This expression is crucial here, for it is also used in Salentine (*parla comu te fice mammata*), and means to talk in a simple, unpretentious way. In this case, it indicates how speaking Griko was discriminated against on moral grounds. He then lifts the metalinguistic comment "it is rude for you (plural) to speak Griko when there is someone who doesn't understand it" out of the inter-actional setting, and by 'animating' this utterance he blends the voice with his own and makes it speak Griko, as it were.

This reveals once again the extent to which this negative perception of Griko was circulated and internalized within the Griko-speaking community. Interestingly, however, Antimino uses the markers *anzi* (on top of that) and '*ndirit-tura* (even) to signal a disassociation from the quoted voice. He ultimately does not take responsibility for the utterance by emphatically reconstructing the dialogue in an animated tone. In particular he stresses the word *scostumatezza* (rudeness) and utters it at a slower pace, mimicking the voice. This points to the dialectical struggle he personally went through, a struggle which was, however, collectively shared by Griko speakers, as Antimino's several pronoun and tense changes indi-cate; to describe the effort to shift to dialect, he uses the first-person singular pronoun *ivò*, and then vacillates between the first- and third-person plural past continuous (*cerkèamo, cerkèane*) and first-person plural past tense (*cerkèsciamo*). This is also emphasized by the utterance, "In short, each of us would speak dialect to the extent he was able," and suggests varying competence in Salantine. Antimino then shifts temporal domains, referring to the current prestige of knowing Griko. Thanks to the revival, he has indeed become a 'star of Griko' because of his perfor-mance of *The Passion of the Christ*. This evaluation renders even more sharply the contrast between the negative experience of speaking Griko at that time and the painful experience of abandoning it.

Uccio's and Antimino's examples, and more generally elderly speakers' recurrent use of constructed dialogue, together indicate how a plurality of voices, of speaking personalities, is always embedded in the dynamic of language ideologies' transformation. The label 'people with two tongues' even-tually evolved into the stereotype 'people with two tongues and two faces': the imagery of the snake with a forked tongue was in fact evoked by monolingual Salentine speakers, epitomizing the stigmatization of Griko speakers, who came to be considered as people who could not be trusted. The practice of cryptolalia certainly favored and reinforced stigmatization by non-Griko speakers, but it also depicted monolingual Salentine speakers' lack of 'power' due to their lack of access to Griko; they therefore felt under threat every time they heard Griko spoken, not just in situations of cryptolalia. Griko speakers, for their part, felt pressure to avoid the stigma of being thought of as untrustworthy, and this played an additional role in mediating the shift away from Griko. Focusing on the practice of cryptolalia and its wider implications we find that Griko speakers were faced with this moral evaluation of the use of Griko as something 'rude and impolite,' which circulated as a moral evaluation of the language itself: Griko becomes indexical of 'rudeness'—a marker of it, as it were—and this externally mediated language ideology contributed to unsettling Griko speakers, who grew to have mixed feelings about Griko. Caught in these local dynamics and immersed in the wider national context, over time Griko came to be internalized as something of which to be ashamed.

The Language of Shame

Uccio Costa (1933–2011) from Zollino gives a telling example of the troubled process Griko speakers went through. He did so during an informal interview on a cloudy November afternoon when I went to visit him at his house. Uccio was a Griko mother-tongue speaker who had left the village when he was twenty-three years old to migrate to southern Germany. After spending about fifteen years working there in various *fabbriche* (factories), Uccio and his wife returned to the village and he opened his own business selling gelato. He lost his wife when their two children were teenagers; his gaze indeed betrayed a touch of sadness. I have always known Uccio to be a man of few words—except when he spoke Griko! He was the father of my sister's best friend and a friend of my own father. Ever since he retired, you could find him each afternoon playing bocce in the village's dedicated area, paired with or playing against my father. Whoever lost the game paid for coffee for the winners! I liked visiting him when he carved wood into beautiful human and divine characters (see Figure 13).

Manu manu ka ìrtane i mèsce	When the teachers came
na mas insegnèsciane ce 'e' mas	to teach us and they couldn't understand us,
anoùane, inghìsamo nu mattèsome uttin	we had to learn the other
addhi glossa, 'o dialetto;	language. We learned dialect,
però kulusìsamo panta na kuntèsciume	but we always kept speaking it [Griko]
'o Griko ros 'in guerra ce puru dopu.	until the War, and afterward too.

Figure 13. Uccio carving

Uccio refers to the arrival in Zollino of nuns from other regions of Italy to run the newly established kindergarten—this was in 1932. Tellingly, he uses the first-person plural to depict a collective experience; his account indicates how the 'turning point' for the shift away from Griko in Zollino is linked to this specific 'trigger,' since children born around that year were, by and large, taught Salentine—note, not Italian—so that they could communicate with the nuns. 'Ndata offers a similar account, reiterating that she only spoke Griko until she went to school. "In school we were meant to speak Italian, but really we learned dialect [Salentine]," she insisted. It might seem ironic that the institution of school—the locus of legitimation of national language ideology par excellence—would instead 'teach' dialect. The situation needs to be read in light of the school system of the time, when teachers themselves were not necessarily very competent in standard Italian, and would often use dialect or a mixture of dialect and Italian in the classroom.[7]

This may seem even more ironic if we take into account that the language policies of the Fascist period had in fact aimed to eradicate 'dialects' and minority languages using public schools to promote and impart linguistic purism. On the one hand, the impact of the school system on language acquisition and use at this juncture should not be overestimated, as my elderly interlocutors had access to education only for a limited period of time; from their accounts it emerged that a large percentage of them did not finish primary school because their parents needed their help at home and in the fields. Uccio, for instance, attended school only for three years. On the other hand, even though the campaign of linguistic purism failed to teach them Italian, as it were, it succeeded in teaching students the 'inferiority' of their own vernacular and in creating and circulating what

---

[7]   See De Mauro and Lodi 1979; Montinaro 1994; Gruppo di Lecce 1979.

Bourdieu (1977b) calls 'misrecognition'; that is, the internalization of the (mis) belief in the superiority of one language over another.

Uccio:

Va bene ka tûpa pròi komu sia ka mas èkanne riprezzo komu sia ka erkamòsto en'iscèro attu statu (hesitation) arabu ka ìmosto a popolo ka 'e' mas karkulèi tispo ce dèsamo oli na mattèsume o dialetto, to italiano ce e' stammèni i ruvìna dikìmma ka i glossa is'alìu chronu leo 30, 40 chronu nde pleo' ka tossu i glossa chasi kompletamente en'echi probbio i' Tsuddhìnu en'echi tipoti pleo'. Ripetèo komu sia ka asce ma mas èkanne, enna skusèsci puru, schifo usi usi glossa ce ene mia glossa ka esistèi asce chijae chronu! Echi jenommèna ricerke de? Ka daveru, ka ci sape tinòn arrikordèi! Ce is alìu chronu imì stasimòsto kapaci ka distruggèsciamo tikanène eh! Mena mu dispiacèi jatì ìane mia glossa de kiui ka ìmì scèramo però motta tin imilùamo ittin glossa quasi ka quasi ka mas èkanne vergogna, en'iscèro manku ti enna po.

Uccio:

To us this language we spoke, as I said earlier, it was as if it gave us disgust, as if we came, I don't even know, from the Arab countries, a people that no one cares about and we all started to learn dialect and Italian and this has been our disgrace, that this language in 30, 40 years—no more than that—the language has completely disappeared, there is nothing left of it anymore in Zollino. I repeat: to us it was as if it gave us—you have to forgive me—disgust, that language and it is a language of thousands of years. Research has been conducted on it, right? Really, who knows how far back it goes! And in just a few years we have been able to destroy everything! I feel sorry, as it was an additional language we knew, but when we spoke it this language almost made us feel shame, I don't even know how to say it.

Ethnographer:

Ce jatì vergogna?

Ethnographer:

Why shame?

Uccio:

*En'iscèro ivò, tòa ìu ìane
Ka ìchamo na mattèsume oli to italiano!*

Uccio:

I don't know, back then it was like that, that we all had to learn Italian!

In this segment, Uccio self-reflexively refers to the lack of attention paid to Griko speakers at the time, comparing the discrimination they suffered in the past to the discrimination suffered by today's 'others'; he identifies them here with migrants who speak Arabic, although he is referring more broadly to the current phenomenon of migration to Italy and Europe as it emerged in other conversations. Uccio seems to imply that Griko speakers started learning dialect and Italian in order to avoid being discriminated against on linguistic grounds. His struggle to make sense of what happened is apparent, for he speaks nervously, playing with a pen throughout our conversation. He then rather bluntly states that learning dialect and then Italian has been a disgrace, and he regrets that in the timeframe of thirty or forty years Griko has disappeared.

He continues his reflection, remembering how Griko speakers felt about Griko, stating that they felt almost (note the repetition of "almost") ashamed of speaking it at that juncture; interestingly, in an escalation of derogatory 'feelings' attached to the use of Griko, 'disgust' becomes 'repulsion' and then 'shame'—*riprezzo, schifo, vergogna*.[8] These descriptions of emotions are important, as they show their centrality at times of perceived sudden changes. Although Uccio keeps using the first-person plural throughout the segment— thus giving his statements a collective agency—he also distances himself from them, apologizing for using the word *schifo* (repulsion), which suggests that he is the animator and not the author of the comment.

Uccio's account ultimately shows how the internalization of the national language's symbolic power prompted a process that, following Tsitsipis (1995, 1998), I call self-deprecation.[9] This led them to internalize these negative perceptions of Griko, which contributed to the already widespread and widely circulated belief that Griko was a 'bastard language'—a corrupted language that included both Greek and Salentine, as we have seen. Uccio then shifts the temporal register and points out that Griko is a language that had been spoken for millennia, one that studies have been written about; this comment shows the effects of the current language revival on self-awareness and understanding— similar to Antimino's comment above about Griko's current prestige—through which it has become a 'language of pride.' Uccio then concludes by taking collective responsibility for managing to destroy 'everything,' and adds that he feels sorry about it, since Griko was an additional resource.

To my question regarding why they felt 'shame' back then, his reply conveys lack of agency: "What do I know?" He continues, "Back then it was like that. We had to learn Italian," ascribing the shift to a fatalistic turn of events. Uccio seems to acknowledge, on the one hand, the internalization of the dominant

---

[8] These terms are Italian loanwords; note that *riprezzo* is the Romance-variety equivalent of the Italian *ribrezzo*; *vergogna* and *schifo* are also used in Salentine.

[9] Tsitsipis first introduced self-deprecation in 1995, building on Hamp (1978) and further developing his notion.

language ideology, implying that they had to speak Italian to be recognized as Italians, "as if this Griko" prevented them from being ascribed a full 'Italianness.' On the other hand, the ironic tone of the rhetorical question seems to contrast this. This vacillation indicates how Griko speakers are still self-reflexively negotiating their own responsibility for Griko's (mis)fortune. Shifting languages and stopping communicating in Griko therefore entailed a troubled decision, while the clash between 'the known past' and the 'changing world' affected Griko-speakers' ideas and feelings about their languages. What is interesting in the case at hand is that this subtle work of 'symbolic domination' (Bourdieu 1991:51) of the national language paradoxically resulted in the perception of Salentine as a resource to get to Italian.

"When Everything Started Changing": Salentine as 'Conduit'

Uccia from Sternatia is a beautiful woman in her late eighties, the sister of Cesarino De Santis (better known by his nickname Batti), who long loved and fought for the preservation of Griko. To improve my Griko, I spent several summer nights with her, her husband Grazio, and a few of their neighbors, sitting in front of the doorstep of their home. Uccia and Grazio welcomed me to their home on various occasions to help me with my research (see Figure 14).

Figure 14. Uccia

Uccia: Until 1950, when my first child was born, it was just normal to teach Griko to children. Twelve years later I had my second child. Well! By that time, people had started abandoning Griko in Sternatia; in the other villages, Griko had already been abandoned. In the previous three or four years all children had been speaking dialect [Salentine]. I said, "What shall we do with our child now? And when he goes to kindergarten and he wants to go to the toilet, how will he be able to say it if he doesn't yet know the dialect?" Like the others in the village, we too decided all of a sudden to teach him dialect too."

Grazio (her husband, interjecting to correct her): Italian!

Uccia: Italian? And who knew Italian back then?

Grazio: Who knew it? Come on, dialect is a sort of Italian, isn't it?

Uccia: We taught him diale—(she hesitates) Italian.

Ethnographer: Dialect or Italian?

Uccia (looking at Grazio): If my husband wants to say Italian, I have to say Italian too, but it is not true. I have to say dialect, not Italian. What Italian did we know? We taught him dialect so that he could communicate with the other children when he would play, and when he would go to the kindergarten. And then he would learn Italian too. We were influenced.

Uccia's words reveal the troubling decision that faced Griko speakers when bringing up their own children "when everything started changing." Elderly speakers indeed often comment that they wanted to prevent their children from suffering the discrimination they had suffered for knowing 'only' Griko: this would render them too inadequate in 'a changed world.' Recurrent statements such as, "I do not want my children to suffer what I suffered" clearly point to the troubles they endured during this process, and their experience of Griko as a handicap (in school, while migrating, etc.). As often happens in the process of language shifts, such statements also show that parents believed that they had to 'choose' which language to transmit, that it was an either/ or decision.[10] What emerges from this vignette is that Uccia 'decided' to teach Salentine, the Romance variety, to her second child to facilitate his entry to

[10]   See Jaffe 1999; also Dorian 1981 for Gaelic and Kuter 1989 for Breton. Uccia from Sternatia made a compelling argument when she told me that her first child, whose mother tongue was Griko, had no problem learning Italian and was first in his class, as he learned it from the 'ground up';

kindergarten and then to school, while the mother tongue of their first child, born in 1950, was Griko. The fact that Grazio confronts her with the contention that they taught their child Italian is an example of the symbolic power of the national language, and of the confusion about the difference between Salentine and Italian. This is one of the many instances in which my interlocutors fought on this issue. When I asked them to which language they shifted, they would initially say Italian; someone would join the conversation and note that they did not know Italian, that they spoke dialect with 'some words' in Italian; someone else would reiterate that they spoke Italian, and so on, until agreement was eventually reached: "We changed the dialect a bit, and we spoke Italian," they concluded.

This last statement points to the relation between Italian and Salentine; linguist Oronzo Parlangeli (1953:37–38) argued at the time that, "If they speak Italian, it will be a strongly Romanized Italian in the more educated individuals and it will be Salentine with a weak Italian flavor in the less educated." Back then, Italian was not an available resource for Uccia and Grazio—or for the others; instead, Salentine came to be considered a resource—a conduit—to access Italian and the world of opportunities its knowledge promised. To be sure, the differences between Salentine and standard Italian are not insignificant; nevertheless, Griko speakers perceived the shift from the Romance variety to Italian as a movement along a linguistic continuum, in contrast to Salentine and Griko and Italian and Griko. The affinities between Italian and Salentine, whether merely perceived or real, ultimately led Griko speakers to consider Salentine 'more valuable' and perceived speaking it—or an 'Italianized' version of it—as a tool of social inclusion in itself, as the vignettes show.[11]

The primary effect of the national language ideology was in fact not only to demote Griko in relation to Italian, but also in relation to Salentine; the internalization of Italian as the 'language of the future,' therefore, unsettled once and for all the local languagescape, as well as the Griko-Salentine power balance. This had been rather stable, and language choice depended on

---

yet her second child, to whom she taught Salentine as a mother tongue, had more difficulty, as he would get confused between Italian and Salentine.

[11]   This brings us back to notions of 'purity' and 'hybridity,' which I discussed in the previous chapter in relation to the 'polluting' effect of the Romance variety on Griko. The same dynamic is at play when it comes to Italian, which becomes 'bastardized/hybrid' for the same reason. My elderly informants still get away with what they define as 'homemade Italian' (*Italiano fatto a casa*), using what they had available, as it were. See Jaffe (1999), who reports the same dynamic at play in the case of Corsican and Italian, where the boundaries between Corsican and Italian are fuzzy, and where speaking Italian meant liberally sprinkling in Corsican. See also Stacul 2001; Cavanaugh 2009.

the language of interlocutor, but in this phase it did not necessarily manifest a distinction in status. In this highly competitive "linguistic market," to use Bourdieu's (1977a:652) terminology, Griko had been devalued not only in relation to Italian but also to Salentine; the consequent difference in status between Griko and Salentine, and the resulting stigmatization of Griko therefore needs to be read as part of the larger picture of the emergence of the symbolic value of Italian.

Yet if we return to Uccia's vignette above, it becomes apparent that the 'decision' not to teach Griko to her second child was 'influenced' by the fact that Griko had been abandoned in the other Griko-speaking villages: "We decided all of a sudden to teach him dialect, like the others in the village." Uccia's neighbor Giglio (born in 1949) similarly emphasized that, "In the '50s the 'fashion' of Italian started; one family would *imitate* the other; it was as if everyone had come to the agreement to stop teaching Griko to their children" (my emphasis). We see here the strength of the hegemony of style (Bourdieu 1984), which led Griko speakers to adopt Italian, since knowing and speaking it was perceived as fashionable in line with the symbolic value that had come to be attached to it. What I want to stress is the notion of 'imitation,' which kept emerging in my informants' accounts. Gaetano noted,

> There was a period in which some families started sending their children to school to Lecce, and they realized the importance of Italian. Some of us who had migrated returned and had learned some Italian. So, the other families started *imitating* them and speaking Italian, well uh, or dialect with a few Italian words" (my emphasis).

In the quotations above, I used the verb "imitate" to translate, in the first example, the Salentine verb *secutare*, which literally means "to follow," and, in the second example, the Griko original *ikopièane*—itself based on the Romance and Italian *copiare*—which means "to imitate," "to mimic." These are the two verbs that recurred frequently in my ethnographic material. Imitation therefore becomes crucial not only in the process of language acquisition but also in language abandonment. The fact that Griko speakers started 'imitating' one another, the decision not to transmit Griko reveals the underlying belief that those who were 'going forward,' as my informants put it—those who were advancing, as it were—would switch to Salentine and Italian. In fact the Romance verb *secutare* (to follow) indicates a movement toward something; this 'something' is the perceived path to modernization.

The Impact of Migration

It was in the context of migration that the 'symbolic domination' of the national language worked at its best, and that my elderly Griko friends came to identify Italian as a tool to access 'a better life,' which they had long awaited. Italian therefore came to be perceived as indexical of progress, of what in studies of language shift has been called the 'prestige code' (Labov 1966), while in symbolic contrast to it Griko became indexical of the hardship of the past, an index of backwardness, of a life before prosperity, also effectively classifying its speakers as inadequate in a changed world. Indeed, my interlocutors identified migration as one of the main (if not the main) reasons for the abandonment of Griko. The extremely poor economic situation of Grecìa Salentina had obliged people to leave their homes in search of 'a better life,' as the locals say.

Migration flows to Northern Italy and abroad, together with the related notion of economic enhancement, had a crucial impact on the perception of Griko; both of these factors affected every village of Grecìa Salentina, and of Salento more broadly, intensifying in the mid-1950s. Although the migration patterns of the villages are rather heterogeneous, the main destinations abroad were Switzerland, Germany, and Belgium, all facilitated by bilateral agreements with Italy; within Italy the main destination was Milan. The length of the migration period varied between a few years and a maximum of three decades. Also fairly common was the pattern of seasonal migration, with some spending a number of months working abroad each year, mainly in Switzerland. At the opposite end of the spectrum were those migrants who had recently retired and returned 'home' to spend their 'old age' there.

My interlocutors consistently refer to the difficulty of communication they encountered when they migrated to the North or abroad in search of jobs. As Gaetano characteristically said, "We were used to speaking mainly Griko, and when we left and migrated we realized that Italian was more important, but we were not able to speak Italian. We wondered how we were supposed to speak now?" Mario (born in 1961) from Sternatia told me, "I could not understand why it was better to speak this way and not the other way. I felt I had one foot in the 'old world' and one in the 'modern world.'" Griko speakers were therefore caught in this transitional moment where contradictions and tensions between the past and present worldviews were encoded in tensions between specific languages. This is the tension that, according to Bakhtin (1981:291, 292) derives from heteroglossia:[12]

---

[12]   In order to describe the tension among languages and language ideologies experienced by speakers through the process of language shift, scholars have fruitfully applied Bakhtin's framework. See Tsitsipis 1998, Hill and Hill 1986, among others.

> The co-existence of socio-ideological contradictions between the present and the past, between differing epochs of the past, between different socio-ideological groups in the present, between tendencies, schools, circles and so forth. All the languages of heteroglossia ... are specific points of view on the world, forms for conceptualizing the world in words, specific worldviews, each characterized by its own objects, meanings, and values.

Heteroglossia—from the Greek *ètero* (other) and *glossa* (language/speech)—is therefore particularly apt to describe the local languagescape constituted by Griko, Salentine, and then Italian, and to highlight the struggle of 'voices'—the speaking consciousness (Bakhtin 1981)—embedded in the process of language shift. Such a coexistence of multiple linguistic varieties and the emerging tension among them engenders what I call 'language displacement': an experiential displacement encoded through language, which unsettled Griko speakers and led them through a complex process to evaluate and negotiate the meanings attached to each linguistic code, and to 'adapt' to them linguistically and existentially. Crucially, displacement refers not to substitution but instead captures the sense of confusion my interlocutors felt about when and why to use a given language. Semiotician Julia Kristeva (1980:27) has also stressed that in times of abrupt change, when identity is unstable, language is unstable too.

The following excerpt from Gaetano offers the most explicit discussion of how the sense of displacement experienced by Griko speakers at the time indeed transcended linguistic competencies. This led them to experience a complex mixture of feelings, which is not 'simply' related to the fact that they did not speak Italian well enough, but which became an 'experiential displacement': shifting away from Griko equally required a shift from a 'traditional' worldview to a 'modern' one.

1	*Ivò motte ìcha dekapènte chronu ìstigga già is Milana*	When I was 15 years old I was/ lived already in Milan
2	*kuindi is dekapènte chronu iane già lu sessantadue*	so when I was 15 years old it was already '62
3	*millenovecentosessantadue*	1962
4	*Ittù en'ene ka iche kaggiètsonta, ittù mesa mesa so paìsi*	Here nothing had changed here inside, inside in the village

5	*javènnane ta pròata, javènnane t' aleàte, tinà*	goats passed by, cows passed by
6	*izùamo ankora me ti ... mi zoì, jènato i zoì ka jènato panta.*	we still lived with life was as it had always been
7	*Isù ìgue (...) ìgue so pornò*	You would hear in the morning
8	*iche kammia strata asfaltata*	there were some paved streets
9	*allora ìgue tus tus trainu*	so you would hear the carts of
10	*t'ampària, plaplapla, te staffe ka staffilèane (...)*	the horses plaplapla the stirrups
11	*Motte èplonne ka so porno ìgue citta ampària*	When you were sleeping in the morning you would hear those horses
12	*probbio ìane mia musika mia*	it was really like music
13	*'na pramma òrio ka finka*	it was really nice and until
14	*chronu ampì poi arikordèome*	a few years back I remember
15	*motte èplonna si ciuriacì ce iche kanèna aghitòniso*	when I'd sleep on Sundays and there was some neighbor
16	*ka ankora iche to traino me to (.) me t'ampàri (.)*	who still had the cart with the horse.
17	*Motte jàvenne mu èrkatto stennù ola ta pràmata*	When it passed by, I'd remember all these things.
18	*tuso ampàri, cisi, cisi musika probbio atte staffe att'ampària*	that horse, that music really
19	*Allora ivò motta pirta is Milana*	So when I went to Milan
20	*àtsikkosa na torìso ka i annamurati*	I started seeing that partners
21	*ghènnane manechùddiattu*	went out on their own
22	*Eh, ma ittù pane manechùddiatu so cìnema*	But here they go on their own to the cinema
23	*guènnane manechùddiattu*	they went out on their own
24	*filèatto mesa si strata*	they kissed on the street

25	*Ce so cìnema 'mbratsònnato, na kapu de [kardu]*	And in the cinema they hugged each other, what the [hell]
26	*Itù manechuddi ittù?*	They live like this here?
27	*Allora me tus kumpàgnu dikummu*	So with my friends
28	*Ma imì motta jenomèsta mali*	But we when we get older
29	*motta èchume pedia imì*	when we have our own children
30	*Eh pos enna kàmome?*	Eh how shall we do it?
31	*Ma ta rotùamo is se ma stesso*	We asked ourselves
32	*Pos enna kàmome? Kundu mas kàmane se ma?*	What shall we do? Like it was done to us?
33	*Na mi tus kàmome nâggune antàma manechùddhiato*	Shall we forbid them to go out alone
34	*o kànome kundu ittù kundu kànnune is Milana?*	or shall we do like they do in Milan?
35	*En'itsèrame manku emì na dòkume mia risposta*	We didn't even know how to answer.

Gaetano's narrative starts with autobiographical references that provide information about the setting (Milan) and the time (1962) of his migration, but he soon shifts and provides a detailed image of village life back then (lines 4–18) showing involvement with his own memory. In 1962, nothing had changed in the village and 'life still was as it had always been,' Gaetano argues, suggesting a notion of time (up to then) devoid of radical changes. Here the use of the temporal adverb *'nkora* (still) allows Gaetano to convey a sense of opposition, anticipating that things did change drastically later on. He goes on to recall how, until a few years earlier, he used to be awakened by the sound of the horses passing by—when he 'still' (*'nkora*) had neighbors with horses—implying this later became unusual; the repetition of this temporal adverb (lines 6 and 16) further builds on the idea of a break from a continuous unchanged past. This sound, which he tries to mimic, this music, as he calls it, catalyzes a nostalgic flashback, and Gaetano "remembered all these things" and evaluates them in light of the present, in so doing dissipating the hardships of the past and portraying the past almost as desirable.

In line 19, Gaetano then takes up the initial theme about his years in Milan, and he stresses how couples would go out on their own, they would kiss on the street and hug in the cinema (i.e. not chaperoned by anyone as was the dominant custom in Southern Italy at the time). This unexpected turn of events gives way in line 26 to thoughts Gaetano reports as an internal dialogue. In line 25, we find a hint of an imprecation (*kapu de ...*). Although Gaetano omits the final part (*de kardu*)—roughly rendered in English as 'what the hell'—this hint effectively communicates his own surprise and a feeling of excitement (mixed with envy) at seeing these couples' behavior in public. This inner speech serves as an attention-getter that prepares the ground for what it is to follow. In line 27, Gaetano moves from his inner speech to including in his thoughts also his friends in Milan, who likewise moved there from the South of Italy. The open-ended problem-solving dialogue introduces the dilemma about how they will act with their own children: whether they will allow them to go out without being chaperoned (like in Milan) or not (like in Sternatia). The opposition between we/them becomes clear. In line 31, Gaetano breaks the constructed dialogue by saying, 'We asked ourselves.' The repetition of the same question, 'what shall we do?' in lines 30 and 32 intensifies their dilemma (line 35).

Thus in a very condensed space, Gaetano epitomizes the negotiation between a past and a modern worldview—and the struggle to adjust to a shifting chronotope. In the first part of the narrative, Gaetano describes village life before he moved to Milan; crucially, in light of the present, he portrays an image of the past free from ruptures/changes. In the second part of the narrative, he describes a mixed feeling of surprise/excitement about the 'different' way in which things were done in Milan. As Elinor Ochs (2004) argues, narratives of the open-ended dialogic problem-solving kind, such as Gaetano's here, encompass raising and responding to doubts, questions, speculations, challenges, and other evaluative stances. Through narrative, Gaetano brings into dialogic consciousness multiple temporalities and multiple perceptions of the self. Shifting throughout the narrative from autobiographical experiences to collective ones, he provides a moral evaluation of colliding views based on an ongoing dialogical negotiation and appropriation of different voices.

As in Gaetano's case, the experience of living in the North of Italy, and indeed abroad, exposed Griko speakers to a reality they perceived as drastically different from their own experiential reality. The temporal divide between 'the known past and place' and the 'changing world'—the clash between the agricultural and the urban environment—became apparent and unsettled them. This is a constitutive part of 'language displacement', which ultimately affected Griko speakers' ideas and feelings about their languages. My interlocutors constantly say that 'they did things differently there'; paraphrasing Hartley (1953), we could say that for them back then, "the future was a foreign country: they did things differently there." They felt displaced by different customs, which they perceived as 'modern' in comparison with their own. This ongoing comparison mediated a self-scrutiny and entailed a number of different emotional reactions, as well as moral evaluations; it entailed surprise and excitement about social and economic emancipation, but also uncertainty, discomfort, and disorientation about colliding values and goals, as we heard in Gaetano's words above.

The formulaic expression *O kosmo kàngesce* ('The world changed'), which elderly speakers use as self-explanatory, therefore refers not simply to the macro changes that followed WWII; rather, these different experiential environments mediated a troubled process of negotiation and self- and group-redefinition that came to be encoded through language. This became evident in another conversation with Uccio from Zollino, who reflected on this transitional moment, saying, "Until then we didn't even have anything to eat, we didn't have money; when we migrated we earned money, we saw how life was elsewhere." This is where I interjected with "*O kosmo kàngesce*"—"The world changed." But, crucially, this is where he replied, "*Si si kàngesce. Kangèsciamo imì. Imì kangèsciamo*"—"Yes, yes it changed. We changed, *we* changed" (emphasis in original).

As studies following a language ideological approach to language shift have shown, language use is indeed linked to the speaker's interpretations of macro-processes and language and social relations, and it becomes attuned to shifting group and world conceptions.[13] In other words, it is how Griko speakers interpreted "the changing world," how they negotiated and internalized it and eventually participated in it, that had an effect on language use. Elderly people still reflect on the implications of change—including its deriving economic enhancement—in light of the present, and still negotiate its meaning and their own personal and group responsibility in shifting away from Griko, but they also admit that change was then welcomed, longed for, and actively pursued. By the same token, the past, whose language of expression is Griko so to speak, may be portrayed by highlighting its hardship—as we heard Gaetano doing in the first chapter—and/or it may be nostalgically reevaluated in light of the present, as he does here, providing evidence of the cultural temporality of language I continue to analyze in the next chapters.

In analytical terms, I identify two language shifts, which concern three generations. Not surprisingly, these shifts are not clearcut, but overlap. The first generation shifted from Griko to Salentine; Griko stopped being transmitted to children as a mother tongue. This shift can be located approximately between the mid-1930s and the end of the 1940s. The Griko-Romance power balance

---

[13]   See Gal 1978, 1979; Woolard 1989; Mertz 1989; Kulick 1992; Hill 1993 among others.

shifted toward Salentine as the 'Italian' language ideology progressively penetrated everyday life. At this stage, however, Salentine became a tool for social inclusion, and was perceived as a 'conduit' to accessing Italian. Griko was still used as the language of intimacy within the household, as the solidarity code in intragroup communication, and for cryptolalic purposes.

The second generation shifted from Salentine to Italian; this process needs to be read in the larger scale of national dynamics, and in relation to the long war against 'dialects,' which used the school system as the means of eradicating them by prescribing and enforcing a form of Italian that had to differ as much as possible from the Romance varieties—what linguist Tulio de Mauro (1979:14) called "dialect-phobia." However, the impact of television in spreading Italian was tangible and more effective than any language planning ever could have been. Notably, Pasolini provocatively wrote in 1964, "Italian is finally born" (quoted in Tosi 2004: 278).[14] Although today the percentage of Italians who speak *only* local dialects is very limited and Italian is the undisputed national language of Italy, it would be incorrect to say that Italians speak only Italian (Berruto 1993). In fact, according to Grimes (1988, quoted in Tosi 2004: 259), Italian is the first language of only fifty percent of the country's population, and according to Lepschy (2002:44), Italy is largely a bilingual country.

Bearing this in mind, the distribution of linguistic resources across generations is as follows: the elderly generation is mostly bilingual, speaking Griko and Salentine along with varying degrees of competence in Italian; the young generation is bilingual, speaking Italian and dialect; and the 'in-between generation' is trilingual, speaking Griko, dialect, and Italian, with varying degrees of competence in Griko. In light of this discussion, it seems more appropriate to talk of 'one shift in two phases' in the case of Griko speakers: the conceptual and existential shift is to Italian, but it is mediated through Salentine. It might therefore be more productive to visualize this process not in terms of oppositions, but in terms of embeddedness within concentric circles, in which one finds Griko embedded in the larger circle of Salentine, which in turn is embedded in the larger circle of Italian. The borders of these circles are fading, a discussion I continue in the next section.

Families' Interactions and the Transmission of Griko

The fuzzy boundaries between codes are clearly demonstrated by the fact that, even within the same household, parents spoke to their eldest children in Griko,

---

[14] Pasolini referred to the spread of a particular type of Italian imposed by the media, commerce, and industry, which he defined as "technological": a language created by capitalism.

and in Salentine to those children who were born "when everything started changing." Indeed, although many of my interlocutors perceived and describe this shift away from Griko as sudden, Griko also continued to be transmitted during this transitional time.

Vincenzo (father)	*Pippi! Tela ittù na su po* (Griko)
	Pippi. Come here. I have to talk to you.
Pippi (eldest son)	*Mino 'na spirì tàta, ste ce èrkome* (Griko)
	Wait a second, Dad, I am coming.
	(Speaking to his younger brother in Salentine)
	Tocca vau, Nucita ca lu tata sta me chiama.
	I have to go, Niceta, Dad is calling me.
Vincenzo	*Nucita, veni cu te dicu puru a tie* (Salentine)
	Niceta, come. I have to talk to you too.

This is how my father, Niceta (1932–2014), recalls a typical conversation between his own father Vincenzo (born in 1901) and his elder brother Pippi (born in 1926). This practice was widespread among families and emerged dominantly from the interview data within households: parents would speak Griko among themselves, they would address their eldest children in Griko, and speak Salentine to those children who were born "when everything started changing": the eldest children would reply in Griko to their parents, but speak Salentine to their younger siblings, and so on. Language choice within the same conversation therefore depended on which child/sibling they were addressing. These intragroup interactions help us to understand how at this stage the transmission of Griko was still assured even as parents 'consciously' decided not to teach it as the mother tongue. In fact, language transmission and socialization go *beyond* parent-child interactions. Just as in the case of my own father, many of my interlocutors were exposed to Griko and learned it by hearing the interactions between their parents and older siblings, as well as interactions between their parents, and between their parents and their grandparents. My brother-in-law Salvatore (born in 1954) from Zollino remembers:

> My auntie, my father's sister, used to live with us and also my grandmother, and they would always speak Griko to each other. My mother and father would also speak it between them, and with my grandmother and auntie. So even if they did not speak it to us, how could we not learn it? Now it is difficult for us to speak it; I have forgotten it.

Moreover, it was common at this time for grandparents to care for their grandchildren when their own sons and daughters had migrated—as elsewhere in Southern Europe. This is important because even if Griko was not transmitted as a mother tongue, children would spend a considerable amount of time with the 'elderly,' and were exposed to it simply because it was the language of the household, of the family, of 'intimacy.' At least partially, Griko was therefore transmitted through this intrafamilial practice. This brings us back to the central role played by affect in language socialization and vice versa, and to the 'affective' function of Griko linked to the speakers' autobiographical memory.

This dynamic, moreover, bears crucial implications for the present and sheds light on the nonfulfillment of Morosi's prophecy about the 'death of Griko,' which I discussed in the previous chapter, and the fact that for more than one generation it has been argued that Griko is spoken by the 'elderly.' Elderly people—those born between the early 1930s and the late 1940s—today are both those who learned Griko as mother tongue and those who learned it through the intragroup practices described above. Those belonging to the 'in-between generation,' as I referred to it earlier, will soon be considered 'elderly' too. As is common in instances of language shift, the degree of competence among speakers varies, and likewise there is currently a high degree of heterogeneity in linguistic competence, to which I will return when discussing contemporary linguistic practice in Chapter 6.

Intragroup Cryptolalia

If the cryptolalic use of Griko—its use as a 'secret language'—allowed Griko speakers to carve out a space for themselves from which those who lacked this resource were excluded, this practice also enforced and reinforced stigmatization by non-Griko speakers, as we have seen. Crucially, however, at a more advanced stage of the shift, Griko was also used for cryptolalic purposes within the family, when parents did not wish to be understood by their children—I have personally experienced it, as my own parents often resorted to this practice. With respect to this, linguist Io Manolessou (2005:106–107) argues that,

> the presence of the Romance dialect has denied the dying Griko the main reason of resistance of all minority languages: communicative situations which require its use. ... In the case of S. Italy, the linguistic roles which confer high prestige are assumed by Italian, whereas the covert prestige belongs to the local Romance dialect, which is the main instrument of everyday communication and social integration. This

leaves no specific role for the Greek dialect to play, except in extreme situations of 'secret' communication.

Manolessou's analysis is in line with research on language shift, which has fruitfully referenced notions variously known as linguistic "prestige," dominance and power for the dominant/high code, and "covert prestige" (Labov 1966) and more often solidarity for the minority/low code. I suggest instead that those extreme situations of secret communication deserve attentive analysis, as they are themselves communicative situations in which the use of Griko is strategically 'exploited.' On one hand, this shows the limits of the intrinsic structuralist paradigm based on high/low, we/they, dominant/subordinate oppositions, which scholars have acknowledged (see Woolard 1999).

This is how my neighbor Giuseppe (born in 1948) from Zollino put it:

> I remember vividly my parents speaking Griko with one another or with my grandparents or uncles/aunties when 'we' young children were not supposed to understand. And yet, that was the moment in which we children would pay more attention to what was said: we would prick up our ears instinctively, and in most cases we would pick up one or two known words and guess the totality of the interaction.

This type of comment came up time and again in my ethnographic material. Indeed, Raffaele (born in 1963) from Zollino similarly recalled,

> When I overheard Griko being spoken by my parents, I knew that something important was going on, something I was not supposed to know ... and this is precisely when a child wants to find out! Sometimes I would get it wrong, but I envied them so much! And when I would get it right, they would be angry at me, but for some reason happy too.

The linguistic practice of cryptolalia is indeed constructed and mediated by a language ideology that sees Griko as an *additional resource* and a valuable asset. Griko is 'practical,' Griko speakers often say.[15] "These extreme situations of 'secret communications'" (Manolessou 2005:107) therefore represent the

---

[15]   My mother's brother Uccio, born in 1921, died fighting in WWII. In 1941, not long after he left home, he sent a letter to my grandmother in which he wrote: "*Manèddhamu, mu vàlane 'es katìne sta chèria ce sta pòja. Sto benissimo mamma.*" The contents of letters were being checked by the authorities before being delivered to the addressee; he therefore used Griko for cryptolalic purposes to say, "Mother, they chained my hands and feet," and then in Italian "I am very well, mother." The practice of cryptolalia is indeed still diffuse, and my informants resort to it in various contexts and for a variety of purposes, including gossiping.

speaker's response to both official language ideologies (Italian) and local pressures (Salentine), ultimately confronting heteroglossia.

As Hill (1993:69) rightly observes, the heteroglossia confronted by speakers is reflected in the ways that

> codes emerge and are reproduced (or not) through what speakers do as they create and deploy a set of interpretive and productive practices that are 'interested,' exploiting the available symbolic materials to try to create those conjunctions of forms and meaning that may be most advantageous.

I therefore suggest treating the practice of cryptolalia as a form of symbolic resistance to linguistic domination. Indeed, Griko speakers experienced self-deprecation, and had internalized the dominant language ideology that considers Griko as a 'handicap' in the changed world; they also experienced stigmatization by Salentine speakers and internalized the notion that using Griko was 'rude.' They had 'mixed feelings' about Griko. The use of 'cryptolalia' within the family, however, ensured the transmission of Griko—although at times only passively so—and, more to the point, it had the effect of reproducing the idea that knowing Griko was 'convenient/practical.' The current recourse to Griko, including by those with a limited command of the language, is an indicator of the internalization of a language ideology that considers Griko as a 'valuable resource' to be exploited when needed, in addition to indexing in-group intimacy (Pellegrino 2019).

Multiple Linguistic Repertoire

Ma, leo 'vò, jatì?	But I ask why?
E mànema ma milìsane grika	Our mothers spoke Griko to us and that
ka cini ìone e glòssama,	was our language,
oli iu milùsamo, ce màsamo o griko ...	we all spoke it, and we learned it.
depoi mas ènghise na milìsome	Then we had to learn to speak Salentine
o dialetto ja ta pedìa,	for our children's sake,
ka o griko 'en ìbbie pleo kalò ...	because Griko wasn't good anymore ...
ce màsamo o dialetto.	and we learned it.
Depoi irta' t'anitzia,	Then our grandchildren arrived,

ka milùne italiano,	who speak Italian
c' ènghise na màsome puru o	and we had to learn to speak
italiano.	Italian too.
Ma arte, leo evò,	But now, I say,
itta loja amerikana,	these American words,
pètemmu pròbbio,	tell me really,
ti katzo mas endiàzzutte?	what the hell do we need them for?
(Griko from Calimera)	(Mudanzia, from the comedy *Loja Americana* by Salvatore Tommasi)

The case at hand points to a complex linguistic repertoire, which is the outcome of the historical Griko-Romance bilingualism described in the previous chapter, and of the shift to Italian. This complex repertoire has been defined in different ways: *triglossia* without trilingualism (Profili 1985); bilingualism with diglossia with three codes involved (Ineschi 1983); some scholars have even called into question the very applicability of the term bilingualism and refer to "a complex situation of cohabitation of linguistic varieties" (Romano et al. 2002:76).[16] As Kathryn Woolard (1999) argues, scholars' approach to bilingualism and multi-lingualism has been influenced by postmodern trends, and has moved away from linguistic theoretical perspectives that, embedded in the monolingual Western intellectual tradition, understood bilingualism and multilingualism to be anomalous.

The case of the Griko-Salentine-Italian relationship contributes to this line of inquiry by showing how speakers, through an admittedly complex process, 'adapted' to different linguistic and existential codes, and how they evaluated and negotiated the meanings attached to them. The quotation above makes this point. These coexisting linguistic repertoires are indeed used by speakers to index multiple social identities in alternative terms, as the fluidity of the code boundaries and their manipulation attest. This confirms Bakhtin's argument that "languages do not *exclude* each other, but rather intersect with each other in many different ways" (Bakhtin 1981:291). As we will see in the chapters that follow, this intersection continues to have crucial implications, as languages remain indexical of specific worldviews, which are temporally anchored and emotionally charged.

---

16   The alternative uses of Italian and 'dialect' have been the topic of debate among linguists; Berruto (2005:205), for instance, distinguishes among social bilingualism, diglossia, dilalia, and bidialectism.

3

The Reappropriation of the Past

ONCE the specter of World War II had abated, and while Griko speakers were 'abandoning' Griko, a second generation of philhellenists recast Griko activism with renewed enthusiasm. Prof. Salvatore Sicuro (1922–2014),[1] from Martano, represented the living memory of postwar Griko activism, as he personally engaged with the cause of Griko throughout his life. He worked as a schoolteacher and was a well-known *cultore del griko* in the local scene and in Greece, where he was often invited to give talks on the topic of Griko at various universities, as well as in Cyprus. I knew him by name but had never met him in person, so I looked up his telephone number and called him. I told him briefly about my research, and we agreed to meet at his apartment in the center of Martano the following Thursday afternoon. I had immediately noticed that he addressed me in Italian using the formal form of address—a practice not necessarily followed locally even when 'strictly' required—but I did not make much of it; I expected that once we actually met he would revert to informal speech, particularly given the generation gap between us. I was wrong. When he opened the door, he welcome me in with a very polite "*Si accomodi, signorina*" (Italian)— "Please follow me, Miss"—he continued that practice over several months of weekly Thursday afternoon appointments, a practice that showed not only his politeness, but also the value that he kept attributing to Italian as the language of 'prestige'.

Entering his apartment, the smell of paper immediately yet gently overwhelmed me: books, encyclopedias, leaflets, magazines, newspapers, pictures. The windows in the living room were high and wide. Though it was still daytime, the shutters were half closed. Prof. Sicuro was a tiny man, very refined and extremely well educated; his Italian was almost old-fashioned, his Modern Greek polished, his Griko very measured. I had the pleasure of appreciating personally his immense knowledge and intellectual curiosity during those months; but he got to the heart of my questions on that first meeting.

---

[1]   The title 'Prof.' in this thesis refers to schoolteachers and reflects the local use of the term.

He began to share his memories: "I recall that after the war, my uncle, Prof. Stomeo from Martano, and Prof. Cotardo from Castrignano started to travel to Greece. Together with Giannino Aprile, they reestablished contacts with Greece and invited professors from the University of Athens and Salonika," he said adjusting his *coppula* ('flat hat'), which he never removed. He was the nephew of Prof. Paolo Stomeo (1909–1987) from Martano, another distinguished Griko scholar who likewise is remembered with pride among activists. They collaborated, giving classes at the University of Lecce in which they compared MG to Griko. "My uncle graduated in Classics from the University of Florence and collaborated with Rohlfs," Prof. Sicuro added with a hint of pride, "and Stomeo also founded the department of Modern Greek language and literature at the University of Lecce, where he was the chair of the department. In 1958, he was invited to talk about Palumbo by the Italian Institute of Culture in Athens; the following year the twinning between Calimera and the city of Athens was inaugurated, and after this many such twinnings and collaborations followed."

Prof. Sicuro would navigate among his hundreds of books with remarkable facility, looking for this or that article he particularly wanted to show me. He handed me his notes for his lessons comparing Griko and MG (which I found enlightening), and added,

> Prof. Angiolino Cotardo was a disciple of my uncle; he graduated in Balkan studies from the University Orientale of Naples with a thesis on Griko for which he was warmly praised by Rohlfs. At university he had learned *katharévousa*, the official language of Greece, but that did not help him much to communicate. In reality when he traveled to Greece he had to resort to his Griko. Funny isn't it? When he and my uncle started to travel to Greece they were mistaken for Cretans [the sound /k/ is pronounced /tʃ/ in both varieties].

He laughed discreetly; he must have realized that I could not stop looking around—I was fascinated by that room filled with memories. Perhaps thinking I was critical of our surroundings, he said, "I know, one day someone will put some order into this mess. Look, here there are some Linguaphon. This is how I learned *dimotikì* [MG], listening to these tapes—old technology now, but I wanted to learn Modern Greek. It was important for us to get to Greece, you know? In Italy nobody cared about Griko. By contrast, Greeks regarded us with great interest, no matter their political orientation, and they helped us." Indeed, in their efforts to maintain the linguistic heritage of Griko, the second generation of philhellenists—mainly from Calimera and Martano, and to which Prof. Sicuro belongs—kept looking to Greece for recognition and support. They tried and succeeded to reestablish contacts with Greece, as he highlights.[2]

On July 4, 1960, an article written by Gino de Sanctis from Calimera—son of the philhellenist Brizio we met in Chapter 1—appeared in the national daily newspaper *Il Messaggero* (The Messenger):

> How amazed and moved my father and his friends and colleagues with him—the *jdalgos* of Apulian Hellenism—would have been if they could have attended the civic fest in Calimera a few days ago. I was there, and I was given room in the gallery of honor. Below me, in a newly planted garden, fresh with young shadows and flowerbeds, with oaks, willows and cypresses reflected in fountains and ponds, the entire population of the village sang in Griko—voices of old people and children, voices of women singing 'fly, fly swallow'—a song that certainly will have lulled the dreams of my father as a boy and of his own father before him. The mayor emphatically spoke claiming [Greece as] the 'second homeland', and after him, an official of the Greek Embassy of Rome intervened. An Attic stele donated by the town hall of Athens to this small and remote Apulian village was inaugurated that day; around the funerary stele named after a fourth-century Athenian girl—a vague Patròclia—stood the bronze busts of Vito Domenico Palumbo, of my father, of Giuseppe Gabrieli, of Pasquale Lefons, the far-from-forgotten patrol of the *Don Chisciotti* of Hellenism."
>
> *Il Messaggero*, April 1960

This is how Gino de Sanctis recalls the day that *la stele*—an Attic marble stone—was placed in the public gardens of Calimera (see Figure 15, below). Indeed, three years earlier, in 1957, Giannino Aprile (1918-1968), the mayor of the village, had sent a letter to the mayor of Athens asking for "an architectonic remain, or at least one stone from the Acropolis as a symbol of the common origin and the ideal continuity of the relations."[3] The mayor of Athens went along with his wish. The 'gift' (dating back to the fourth century BCE) had come from the National Museum of Athens: the symbolic nature of the funerary monument, which represents the embrace between a mother and her dead daughter—mother/Greece, daughter/Grecìa Salentina—points

---

[2] Thanks to these contacts, the first cultural exchanges with Greece were also to follow in the 1970s.

[3] www.ghetonia.it/pubblicazioni [06/22/2011]. Link expired; see archived version at https://web.archive.org/web/20160913045811/www.ghetonia.it/pubblicazioni (most recent archived version: 09/13/2016).

to the attention that Greece would start to pay to this enclave. In the 1980s the marble stone was located in an aedicule, and the following phrase was carved on its façade: "*Zeni sù en ise ettù sti Kalimera*," "You are not a foreigner in Calimera."

Figure 15: The Attic marble stone, Calimera

The activism of these intellectuals represents the ideal continuation of the activism initiated by Palumbo and his philhellenic circle; they indeed adopted the same modus operandi, writing linguistic contributions on the topic and continuing to preserve the 'oral tradition.' These *cultori del griko*, like their predecessors, had been educated in the most active centers of Italian culture, and effectively continued their legacy. Their discourse is permeated with references to the glorious Hellenic past, and to Greece as the 'motherland.' They equally perpetuated the "performative contradiction" of the first generation of philhellenists, which highlighted the distance between their explicit language ideology and their communicative practices at large. Yet in so doing, they ironically contributed to building a sense of popular 'skepticism' that risked producing an effect opposite to that desired.[4] As we have seen, Griko speakers were undergoing a complex process through which they came to identify a language shift away from Griko as a way to get to 'modernity' and its promised advantages. They did not understand why they were asked to keep speaking Griko by those who did not practice what they preached.

---

4   See Pipyrou 2016, for Calabria.

Beyond Activism: Griko-Greek Encounters

Parlangeli (1960) had stressed how common Griko speakers were typically monoglot, insofar as they completely ignored Greek as the language of culture. The long period of coexistence and the integration of cultures and languages had washed away whatever account of their distant past they might have had. To use Giorgio's words, "The elderly thought they were the 'Greeks.' They were called and called themselves *Greci* ['Greeks' in both Salentine and Italian], but many did not even know that Greece existed. When they met the Greeks elsewhere, or when the Greeks from Greece started traveling here, [the elderly] were surprised they spoke a language similar to theirs."

Indeed, the elderly use the term *Griko* in Griko, but in the Romance variety they translate it as *Grecu* or *Greco*—'Greek,' though by that they do not mean Greek of Greece. For instance, Franco (born in 1932) almost proudly pointed out, "My parents knew there was Greece, but that was it. My father could read; he even went to school for two years." His wife Concetta joined the conversation and said, "My father could not read. Anyway, some Greeks must have stayed here if the language continued, right?" Franco replied, "Did they come and stay here? Did they die here? How can you go back in time? Who is here to tell us?" He stopped, sighed, and finally asked me, almost provocatively, "You study these things. Do you know?"

The absence of historical speculation emerges clearly here. The emphasis given to being able to or unable to read brings us back to the divide between the intellectuals and the lay Griko speakers. If on one level it strengthens the authority given to those who can read—quite literally—it also seems to challenge that modus operandi. The past, and the knowledge that comes with it, is not something you read but something you live and experience.[5] What they relied on were their own memories and the memories of the people they knew. 'Ndata from Zollino told me,

> We did not know anything. From the fields we could see the mountains of Greece [Epiro] when the day was clear. What have we got to do with Greece? I don't know. Does it matter? They were Greeks, but we have always been here. I met the first Greek person in my life after the war,

---

[5] Papagaroufali (2005) makes a similar point when discussing the perception of local history among the inhabitants of Palaea Fokaea, a village near the city of Athens. They belong to those Greek-speaking Orthodox Christians who were relocated to Greece from Asia Minor as part of the population exchange in 1922. She argues that for them, "history is something that must be 'really felt'" (2005:337), as their knowledge of history and the past is at a sensory-affective level.

in the hospital of Scorrano. Now Greeks come here, but back then, who even saw them?

From my data it transpires that the image of Greece as the 'motherland' had no currency as such. 'Ndata refers to the first time she *met* a Greek person. This emphasizes that it is through personal encounter that the notion of 'the Greeks' enters a person's experiential reality. Interestingly, if migration to the North of Italy was crucial for indexing 'Italian' as a language of 'opportunities,' migration abroad crucially allowed Griko speakers to come into direct contact with Greek migrants, and to realize that Griko allowed them to communicate— although admittedly on a limited level—with Greeks. My mother recalls one such instance. When my parents migrated to Switzerland in 1955, my mother 'Ntina worked as a tailor in the textile industry in Zurich, and there she met Soula from the Peloponnese. On her first day at work, Soula could not speak or understand Swiss German. "I could see she was totally lost, so to help her I said in Griko, "*Piako to velòni. Piako to dattilìdi*"—"Take the needle, take the thimble"— and that's when her face changed; it looked like those few words changed her world," my mother often recalls proudly.

The identification of a few common—or at least mutually intelligible— keywords assured some basic level of communication. And, at times, familiar sounds can be enough to create a connection, especially when living in an 'unfamiliar' place, as Switzerland must have been for them. These encounters ultimately contributed to the ideology of Griko as a 'resource,' for it became apparent in a 'firsthand' sense to Griko speakers that Griko was not 'just' what they had come to internalize as a 'bastard language' and 'the language of shame,' but that it shared common origins with a national language.

The most characteristic example of this phenomenon is Cesarino De Santis (1920–1986) from Sternatia; he was a peasant, a migrant, and a poet, who spent forty-four years working in Germany and Northern Italy. During his years in Germany he got to know Greek migrants from Corfù, and through these encoun- ters he started realizing the value of Griko. After returning to Sternatia, he spent the rest of his life engaging with the cause of Griko. He restlessly tried to encourage his co-villagers, old and young, to keep using the language—at the time his efforts were not fully appreciated locally, although his knowledge of Griko was highly valued by the linguist Rohlfs, who visited the De Santis's house regularly. The value of Griko as a means to establish relationships was an additional reason to consider it a 'resource'—a realization that in itself did not, however, stop the overall shift away from Griko, as we have seen.[6]

---

[6]   While the intellectuals' efforts to give prestige to Griko had so far remained distant from lay preoccupations, the experience of fighting in Greece represented the first 'real' contact with

The Middle Revival: The Seventies and the Eighties

Reviewing linguistic and cultural activism effectively means tracing how locals have been redefining the meanings they attach to their language and to their past. What for analytical purposes I have referred to as the 'first ideological revival' of Griko stretches from the end of the nineteenth century to the mid-1970s; this was followed in the late 1970s and '80s by the 'middle revival,' while the current one began in the 1990s. The distinction is clearly not merely temporal; I decided to adopt a diachronic approach because I was interested in understanding and analyzing the different sociocultural and political landscapes of each phase, and the shifting ideological structures upon which locals' efforts to reevaluate, preserve, and/or promote Griko—and the past—were articulated.

Language activism and cultural revival emerged as a relevant social force in the mid-seventies, once locals had undergone the linguistic and existential shift discussed in the previous chapter; that is, upon fully embracing modernity and Italian. At this juncture, a group of young, educated local people initiated a process that once again subverted the state of things, promoting a reevaluation of the past, of what functioned as indexical of it, and articulating it as a defense of the language and its manifestations. This overall shift led cultural activists to repropose and thus enact yet another historicity; crucially in this case this movement was not linked to the Hellenic past, which the very Griko speakers could not identify with. The cultural activists of the middle revival instead reproposed a recent past linked to local practices; similar to elsewhere in Italy, they promoted a discourse aimed at legitimizing locality and its differences: the reevaluation of a past linked to the agricultural cosmology that Griko speakers had inhabited until not too long before. The 'redemption of the past' meant respecting local cultural specificities and its values, which were at risk of being erased through the 'race' to modernity.

The activities promoted by the cultural activists of the 'middle revival' were articulated on two quite separate fronts: the teaching of Griko, and the emergence of cultural associations engaged with the preservation of Griko and popular culture. The teaching of Griko dates back to the 1970s. At that time, Prof. Paolo Stomeo from Martano was an inspector at the Ministry of Education, while his disciple and follower Prof. Cotardo from Castrignano was a teacher in the primary school of the village. In the absence of legislative measures regarding minority languages at the national and regional levels, they requested and obtained an inspection of the local schools by the Italian Ministry of Education.

Greece and with Greeks. It is common to hear that Griko speakers fighting in Greece learned MG in the span of few months (see Pellegrino 2013).

This inspection assessed the conditions for teaching Griko in kindergarten and primary schools in the area, and the attendant lobbying resulted in the first law to safeguard Griko: Law 820 (enacted in 1971), which supported the teaching of Griko. However, such teaching was to be part of supplemental activities carried out in the context of after-school care (Nucita and Cotardo 1985:61–62); this factor highlights the different 'appeal' of the minority language and its 'status' as an undervalued subject in school.[7]

The teaching of Griko was conducted by Prof. Cotardo himself in the primary school of Castrignano. He developed his own method—known as the Cotardo Method—which consisted in teaching Griko and MG comparatively, providing a one-for-one translation. The positive evaluation by the Ministry of Education in 1976 brought about a new ministerial memorandum aimed at "the conservation of the linguistic and cultural heritage of the Salentine-Greek language" (Nucita 1997:13). This in reality refers to the experimental teaching of MG, and it therefore 'presupposes' knowledge of Griko rather than 'promoting' it; in other words, it considers Griko as a resource with which to learn MG. Indeed, "Recent studies ... establish that the knowledge of Griko facilitates the learning of MG and this can facilitate the commercial and touristic exchanges with neighboring Greece" (Nucita 1997:94–96). Local activists effectively inverted the relation of Griko/MG by giving centrality to MG, which appeared to them as an 'agent of renewal' and a means to build relations.[8]

In the 1985 book *Ten Years After: Language, Culture and Folklore in Grecìa Salentina*, Prof. Cotardo and Prof. Ada Nucita—the latter being the principal of the Castrignano schools from 1979 to 2003—reflect upon the first decade of this experimental teaching program. Their words reveal how heavily they relied on 'folklore,' popular traditions and popular memory as a pedagogical method. This emerged clearly from my conversations with Prof. Nucita, who, after Cotardo's death, continued to follow his method and engaged in Griko activism. She told me, "Prof. Cotardo would go around in the village with the school children and talk to the elderly, who would tell stories, anecdotes, proverbs, etc. Once back in the classroom, the terms collected would be put together. Field research was our method." These 'data' would then be turned into dialogues and sketches, dramas and plays in Griko. The end of each school year was in fact celebrated with a theatrical performance in which the children were the

---

[7] See McDonald (1989) and Jaffe (1999) for similar remarks concerning Breton and Corsican respectively.

[8] Furthermore, the lack of 'qualified' teachers, with the required linguistic and methodological training (who, according to the memorandum, had to be competent not only in Griko but also in MG), posed serious constraints to the school principals in the application of the memorandum. I will come back to the issue of the teachers' training in Chapter 5, as it is still an important one in the current revival.

'actors' of the 'Griko world'. Nucita clearly defined the aim of their experimental teaching: "Far from the pretension to revive the minority language at a social level, our aim was to render it an object of teaching, linking Griko, the language of our fathers, to a living language, Modern Greek" (Nucita 1997:28).[9] They state explicitly that their aim was not to 'revive' spoken Griko, while simultaneously making a claim to modern Greece as well as ancient Greece.[10]

Nucita (1997:14) hints at "widespread contrasts in public opinion" with regard to the experimental teaching of Griko, contrasts that she argues they had successfully laid to rest through their activities. She then stresses the popular positive reception their language teaching enjoyed, and the unconditional engagement and support of the children's families and the wider community for their efforts. The analysis of the popular reception to the teaching of Griko provided by The Lecce Group (1979) complements, yet to some extent also contrasts with, this self-celebratory attitude. These researchers from the University of Lecce carried out a survey in Sternatia, and noted that the practical implementation of the classes had provoked unanimously negative reactions. The people interviewed expressed mistrust over the selection of teachers and their competence, and doubts as to the validity of their teaching method. The data provided in the survey indicates a general lack of expectation regarding the intervention of official institutions (the town hall or even the Ministry of Education) for the cause of Griko. The authors write, "There are those who suspect that the community of Sternatia did not embrace the teaching of Griko in school, because it is considered a subject in contrast to the traditional seriousness of education" (The Lecce Group 1979:170).

This last point is important: the diffidence in the popular response can be explained by bearing in mind that the teaching of Griko is articulated within an 'institutional' sphere (the school), whereas the movement of cultural associations is enacted explicitly and purposely outside it. Paraphrasing McDonald (1989), who refers to the case of Breton, schooling and Griko evidently do not mix easily. This skepticism toward language planning is an instance of 'passive resistance of separation'; according to Jaffe (1999), who analyses the Corsican case, this is based on the local language ideology, which separates the meaning and value of the minority language from the official domains of the dominant language. This resistance thus defended the "alternative linguistic market associated with the minority language" (Jaffe 1999:160).

To be sure, the teaching of Griko was also criticized by teachers of non–Griko-speaking villages, who considered it "a romantic ambition to revive

---

[9]   Prof. Nucita is also the author of *Twenty Years After: Language, Culture and Folklore in Grecìa Salentina*, published after Prof. Cotardo's premature death in 1987.
[10]   See Pipyrou 2010 for Calabrian Greek.

impossible past glories" (cited in Nucita and Cotardo 1985:103). Similarly, in an article that appeared in a local newspaper in July 1976, Prof. Rizzelli, a teacher from the village of Galatina, contests such teaching, calling it an imposition, "a new tool of torture for the new generations and of self-gratification for the learned advocates ... It is absurd to expect to awaken the love for the language of [one's] origins after centuries of brainwashing" (Rizzelli 1976, cited in Nucita and Cotardo 1985:103). This is Prof. Cotardo's reply to that article:

> To teach the new generations how to know their own history, tradi-
> tions, the language of their fathers, means to teach them how to fit
> in with the social environment with confidence ... To know one's own
> history means to free oneself from the centuries-long slavery and from
> being considered 'inferior.'
>
> Nucita and Cotardo 1985:103

One is reminded of de Martino's concept of "inroads into history" and "the expansion of our own-self-consciousness in order to direct our actions" (de Martino 1941:12). For de Martino, self-consciousness is required to shape history, which is seen as the struggle for freedom. In our conversations, Prof. Nucita always stressed the importance of popular memory and the role of tales, songs, customs, and dances in building consciousness of the values of tradition and of local history. Popular culture and folklore were therefore not only conceptualized as the means to access the language, but crucially also as consciousness-raisers. This was the dominant discourse permeating the activity of cultural associations, which I now turn to discuss. Interestingly the centrality given to Modern Greek—and consequently to Modern Greece—that emerges in the experimental teaching of Griko is by and large absent during the first years of the associations; this was to develop during a second stage.

Beyond Griko: Cultural Associations and the Reproposal of Popular Traditions

The majority of the cultural associations were established in the second half of the 1970s, and tellingly all their names save one are in Griko. Most of these 'historical' associations have worked unceasingly to bring the issue of Griko to the fore, each of them focusing on different aspects. Among them Argalìo ('Loom,' Corigliano) privileged music; Chora-Ma ('My Village,' Sternatia) the 'intellec-tual' aspect, through book and art exhibitions; and Ghetonìa ('Neighborhood,' Calimera) editorial activities; whereas La Bottega ('The Workshop,' Zollino) and

Glòssama ('My Language,' Martano) were more diverse and versatile in nature.[11] By reviewing the activities promoted at the time by these associations, it transpires that they were not aimed specifically at language practice or planning, nor were they restricted to 'language' as a monolithic entity. Their *trait d'union* was instead their renewed commitment to Griko, and the reevaluation of the past it indexed and the world it represented. To this end, their attempts mainly focused on documenting and 'reviving' popular traditions that had fallen into disuse. 'Revival' is, however, a term these activists do not typically use. Instead, the terms that dominate are *recupero* (recovery) and *riproposta* (literally 'reproposal'). As we will see, the difference between them is not simply semantic.

* * *

I heard that Giovanni was around and I called him to catch up. I was looking forward to meeting with him since I never tire of listening to him recount tales of activism during the late 1970s and early '80s; his personal contribution to the middle revival cannot be stressed enough, although his bright and far-seeing mind was not fully appreciated at the time. "Come over for dinner on Saturday! We'll light the fire and eat something. What shall I prepare? Some wild vegetables?" How could I deny myself the pleasure? Food is always involved when meeting him, always locally produced—zero-mile food indeed. Giovanni Pellegrino from Zollino is more than a simple *operatore culturale*; socially and politically engaged, he has also invented groundbreaking novelties in the realm of what he calls 'popular technologies'—his vocabulary is highly idiosyncratic. "I am an intermediate technologist, a technician of that technological know-how almost abandoned by the modern consumerist and destructive tendencies of the environment," as he describes himself. In this capacity he has given his best, designing assisted pedal bicycles for instance, and inventing stoves that run on agro-industry waste products, as well as some ergonomic agricultural tools. Indeed, everyone knows him in the village as *l' inventore* (the inventor). Even now, as he approaches his eighties, he keeps moving and is very difficult to pin down. It is hard to know whether he is living in the next village or has gone to another country to embark on yet another of his many projects. "OK, I

---

[11] The association of Glòssama (My Language) was the first one to be established in the early 1970s. The centrality given to contacts with Greece differentiates it from the discourse that permeates the activities of the rest of the associations. Moreover, its founder, Prof. Sicuro, had engaged with Griko activism much longer compared to the activists of the middle revival. Among the initiatives promoted by the association we find *radio Glòssama*, which for a few years broadcast daily lessons in MG, and in so doing compared it to Griko. Equally important is that, thanks to Sicuro's activity, the first cultural exchanges with Greece were organized in the early 1970s. These involved schoolchildren.

will bring a bottle of red wine and some cheese. See you there, Uncle Giò," I said, calling him by his self-assigned nickname.

We met on a chilly February night, and Giovanni hurriedly collected some wood to light the fire, chatting all the while: "At the time there was no sensibility toward traditions, as they were considered to be antiques to be overcome in order to enter with unfurled sails into modernity. *I Passiùna tu Christù* [*The Passion of the Christ*] it is just the emblematic example." The reproposal of this tradition is indeed one of his most successful *operazioni culturali* (cultural operations/interventions), which he promoted as part of the association La Bottega del Teatro, based in Zollino. The Passion of the Christ is a form of popular theater in Griko, which narrates the death and resurrection of Christ, and used to be performed by local peasants during the week preceding Palm Sunday, and again on Easter Saturday. It is a tradition strongly held in the village of Zollino, and it was once widespread in most of the Griko-speaking villages. Considered to be one of the strongest cultural manifestations in Griko, it holds strong symbolic meaning as it represents a spring propitiatory and purifying rite (The Lecce Group 1977). It consists of sixty-six stanzas performed alternately by two singers accompanied by an accordionist or organ grinder. It used to be performed on the villages' crossroads and squares, as well as on manor farms and tobacco farms. A third person would hold an olive branch or palm decorated with colorful ribbons, sacred images, and/or oranges—symbols of fertility. At the end of the performance, the singers would collect eggs or money in a basket and move on to the next crossroads or village. The tradition had fallen out of practice by the mid-1950s (see Figure 16).

Giovanni moved across the kitchen and, while turning the greens in the pot and filling the room with an intense smell of garlic, said, "It was the expression of the people—*del popolo*—which had been silenced during the post-war years. It was quite literally a tradition obstructed by the priest[s] and by local authorities in the name of modernity. Can you believe it?" His eyes still redden at this memory. He then adjusted his glasses, which normally rested on top of his head, and added, "When we decided to perform the Passion again, it had not been performed for over twenty years, so young people did not know about it. At that point, it was difficult for it to reemerge from below. It needed us."[12]

Indeed, in the early 1980s, La Bottega approached Tommaso, a Griko speaker from Zollino, to be the new *cantore*, since his idiosyncratic voice resembled that

---

[12] In Zollino in particular, he argues, there was strong opposition to this initiative. On the one hand, the Catholic church was quite literally annoyed by this tradition, which was considered to be an invasion by unauthorized people into themes that were primarily religious and thus the domain of the clergy. On the other hand, the local administration did not appreciate any initiatives that came from 'Communists,' and did not tolerate their intrusions well.

of another performer who had died. He was to sing together with Antimino (whom you met in the previous chapter). I told Giovanni that incidentally the day before I had visited Antimino; he had been waiting for me to go and collect some lemons from his garden. "He sends you his love," I said, adding that Antimino had rightly predicted that we would talk about him and the Passion. In reality, it is Antimino who does not miss any occasion to mention the topic! That morning he had added a detail, and recalled enthusiastically the time they performed in Bova Marina in Calabria in the early 1980s. "I started singing the Passion when I was fourteen years old. Then everything changed, everything stopped. Giovanni contacted me [in 1981] and since then I have been singing it every year with all my heart," he said, before emphatically adding, "Even in mother's womb I sang the Passion. Some people call me 'the father of the Passion' (*O ciùri atti' Passiùna*) [he laughs]. I'll keep singing it until I die."

Figure 16. The performance of *I passiùna tu Christù*

The reproposal of *The Passion of the Christ* was just one of many festivities that became the object of interest for the cultural activists of the middle revival.[13] Scratching his bald forehead, Giovanni added thoughtfully, "People were losing

---

[13] Among those Giovanni also mentioned are the Carnival of Grecìa Salentina and the Focare de Sant'Antoniu (Saint Anthony's Fires). These were, effectively, pagan festivals celebrating the winter by symbolically defeating the bad weather. The bonfires were lit on the commemoration day of Saint Anthony Abate, for instance. Giovanni and La Bottega reintroduced this tradition and gave life to the La Festa de lu focu (the Feast of the Fire) in 1978 (reenacted yearly ever since), which anticipated the traditional one to December 28, when migrants would return to the village for Christmas celebrations.

their traditions. They were losing themselves, their memory of themselves as a community, the sense of place where they created community. It was essential to feel part of the environment again, to go out to the fields, to respect the old rhythms of nature. This is why we choose those festivities linked to the time of the year, and to the place, the environment that gave it a meaning." While searching for the salad he had meticulously prepared, Giovanni went on to recall, "Take *La festa di San Rocco* in Torrepaduli, for instance. It was not dead yet, but it was dying out. In the last few years, you would never see more than five or six tambourine players. We understood the values behind that practice, the very sense of the *ronde*."

Here, Giovanni is referring to The Feast of Saint Rocco in Torrepaduli, a small town near Ruffano. This feast was traditionally linked to the healing saint of plague, Saint Rocco, and to the agricultural market-fair held on the sixteenth of August. On that occasion, people from the nearby areas would arrive the day before and stay overnight to wait for the trade to begin and the first mass. In front of the sanctuary of Saint Rocco, locals would perform the *danza delle spade* (sword dance), also known as *danza dei coltelli* (dance of the knives), a performance that combines martial arts and dance, and is accompanied by the beat of tambourines. Danced in the form of a *ronde* (circles), it used to be performed with knives—or with the hand and fingers mimicking knives—in order to resolve conflicts that were typically either linked to disputes over women or family.[14]

By the end of the 1970s, the last remaining tambourine players were almost all elderly, and the celebration of the feast of Saint Rocco was indeed dying out. This dance belongs to the tradition of *pizzica* (literally 'pinch'), the Salentine version of the tarantella (more on this later), which likewise is an index of the past that locals had internalized as a marker of their subalternity. With La Bottega, in 1982 Giovanni organized an event called *Il ritorno a San Rocco* (The Return to Saint Rocco), which was to have far-reaching effects lasting into contemporary times. For Giovanni, the *festa di San Rocco* indeed had a very specific meaning, as the dance in the *ronde* respected a choral rhythm, he argued. "This modality of relation that comes from the past reassured people and helped the community form and maintain its identity; otherwise we lose direction and get lost," Giovanni kept repeating. The initiative involved identifying and approaching those remaining musicians and dancers in the surrounding villages, since there were only a few left and most of them did not even own a tambourine anymore. In another conversation, Uccio—another member of the association—told me that, together with Giovanni, he had bought about twenty-five tambourines, and had gone around distributing them to players.

---

[14] See Lüdtke (2009).

Giovanni stood up all of a sudden and disappeared into the next room, to return with an old newspaper—a copy of *il Quotidiano* dating back to 1981 wherein the ethnomusicologist Diego Carpitella made his plea about the tambourine. The title read, "*Il tamburello simbolo vivo di una civiltà. Non lasciatelo scomparire così.*" (Italian: The tambourine is a living symbol of a civilization. Do not let it disappear this way). Giovanni had indeed traveled to Rome to meet him. Repeating himself, he said, "Something needed to be done; the tradition of the tambourine and pizzica was disappearing among the general indifference. It was also important that someone respected and passed on the message to keep it, to value it. They would not pay attention to me. They listened to Carpitella, though!"

Figure 17. Festa di San Rocco, Torre Paduli, one *ronda*

Indeed, scholars have paid crucial attention to the phenomenon of tarantism—albeit with divergent results—attention that prompted Caroli (2009:259) to define Salento as an "ethnologized place." The University of Lecce had even promoted a project on tarantism in 1981, by the title *Il Ragno del Dio che danza* (Italian: The Spider of the Dancing God) all geared toward a final performance, which, however, never took place.[15] Among the researchers and scholars involved were the ethnomusicologists Diego Carpitella and George Lapassade. "The rest is history," Giovanni concluded, reflecting on the unpredictable repercussions that the middle revival was to have, even to the present (see Figure 17). Indeed,

15   See Imbriani (2015) for an overview.

his own initiatives further launched the tambourine and *pizzica*, contributing to the 'return of the *pizzica*' and its contemporary revival. Five hours had passed since I arrived at his home. It was late. *"Kalinitta, zio Giò"*—"Good night, Uncle Giò," I said teasing. "Sleep well, Manuela," he replied smiling.[16]

In reality, ethnomusicologists soon paid attention to the rich folk music repertoire that included *pizzica*. As early as the mid-1950s, Diego Carpitella and Alan Lomax had conducted a yearlong study on local lullabies, funeral laments such as *moroloja* (the Griko equivalent of what Greeks call *miroloja*), but also songs about work and the therapeutic music of tarantism (Carpitella 1986:79). Moreover, in 1959 the father of Italian anthropologist Ernesto de Martino had conducted fieldwork in Salento to investigate the phenomenon of tarantism, the spider (*taranta*) spirit possession cult in Salento. The *Tarantate* were women who claimed they had been bitten by a tarantula while working in the fields, and who were cured through the music of *pizzica tarantata* along with dance and color symbolism.[17] In his most famous book, *La Terra del Rimorso* (The Land of Remorse), de Martino detached tarantism from the interpretation that had prevailed in medical investigations since the Middle Ages. For him, it was not a hysterical mental disorder or an illness caused by the poison of the tarantula. Instead, he linked tarantism to female existential and social suffering, and regarded it as a manifestation of class and gender inequality. To use the words of Giovanni Pizza, de Martino's book revealed "profound contradictions: the wounds of the war, the social suffering, the material poverty, emigration, [and] the authoritarian tendencies of the post-fascist democratic governments" (Pizza 2005:n.p.; see also Pizza 2015). The folk music repertoire was to play an important role in the dynamics of the middle revival, and eventually became central in the discursive management of the current revival, as we will see.

Reappropriating the Past

As in the case of La Bottega, so too the other cultural associations that emerged in the mid-1970s primarily engaged in reproposing—relaunching, as it were—local traditions that had fallen out of practice. Within the association named Argalìo (Loom), based in Corigliano, there operated—and to a lesser extent still does—a laboratory comprised of both elderly and young singers who focus on

---

[16] Giovanni never stopped engaging with Griko and the local culture; most recently he founded the cultural association Fonè (Voices) in Zollino in 2015, which gave indeed a 'voice' to locals' concerns about environmental, political, and cultural issues.

[17] They would go to the Church of Saint Paul in Galatina on June 29 (Saint Paul's day) to ask him to help them recover. At the front of the church, as well as outside, they would convulse, and the music of *pizzica tarantata* was used to cure them.

the reappropriation and revitalization of folk music. This is one indicator of the significant role played by music groups in the promotion of language. Moreover, the very name of the association is telling, since it set out symbolically to weave together the past and the present, the elderly and the young.[18] When I met Michele—the son of Luigi, a central figure of Argalìo—he proudly remarked on the organization's achievements. Not only had the group become well known in Greece, but Michele stressed the contribution of the elderly members of the association to the studies of local and foreign scholars of folk music.[19] In particular, the association is linked to the *riproposta* of a tradition that had fallen out of practice, Le Strine (Salentine: The Gifts). A religious-pagan song sung during the collection of alms, its performance accompanied the arrival of the New Year. Traditionally, groups of musicians with tambourines and diatonic accordions would perform it by moving from *masseria* to *masseria*, from house to house, collecting mainly eggs and cheese as payment for their music making. Most likely it was an ancient pagan song of propitiation (which included the blessing of tools, plants, and animals) to which was subsequently added the tale of Jesus Christ's birth.

Michele told me, "The original text is in Griko, and there is also a version in Salentine, although it is not a faithful translation. It was a song wishing good harvests, abundance, and good fortune to all people." Indeed, it is a tradition strictly linked to the agricultural world, and it bears a strong resemblance to the Greek *kàlanda*. "Here in Salento and Grecìa Salentina, people had grown distant from their own traditions, so it was necessary to do something about it. It was time to express ourselves again through our traditions," Michele concluded.

Donato Indino, the founding father of the Chora-Ma association in Sternatia, similarly stressed, "At the time people did not realize their own 'treasure' and they were ashamed of Griko. We wanted *to awaken* them [my emphasis], to make them realize the importance of the language and their culture." In their self-assigned function as consciousness raisers, the activists of the center were not restricted to the cause of Griko. When I met Donato, he was about to retire from his job as a librarian at the University of Lecce. He suggested I help him go through the numerous pictures of the events organized by the association over the years; it was the thirtieth anniversary of its founding. I therefore spent quite a few afternoons chatting with him while selecting pictures and crucially gaining an overall idea of the activities the center promoted.

For the exhibition, the white lime walls of the center were plastered with pictures of art exhibits of the most prominent Salentine contemporary artists,

---

[18] Argalìo was officially founded in 1981, although its activity dates back to the early 1970s.
[19] The group of the elderly of Argalìo acted as a precious resource for the research carried out by il Canzoniere Grecanico Salentino, as we will soon see.

of music concerts, poetry competitions, and book presentations. There were also pictures of Paniri tu Tirì (Griko: the Cheese Festival), which was organized to gather funds toward the restoration of a Byzantine church that was close to collapse, Saint Vito in Sternatia. I found particularly interesting the event *La mostra delle cose perdute* (the Exhibition of Lost Things), an exhibition of material culture that had been disregarded by locals (old craft tools, handlooms, iron beds, etc.) as an index of the past. The exhibit recreated each room of a traditional house. Donato proudly labeled it a success, and noted it had managed to sensitize people to the value of their material culture: "People wanted to get rid of all those things! Plastic was in vogue, you know? But they participated in the event and stopped throwing [their stuff] away. It was a marvelous exhibition," he remarked.

Cultural activists belonging to the middle revival therefore centered their activities around a broader reevaluation of the past; indeed, their attempts focused on documenting and reproposing local traditions that had fallen out of practice. They promoted a reevaluation of all things past, including material culture, as we heard from Donato and from Giovanni above—this referred to all those objects that had been rejected in people's efforts to adopt middle-class material culture at a time when only what was new was valued. The activists' aim was therefore to reappropriate the past, and those cultural objects and manifestations that locals had internalized as being embarrassing, and as indexical of their inferiority and backwardness. In the process, they reinterpreted the recent past in which Griko still 'survived' as the linguistic and existential code; crucially, however, the activities they promoted transcended the boundaries of Griko to incorporate cultural expressions of Salentine at large. By including popular traditions and folk music in Salentine, they effectively avoided the exclusionary logic held by the intellectuals of the first revival and its limits.

The reevaluation of the past promoted by the activists of the middle revival is in fact embedded in the specific historical moment that sees the articulation of the protest of radical progress, urbanization, and of established social and cultural hierarchies. This was a widespread phenomenon in Europe. Jeremy Boissevain (1992:9) describes this as being linked to international political and socioeconomic processes, namely, modernization, migration, and tourism, through which "pressures from subordinate classes and regions ... have brought about a shift in power and led to a redefinition of legitimate culture. This has permitted long-suppressed or denigrated regional and popular culture to flourish."

The activists of the middle revival participated in this politicization of local movements occurring in Italy and Europe; theirs was inherently a political act with a political message that formulated claims to local specificity—which included Griko but did not do so in an exclusionary way. Tommaso from Zollino, born in 1947, says,

> You have to understand that my parents' generation was raped, as it were. They were led to believe that their culture, language, lifestyle, everything was inferior. That Italian had to be their language and the hegemonic culture was what they had to strive for. Salento was 'the end of the world,' you know? This was *La terra del rimorso* [the land of remorse]; it is true that people largely improved their economic and social conditions, but they lost so much on the way. You can never forget who you were, and you must not! Be careful: you can never be ashamed of your past. You can only be ashamed of what you lose.

These words summarize the discourse of the activists. They belong to what I referred to in the previous chapters as the 'in-between generation': they were born in the 1950s and '60s, and had grown up between the 'past' and the 'modern' worldviews; beyond their different occupations—among them professors, government employees, librarians, employees of the local municipality—most of them were and are politically sensitive and engaged. Crucially, they are the children of the upwardly mobile peasant and merchant classes who were moving up the social ladder. Their education and political orientation led them to advance claims to the local cultural identity, and to reclaim its centrality as an expression of the people through its own modalities, including songs and traditions, tales, etc. Their aim was to rebuild self-awareness and at the same time to denounce the arbitrariness of the attribution of social inferiority as a so-called 'subaltern' culture.

In contrast to the first revival, the 'addressee' of the middle revival was not Greece but Italy, in the demand for valorization of their specific local history, shifting it from the margins to which the dominant and hegemonic culture had relegated it. Giovanni summarized their activities succinctly: "resistance was a way of being in those times when we were losing important values, values which were wrongly considered obsolete."

The Reproposal of the Folk Music Repertoire

Roberto Licci from Calimera joined Il Canzoniere in 1971 as a singer. When I first met him by chance in Athens, he had seemed shy but also direct. It was now September of the following year, but the heat and humidity of 'this land of dirt mixed with water' (as I call Salento) dominated the air that afternoon. We had agreed to meet on the main square in Calimera and there we sat and drank our coffee, chatting. My first impression was confirmed by that encounter, Roberto was indeed not a showman. "My musical background is really *musica leggera* (pop music); then, in 1974, I met Rina Durante and we founded Il Canzoniere Grecanico Salentino, which was a merger of Il Canzoniere del Salento and Il Canzoniere di Calimera. I was part of it until 1989. That was before we founded Ghetonìa."

Il Canzoniere Grecanico Salentino (the Salentine-Greek Songbook) is the first folk revival group founded with the express intention to preserve the local folk music repertoire. What is now an internationally recognized band that often performs abroad emerged in 1975 as the project of the local writer Rina Durante from Melendugno (a non–Griko-speaking village situated five kilometers from Calimera), who, together with her cousin Daniele Durante—a guitarist—initiated a process of research, documentation, and *riproposta*.[20] Roberto, continuing to talk about music, paused and interjected, "In the end it all started earlier with Griko. Here in Calimera there was at the time a schoolmistress, Angela Campi Colella. She was very good and she could write in Griko. There is a nice song written by her. She really was the first in Calimera to start the research." From the way Roberto described her, it seemed evident that she still holds a place of great affection in Roberto's memory, revealing the crucial role played by sensitive school-teachers in transmitting the 'passion' for Griko.

"The first time we [Canzoniere Grecanico Salentino] went to perform in Greece, we had been invited by the Communist party; it was 1976. It was at the time of local elections and we ended up playing at an electoral campaign event!", Roberto said laughing. I had been told many times that it was a common practice for them during the concerts to *fare un comizio*—that is, to turn their concerts into political meetings by giving a political speech. "We wanted to pass on a message, the message that music itself carries. You know that in the past merchants used to leave the village at night to travel and sell products, right? One caravan after the other, they created a sort of chain, and the first caravan would start with a strophe of a song and the following caravan would sing the second and so on; and then they'd start over. That way, the entire caravan kept in contact. We wanted to do the same, to pass on a message, to recreate community," Roberto concluded.

The aim of the Canzoniere was in fact to create consciousness around the Salentine culture through its music and songs, and "to use traditional lyrics and melodies from a political point of view, in line with what was happening

---

[20] The pivotal contribution of the Canzoniere in the current folk revival is largely acknowledged, as the majority of the repertoire of recent folk groups draws on this initial research and subsequent reintroduction (*riproposta*). Collaborators such as Brizio Montinaro and Luigi Chiriatti from Calimera attest to the ethnographically oriented methodology of their research, which involved direct contact with the bearers of this rich tradition. See Montinaro (1994) and Chiriatti (1995).

in the rest of Italy with the various regional songbooks and with the Italian songbook," as Vincenzo Santoro and Sergio Torsello argue (2002:91). Their protest, however took a specific form in the context of the longstanding tradition of the subalternity of the South. The Southern Question, which concerns the contrasting economic, political, and cultural/social relationships between the North and the South, lingered with these activists. The activists of the middle revival longed for the 'redemption' of a long stigmatized South, of *La terra del rimorso* (the land of remorse),[21] and were committed to breaking with their parents' self-deprecation and subalternity.

The following excerpt is taken from the website of the Canzoniere Grecanico Salentino, where they argue for the need

> to locate those roots of the popular culture which are still alive and to identify those essential traits which survive; we have to take into account how they transformed themselves and how they could transform themselves in the meeting-synthesis with other cultural expressions: this is the only way in which this culture can be revitalized.[22]

Having realized that their position between the old and the modern world, as it were, was powerful in some sort of way, they presented themselves as *cerniere generazionali*—"generational connectors." Their discourse and the claims they put forward were far distant from the rhetoric employed by the intellectuals and *cultori del griko* of the first ideological revival of Griko, which would have linked them to a distant albeit glorious Hellenic past; the cultural activists of the middle revival instead engaged in those traditions that were expressions of the people and their locality—traditions that had been partially forgotten but not erased. Griko was if not the first and main element, then certainly the most disruptive among the local codes, and crucially the language of expression of a world that had been silenced by modernity. The explicit aim of the activists of the middle revival was to 'give back' to the people a pride in their own cultural distinctiveness, to restore the broken memory of the local past and with it the best values it carried—turning what used to be considered a reason for shame into a reason for pride. In the process they linked Griko to a local chronotope promoting a specific cultural temporality of language.

---

[21]   De Martino's book was translated into English by Dorothy Louise Zinn (2005). Studies in this field have proliferated in recent years, particularly around what has become known as neo-tarantism, a contemporary reappropriation of tarantism. The bibliography is extensive; see Pizza (1999, 2004, 2015) and for a recent treatment in English, see Lüdtke (2009). For a review of the bibliography related to tarantism, see also Mina and Torsello (2005). For a thorough consideration of de Martino and spirit possession in English, see Lewis (1996).

[22]   www.canzonieregrecanico.it (Accessed 06/30/2011; link now expired.)

The Past on Stage: The Spectacle-ization of Popular Culture

Yet these cultural activists did not limit themselves to 'restoring' the past, as the term *riproposta* (reproposal) might indicate. Instead, they re-storied it, reproposing folk traditions by reinterpreting those cultural practices; ultimately they reappropriated the past inhabited by their parents: "Through our initiatives we reproposed the best values the past carried for the present and the future," Giovanni summarized. It was not a mere act of reviving something, to restore life to the past, language included, but an act of interpretation, reappropriation, and reproposal. Through it, the cultural activists of the middle revival redefined the relationship between the past and the present; the past was 'redeemed' and crucially it became a route into a new future.

The very act of restoring/re-storying and reproposing is a performative act in which the activists of the middle revival performed as social actors in front of an audience. The success of the 'reproposal' of local traditions was therefore clearly dependent upon the responses of the audience, who are the bearers of that very culture; this points out the interactional aspect of the dynamic at play. Such traditional practices certainly struck a chord in people's memories, memories that were still alive: "For a long period of time no one sang the Passion. I had missed it a lot," said Lina from Zollino. "And then, after years of silence, it started being sung again. It was so nice to hear it again."

From the accounts I collected, however, there likewise emerged an initial reluctance, as these practices also reminded people of the hardships of the recent past; the self-deprecation suffered by locals still lingered in their self-perception, and had not yet washed away the feeling of shame they had long internalized. Cultural activists had to gain the locals' trust, as they were suspicious about the motives behind the reintroduction of popular traditions. Particularly diffident were locals who were called on to take part in the process (singers, performers of the *Passion of the Christ*, etc.) and their initial diffidence was overcome through time and thanks to the direct involvement of the activists. The ways in which popular traditions were reproposed initially created tension. Antimino, for instance, complained,

> The Passion used to be sung only at Easter time, then we started singing it at any time of the year. In any case, *it was different* [my emphasis]. We also used to sing the Passion to earn some money or to be given some eggs; my mum would then sell them to buy some cotton and patch our clothes.

The danger of decontextualizing cultural practices lingers, as the organization required to 'revive' traditions may entail a change in the social context and cultural setting associated with them. Let me clarify here that I do not take 'context' to be something unchanging, nor am I implying that one, and only one, context is the right and correct one. A 'context' is "an empirical phenomenon, an observable situation" (Stewart 1994:206) that is defined by different kinds of activities, practices, and performances. Even though the boundaries of such a context cannot necessarily be delimited, people do recognize when they shift. Decontextualization, therefore, does not mean that a practice is to be taken out of context, but that those characteristics that define it have been altered; it ultimately means cultural and ideological change, change that locals may initially find disconcerting and uncomfortable, as Antimino's words reveal. Singing *The Passion of the Christ* was a practice in context in the past, as it were; reproposing it, with its language and music, entails repositioning them in the 'context' of the present. Antimino's is ultimately a comment on change and its perception. Similarly, this is how Michele from Argalìo reports his father's reflections on the changes of the modalities of traditional singing:

> The musical group was a *spontaneous* [my emphasis] initiative which kept the traditional forms; with the first staged musical performances, the 'tradition' became an 'exhibition'; my father and the elderly of the group actually hated it, and they hated being recorded or filmed.

This comment points to the shift from a 'spontaneous' and thus unreflective practice to one in which the locals (the singers, in this case) are very conscious of what they are doing, one in which they 'exhibit' their knowledge. The elderly members of the Argalìo were indeed reluctant; they feared they would potentially be turned into performers of themselves (cf. Sant Cassia 2000:290). Cultural activists of the middle revival instead considered performance itself as the medium through which to denounce the subalternity imposed on popular culture. Their activities gradually led to the spectacle-ization of language and culture; they were, however, aware of this possible consequence and ready to take the risk. In an interview from the late 1970s, Rina Durante from Il Canzoniere said,

> The recovery of popular culture today goes through the acquisition of a political consciousness. When it is done this way, it becomes a serious matter; what counts is whether this operation at the level of awareness works or not, it does not matter whether the recovery goes through spectacle-ization (*spettacolarizzazione*). What matters is whether the

political work we carry on with this discourse on popular culture brings the results it should.[23]

Their primary aim was to raise political consciousness. Not coincidentally, the term *operatore culturale* takes the explicit dimension of activism. *La riproposta* (the reproposal) of the local past at large—with its practices and values—needed the active intervention of cultural activists; their cultural operations were needed. In one of our conversations, Giovanni from Zollino had pointed out,

> When popular culture has been misrecognized, repressed, marginalized for such a long time, you need a phase in which those who own the cultural practices pass them on to the younger generation; you then need an intermediate phase where elderly and young perform together on stage, and then a third stage on which young people move. You need people like me to facilitate this.

This process indeed generated tensions between the old generation, which 'owned' these practices, and the 'in-between generation,' which reappropriated them. It also opened up internal contradictions as to how to define the 'authenticity' of cultural practices and the 'authority' (owners versus interpreters) and 'control' over them, which needed constant renegotiation. Members of the association Argalìo recall, for instance, the heated debates around these issues between the elderly and the younger members of the association/music band. Through the dynamics of the middle revival, interestingly, the social gap that dominated the first revival becomes an intergenerational distance in the choice of the very modalities through which to repropose practices, which were then constantly debated and renegotiated.

The interpretation, appropriation, and redemption of the past by the activists of the middle revival (the 'in-between generation') ultimately led to the objectification of traditional practices, and of language. Crucially and inadvertently, this paved the way to their commodification, turning de Martino's land of remorse into 'the land of resource,' and to the consequent multifaceted and contradictory effects that characterize the current revival.

---

23 Zollino Channel, http://www.youtube.com/watch?v=SYq8aVceT3Y.

4

From "the Land of Remorse" to 'the Land of Resource'

THAT August day was cloudy—not exactly the kind of day you would want to spend at the beach. Yet that is precisely what my longtime friend Antonio proposed when he called me. "Let's drive along the coast. I'll call Massimo too!" He didn't have to persuade me. The three of us regularly make the short trip along the Adriatic coast to admire the views. Driving south from Otranto toward Santa Maria di Leuca, on the heel of the Italian boot, the road gets narrower until it suddenly turns into hairpin bends embracing the coast. To one side is the beautiful countryside and its *masserie* (Italian); on the other, the marvelous coast with its Norman watchtowers, some majestic, some understated. "It is not busy at all today for a change. What a relief," Massimo reflected. It was true. Because of the overcast skies the road was indeed not busy as it often is at summertime, when locals and tourists race to the best sandy and rocky spots. "Guys, why don't we stop here instead and enjoy the *rusciu de lu mare?!* [Salentine]", Antonio exclaimed. "The sound of the sea" refers to the music of the lapping and crashing of waves. Not incidentally, this is also the title of one of the most well-known folk songs in Salentine, a lullaby whose rhythm increases bit by bit, so that it morphs into a pizzica song. Before Massimo and I could agree, Antonio stopped the car in a beautiful spot not far from Porto Badisco, the port where legend has it that Aeneas first landed on his escape from Troy. We all put our sun chairs in the middle of the fields facing the sea. Indeed, the view is overwhelming; you can see that slight curve in the horizon.

"Do you remember that old tape of traditional music you copied for me ages ago?" I asked Antonio, who immediately replied, "I do! Who knows where it is! But I've got the CD of the live concert of *La Notte della Taranta* with me, the 2003 edition of the festival, the one directed by Stewart Copeland." He put the CD on and left the car windows down so we could listen while staring at the sea. The first performance of "The Night of the Tarantula" took place in 1998 and was rather an intimate event. This folk music festival, whose title clearly references tarantism, and in which the music of pizzica dominates, has meanwhile become a major annual event on the global music scene, attracting as many as 200,000 people from all over Italy and the rest of Europe. Over the years it has been directed by well-known Italian and foreign musicians, including the aforementioned former drummer of the English band The Police. At my request, Massimo then advanced the track to *Kalinìtta*, the song in Griko, which is always, almost ritualistically performed as the grand finale of the concert. Originally titled *Matinàta*, it is a poem in the oral tradition that was reworked by Vito Domenico Palumbo and then set to music. It is now the de facto 'anthem' of Grecìa Salentina (GS).[1]

When the song reached its refrain, Antonio started singing, but soon stopped: "I'm terrible at languages ... and when I went to Greece I wished I knew more Griko." His knowledge of Griko is indeed limited to only a few words and expressions. The previous year he had traveled to Ioannina together with a few people from Zollino as part of a trip organized by a Griko activist from Corigliano. "You're old! You should know some more Griko," Massimo intervened, teasing Antonio as usual for the eleven-year age gap between them. He added, laughing, "Your nephews will soon know more Griko than you now that it's taught at school." Antonio, who is approaching his fiftieth birthday, adjusted his posture on his sun chair and replied, "Yes, yes, I am old. And yes, I used to hear it all the time as a child and I don't speak it. But mind you, I can still tell you to shut up in Griko!" We all laughed. He continued, "Seriously now, take Cosimino for instance. Griko helped us get by when we were in Greece, and he has also been taking MG classes." Massimo shifted the conversation, suggesting we take a trip to Greece through Albania—he is always buying musical instruments from abroad—when all of a sudden the sky turned black and the first few raindrops fell. We quickly put the sun chairs in the back of the car and said our farewells to the sea and the music of its waves. It was time for coffee.

As we saw in the previous chapter, cultural activists of the middle revival had advanced claims to the linguistic and cultural heritage of the area in the context of Italian national politics, but they lacked a framework of articulation that would legitimize those claims. The Italian state's legal recognition of Griko that they had long fought to achieve was reached only in 1999, when Law 482 recognized Griko together with Calabrian Greek among the twelve historical minority languages on Italian soil. Consequently, as Massimo mentioned above, Griko is now officially taught in local schools. Meanwhile, in 1994 the Greek Ministry of Education began sending teachers to Salento and Calabria to teach MG in schools and cultural associations. Indeed, Cosimo from Zollino

---

[1] The rhythm accelerates at the end of the refrain—a strange addition, some locals complain, since the lyrics describe a sad love story.

had benefitted from these classes, and Antonio's trip to Greece was the result of collaborations between local cultural associations and Greek ones, which had intensified in the 1990s.

The current revival is partly the outcome of the ceaseless activity of cultural associations, but it crucially points to this interplay of transnational and national language policies and ideologies, and the impact of the rights discourse on the articulation of group claims.[2] The global attention toward 'endangered languages' and the climate of support for minority languages nourished by the European Council gave renewed opportunities to local activists, who felt that their efforts to save and foster Griko were finally being legitimated. Indeed, the European Bureau for Lesser-Used Languages was established in 1982 to represent their communities in their dealings with European Union institutions. Throughout the 1990s, it funded several projects by local cultural associations that resulted in the publication of books, CDs, and grammars of Griko. The resources made possible by the new interest in Griko were instrumental in sustaining the efforts of *cultori del griko* and activists, and in fostering a dynamic process that actively involved part of the local population. Yet it will become clear how their centrality would be eventually overshadowed by the activity of local politicians who effectively made the best of the availability of protected rights and financial resources at the national and European level; crucially, they blended Griko and folk music, and successfully 'marketed' the territory. By the end of the first decade of the twenty-first century, *La Notte della Taranta* and *Grecìa Salentina* not only had entered locals' vocabulary, but, together with catchy terms like *pizzica* and *Griko*, had become familiar well beyond the borders of this cultural island. Indeed, it would be impossible to appreciate fully the dynamics of the current revival of Griko without also considering the revival of folk music, as the two causes are in a metonymic relationship. Likewise, it would be misleading to refer to their repercussions in Grecìa Salentina in isolation from the Salentine surroundings. *La Notte della Taranta*—the jewel of local policymakers, as Lüdtke (2009:110) defines it—effectively inserted the whole of Salento into the circuit of cultural tourism. Songs such as *Lu rusciu de lu mare* and *Kalinìtta* are now widely known. Pizzica, hand in hand with Griko, has been turned into the symbol of the local identity, as well as the trademark of Salento.

In this chapter I analyze the emergence of the current revival and the dynamics it generates, and I show how it is embedded and oriented toward a global discourse wherein the celebration of diversity catalyzes the articulation of local claims. Discourses of cultural difference, however, become the humus for political entrepreneurship, allowing spokesmen to communicate on behalf

---

[2]   See Brown 1998; Goodale 2005; Wright 2004, among others.

of others and initiate polarizing debates, which ultimately limit the options of the followers (Barth 1995:65). In fact, local politicians' managerial approach to the local cultural heritage has created ambiguities and contradictions *within* the community. Moreover, I argue, the application on the ground of the national and regional laws for the safeguard of Griko reveals local tensions about the division of labor and access to resources, as well as fears of losing control over cultural and linguistic ownership.

The Nineties: The Intensification of Contacts with Greece and the Teaching of Modern Greek

One of the features that distinguishes this phase of the revival is indeed the intensification of contacts with Greece, and the collaborations between local cultural associations and Greek ones. As a result, almost every village of GS has a representative who fosters contacts with Greek associations, welcomes Greek tourists, and guides them through the Griko-speaking and surrounding villages; these encounters often result in mutual friendship and collaboration. Antonio Anchora (1950–2016) from Corigliano is a characteristic example; his active engagement with Griko, however, started in the late 1980s, when he was contacted by a Greek association that wanted to collaborate with the Griko-speaking villages. Antonio would travel to Greece as often as every two to three months, and during his years of activity, he coordinated study trips in Greece involving, in total, about two thousand people, including children, students, musicians, academics, artists, and elderly people from Grecìa Salentina. As a result, in 2001 the Greek government, through the Athens prefecture, nominated him 'ambassador of Hellenism in the world' as an acknowledgement of his engagement and activity. His title should not mislead the reader into picturing him as an institutional figure; his jovial and easygoing personality made him highly regarded on both shores. Locally he was referred to and is still remembered as 'the friend of Greeks.'

The same applies to the other representatives who welcomed Greek visitors. Since the late 1980s, the cultural association Chora-Ma has also regularly hosted Greek scholars and groups of tourists, intensifying its relations with Greek cultural associations. More crucially, it has invited Greek religious and political authorities to visit the area. The survival of Griko without any institutionalized support—or maybe because of it—generally strikes a chord with the Greek population at large, as it offers both a reason for and proof of 'national pride' (see Chapter 7). Indeed, while on Italian soil Griko activists' attempts to draw attention to the situation of Griko had to this point fallen on deaf ears, they found an attentive audience in Greece. Local Griko activists always acknowledge Greek aficionados of Griko for taking the issue of Griko to heart, and perhaps most importantly for giving visibility to the Griko cause by alerting the Greek media to it and thereby informing Greek public opinion.[3]

As it was in the first revival, Greece continues to be perceived as 'an agent of recognition'—a recognition that the Italian government would not grant despite the activists' lobbying. However, the current revival expands beyond merely the intellectual audience and reaches out to the Greek population at large thanks to the activity of Greek cultural associations. These effectively became the spring-board for the articulation of Griko activists' claims; local Griko activists saw in Greek aficionados of Griko someone to amplify their voice, and to this end they appealed to and capitalized upon the Greeks' affection for their own cultural heritage, almost in a strategic manner. Interestingly, they always stress the pivotal role Greek cultural associations played, for instance, in advocating the teaching of MG, which they proudly consider the direct result of their continued lobbying. Over the years, local Griko activists had indeed repeatedly approached the Greek consulate in Naples, requesting its mediation and intervention; this eventually led to the Greek consul sending a professor from the University of Naples 'L'Orientale' to study the situation of Grecìa Salentina, after which the advocates' request was granted.

How MG would be beneficial to the preservation of Griko is locally contested. This topic always prompts yet another ideological debate (see Chapter 5), which creates internal tensions among activists and speakers alike: those who are in favor of MG and its teaching perceive it as an 'agent of renewal' of Griko, in that it would enrich Griko's limited vocabulary; and those who see MG instead as an 'agent of contamination' fear that it would erase the historical peculiarities of Griko. I will return to these issues in the next chapter.

Cultural Associations

While the activity of the cultural associations such as Chora-Ma, Bottega, Glòssama, Ghetonìa, and Argalìo continued over the years, newer cultural associations were established throughout the 1990s. Grika Milùme (We Speak Griko) in Martano is the only one that focuses specifically on language issues; Nuova Messapia (New Messapia), created in Soleto in 1995, focuses not only on language but also on local history, art, and environmental issues, as Francesco

---

[3]   Professore Sicuro (whom I introduced in the previous chapter) was one of the founding fathers of CONFEMILI, the 'Federation of Linguistic Minorities of Italy' established in 1984. It is the acronym for Confederazione Italiana delle minoranze linguistiche, "Italian Confederation of Minority Languages." It subsequently became the Italian division of the Bureau for Lesser-Used Languages of Brussels (EBLUL).

explained (see Chapter 1). Significantly, in the 1990s, the Griko cause and that of folk music joined forces. Avlèddha (Little Courtyard), for instance, began its life more broadly as a cultural association, one set up in 1991 by the brothers Gianni (1958–2015) and Rocco De Santis (b. 1964) from Sternatia, both mother-tongue Griko speakers. As a musical group, they specifically relaunched the local music repertoire in Griko and Salentine, and added a number of new songs. As the children of Cesarino De Santis, whom I referred to in the previous chapter, the brothers had inherited their father's passion for the language and followed in his footsteps. As they like to recall, they grew up surrounded by scholars such as Gerhard Rohlfs and Anastasios Karanastasis, who benefited from Cesarino's invaluable collaboration.

The name of the association recalls the layout of typical local houses—*case a corte* (Italian). "We chose this name because the courtyard was simultaneously a closed and an open space, a right of way [Griko: *jusso na diavì apù 'ttù*], a place we share," Gianni explained. Sharing their love and knowledge of Griko has been Rocco's and Gianni's aim ever since, a goal they have accomplished using music, poetry, and theater as their preferred means. Among their albums, *Otranto, Senza frontiere* (Otranto Without Borders) and *Ofidèa* (Snake) are well known locally, as well as in Greece. The late Gianni had been a very charismatic and entertaining man, a real people person. He knew an astounding number of lay people, intellectuals, and activists, and was typically the 'middle man' who facilitated relations between people. He recalled how, when he returned to Sternatia after over twenty years working near Milan, he felt the need to reacquaint himself with and treasure all the things he had missed. "My contribution has been to involve people in this experience; I have the gift to carry people away!" he would say smiling. Of the two brothers, Gianni was typically the one who wrote the lyrics in Griko, while Rocco wrote the music. They also set to music some of their father's and siblings' Griko poems. "Music travels on different wavelengths," Rocco argued, "so in our songs we tend to use Griko."

The marriage between the different skills of the De Santis brothers was to prove successful. They started singing in two taverns in the village—at Mocambo every Friday and at Pizzeria Lu Puzzu (The Well) every Tuesday (see Figure 18). The engagement of the respective taverna owners and the active participation of Giovanni, whom we met in the previous chapter, were vital in gaining visibility for these events, as these were the key people who more generally were championing the recovery of local practices. These music nights became regular features; in particular, what was to become well known as *Martedì Lu*

Puzzu (Tuesdays at Lu Puzzu) became a key event and a catalyst for local folk music amateurs.[4]

Figure 18. *Martedì Lu Puzzu,* 2008

In one of our many conversations, Uccio told me that local people interested in the local music started meeting at his pizzeria, and that by getting to know each other, they became collaborators. "Some of them could not even play tambourine or diatonic accordion! Ninety percent of the folk music bands that are famous today actually started to perform within the walls of my tavern!" he says proudly. Vito echoed his words: "They would arrive here and ask me, 'Would we be disturbing you if we played our music?' And now they have all become famous!" Word spread, and quickly these locations became the meeting point for local folk music aficionados and the point of contact for Greek people traveling to Grecìa Salentina. These regular events effectively created a space for emerging musicians who were to become the VIPs of the current revival.

These local taverns show how the spark of the music revival was lit by a rather spontaneous and genuine reappropriation of folk music in a relaxed and festive environment. According to Gianni, "this spark was constantly fueled to eventually produce an explosion." He also stressed how these regular musical

---

[4]   In the wake of Avlèddha, an analogous association emerged in Sternatia called Astèria (Stars), founded in 1993 by Giorgio Filieri; he is a Griko teacher and one the finest connoisseurs of the language, which he has been actively researching and documenting for years. He is often invited to perform in Greece.

events were followed by local emerging politicians, and particularly by those who later became the mayors of the Griko-speaking villages. "They were young and ambitious. It was quite simply a fortunate and successful combination of the right people. Our contribution was to bring them together. Just imagine: it was at Mocambo that the cast of *Pizzicata* (Bitten) was gathered," he added. Further visibility for the area was provided by the work of Edoardo Winspeare; despite his non–Italian-sounding surname, Winspeare is a Salentine screenwriter and film director who sets his movies in Salento, featuring the local music repertoire and the Salentine landscape.

Music proved to be an additional driving force: "Music has wheels and travels, Griko does not," as one of my informants put it. In other words, it functioned as a vehicle that found a vast audience when compared to the niche audience of Griko aficionados, and it served as a powerful magnet for the recruitment of new young singers and followers. New music bands started popping up like mushrooms in the 1990s, some of which have meanwhile become known well beyond Salento and Italy.

The Union of the Municipalities of Grecìa Salentina and La Notte della Taranta

The 1990s were years of turmoil in Grecìa Salentina. While local politicians had historically been insensitive to Griko and the local cultural heritage, the Griko-speaking villages were now administered by smart and farsighted left-wing mayors. Having come to appreciate not only Griko's cultural but also its economic potential, these mayors joined forces to develop the area, diving in to make the most of the availability of legal instruments and financial resources at the national and European level. Following a national decree, which encouraged administrative integration among the municipalities, in 2001 they established the Union of the Municipalities of Grecìa Salentina (Unione dei Comuni della Grecìa Salentina, UCGS hereafter). If the UCGS has so far failed to provide integrated services such as transport, local police, and law and registry as had been hoped for with the national decree, it has succeeded in prioritizing the 'cultural' over the 'administrative,' although Griko and folk music are not mentioned in the UCGS's statute.

Significantly, the availability of European Union financial resources prompted local mayors to access specific EU INTERREG programs aimed at stimulating interregional cooperation between Italy and Greece. These cross-border cooperation programs further boosted the intensification of contacts with Greece, and facilitated both informal and formal exchanges and partnership between the two countries. Specifically, Grecìa Salentina has so far benefited from five such Italy–Greece programs. These are aimed (among other things) at the "Promotion, Restoration, and Development of the Historical and Cultural Environment of Common Interest." A variety of projects, including the restoration and renovation of numerous monuments and historical centers in each village, have been carried out over the years thanks to these resources.

This favorable intersection of events at the local, national, and international levels led to unpredictable repercussions beyond the Griko-speaking villages, and from there to what has been defined as the Salentine 'renaissance.' The UCGS furthermore launched a marketing campaign of the area that incorporated different strategies (advertising, public relations, direct marketing, and large-scale events). The logo of Grecìa Salentina has been one of the key visual means by which the territory has been marketed. This logo is visible at the entrance of every village that is part of the UCGS, and includes a message of welcome written in Griko—*Kalòs ìrtate* (Welcome)—which is also translated into MG, English, French, and German.[5]

Figure 19. The welcoming sign at the entrance of each village

The logo features a symbol—the letter *alpha* (α) of the Greek alphabet, except turned upside down—along with nine colored bands representing the nine historical Griko-speaking villages, with a blue-sky background and an olive

---

[5] Strikingly, this sign contains a mistake. A Griko scholar pointed out to me that the Griko equivalent word would be *kalòs ìrtato*. This is most likely a mirroring effect of the MG *kalós írthate*.

leaf symbolizing the fruits of this land.[6] The logo appears in every publication related to Griko, but at its root is simply "in honor of Grecìa Salentina," as the ex-mayor of Zollino clarified for me, since it does not necessarily indicate a financial contribution by the UCGS. Riding the wave of the moment, the word 'Salento' itself became a catchword. At the peak of this wave, a proliferation of commercial brands entered locals' everyday lives, such as Salento d'amare (Salento to love), Salento 12, and Salentomania; all draw upon dominant features of the place, merging material with immaterial and symbolic elements. An epidemic of 'Salentinity' was the result.[7]

Dancing and singing the revival: The Night of the Tarantula

Yet it was the folk music repertoire in Salentine, and to a lesser extent in Griko, that was to prove the most effective marketing tool for the area. The folk music festival The Night of the Tarantula was indeed central in this process, and in developing what Paolo Apolito refers to as "anthropological tourism" (2007:13, 14). The name of the festival itself clearly references the phenomenon of tarantism investigated by Ernesto de Martino in the late 1950s. The touring festival (*festival itinerante*) takes place during the month of August and includes concerts in every village of Grecìa Salentina, while the grand closing concert (Italian: *concertone*) takes place in Melpignano, usually on the last Saturday of August. Sergio Blasi, the mayor of Melpignano from 2000 to 2010, often remarks proudly that he was the idea-man behind the festival. He was also one of the promoters of the founding in 1997 of the Istituto Diego Carpitella, to which the festival is tightly linked. Named after the ethnomusicologist who was part of Ernesto de Martino's team, the institute's overall aim was to research, recover, document, and promote the cultural and artistic heritage of Salento, and in particular, as its charter says, "to foster every form of artistic creativity inspired by the themes and expressions typical of the Salentine culture." In addition to the financial support of the UCGS, in 2002 the province of Lecce and in 2005 the region of Puglia started investing in this festival. Finally, in 2008 they joined their efforts, together with the Istituto Diego Carpitella, creating La Fondazione della Notte della Taranta (the

---

[6]   I attended Griko lessons in primary school, where the teacher explained to the children the symbolic meaning of this logo; the blue is also a symbol of the sea that unites the two lands of Grecìa Salentina and Greece; the olive tree leaf—put in place of the accent—symbolizes peace and friendship between the two countries, in addition to being the predominant plant in both countries.

[7]   The slogan *Salento d'amare* was commissioned by the Province of Lecce as the official sponsor of the Lecce Sports Union, appearing on the T-shirts of the Lecce football team. However, it was also used in conjunction with all institutional activities of the province.

Foundation of the Night of the Tarantula) to guarantee the financial and logistical sustainability of the event.[8]

The music revival burgeoned in the first decade of the twenty-first century and has become a mass movement that transcends local boundaries, not only of the Griko-speaking area, but of the Salentine peninsula overall, and has become a globally known phenomenon. *Il fenomeno della pizzica* (the pizzica phenomenon), as it is called, has resulted in the establishment of countless new music bands and pizzica dance schools in Salento and throughout Italy. The tarantula has become contagious, biting everywhere and making national and international headlines. The tourism industry has boomed all over the Salento area, and its unprecedented 'fame' has boosted the local economy: locals have converted their country houses into bed and breakfasts to host tourists mainly in the summer season; traditional houses have been revalued, restored, and sold for large sums; restaurants, 'traditional taverns' selling traditional food, and touring offices have popped up like mushrooms, offering locals occupational relief. Salento is now in the spotlight and has indeed become one of the preferred destinations for tourists in Italy and beyond, and the flow of tourists continues to increase. Local cultural heritage is indeed no longer perceived as a hindrance—as it had long been viewed—but as a source of economic possibility and social redemption. De Martino's "the land of remorse" has been transformed into the 'land of resource'.

An identity to live and to sell

To be sure, The Night of the Tarantula capitalizes on the spectacular phenomenon of tarantism and its seductive myth while sharing nothing with it—the existential suffering and psychological discomfort described by de Martino here becomes a big party. Tarantism is therefore decontextualized and recontextualized, in order to be detached from its negative connotations, and to become a positive symbol of local identity. This phenomenon has attracted the attention of a remarkable number of Italian and foreign scholars of various disciplines, investigating what has become known as 'neo-tarantism'; that is, the contemporary reappropriation of tarantism.[9] According to Karen Lüdtke (2009), the contemporary use of pizzica serves multiple aims that prominently include the search for and celebration of a local sense of identity. The myth of the tarantula, she argues, has now become a

---

[8]   See Imbriani (2015) on the creation and production of the musical event *La notte della taranta*.

[9]   Studies in this field have proliferated and the bibliography is extensive; see Pizza (1999, 2004, 2015) and Lanternari (1995, 2000) among others; for a treatment in English see Lüdtke (2009). For a review of the bibliography related to tarantism, see Mina and Torsello (2005). Among local scholars, see Chiriatti (1995, 1998); De Giorgi (1999); and Giorgio Di Lecce (1994, 2001).

performance that celebrates a local sense of identity, as well as a trendy form of entertainment that advertises and promotes Salento with its exotic features. The myth of the tarantula is part of a wider phenomenon of the renaissances of local identities worldwide emerging as a response to globalization; crucially, it points to the successful mechanism of cultural politics, as it were, involving local politicians and scholars (see Figures 20 and 21).

Figure 20. La notte della Taranta, touring festival 2008, Zollino

Giovanni Pizza (1999, 2004:202) soon drew attention to the commodification of tarantism facilitated by the collaboration between local cultural producers and political and heritage institutions. The rediscovery of de Martino's pivotal work by Italian anthropologists in the mid-1990s (three decades after his death) has inadvertently played a role in this process. Local scholars—"self-proclaimed anthropologists" (Pizza 2004:201)—and ethnomusicologists participated in the renewed academic attention and contributed to the anthropological debate that originated with de Martino's work, ultimately disconnecting tarantism from its negative stereotype and reformulating it. De Martino considered tarantism a cultural phenomenon in which the symbolic bite of the *taranta* occurred when the victim experienced stress and difficulties; it was therefore linked to the "crisis of the presence," that is, "the existential drama of being exposed to the risk of not being here" (de Martino 1948:141).[10]

---

[10]   De Martino's 'presence,' as Saunders (1993) argues, is grounded in the ideas of Heidegger and Hegel, and is akin to that of Hegel's 'sense of self' as a kind of 'self-consciousness': "Being in the

In the moment in which autonomy and freedom are threatened—in this case by economic and social marginalization and lack of political power—the ritual of tarantism represents the victims' attempt "to be there," to redeem their own presence. "The redemption of the presence" means in fact that one takes control of one's own existence in order to "enter into history" (de Martino 1949:248).

Figure 21. The dancing audience, Zollino

As Pizza argues (2004: 205–206), crucial in the contemporary reformulation of tarantism has been the legacy of the work of two French scholars, ethnomusicologist Gilbert Rouget and anthropologist Georges Lapassade, who conducted fieldwork in Salento in the 1980s. Rouget (1980, 2000) does not consider tarantism to be a healing ritual (exorcistic) allowing for the expulsion of an evil that the *taranta* symbolically represents. He instead suggests considering tarantism as a possession cult, in which, through trance, the identification between women and the spider occurs (an adorcistic ritual). The *tarantate* in fact imitate the spider assuming their posture and behavior in their dances: Rouget argues that this identification is an act of alliance with the spider through which the *tarantate* obtain protection against the evil, thus transforming and empowering

---

world, that is maintaining oneself as an individual presence in society and in history, signifies action, the power of decision and of choice according to values" (de Martino 1959:98; I have used the translation by Saunders 1993:884). See Stewart (2012, 2013) for an application of the notion of the 'crisis of the presence' with reference to his study of the outbreak of dreams on the Greek island of Naxos. See also Farnetti and Stewart (2012).

themselves. Lapassade (1994, 2005) attempts to combine de Martino's inter-pretation with Rouget's arguing for the coexistence of both rituals: for him tarantism is an adorcistic ritual, which has lost the conscience of itself, as it was 'masked' as a healing ritual to avoid entering into conflict with the Catholic church. We see how, while de Martino's *tarantate* are victims who suffer for 'not being there' and who need healing, for Roget and Lapassade they become subjects who 'escape reality,' through trance, and who thus empower them-selves. These scholars were instrumental in the reversal of de Martino's inter-pretation of tarantism by local scholars with whom they collaborated.

Local scholar Pierpaolo De Giorgi (1999), for instance, is the author of the book *Tarantismo e rinascita* (Tarantism and Rebirth), while Paolo Pellegrino (2004) wrote *Il ritorno di Dioniso* (The Return of Dionysus); the titles of these books are a clear indicator that they trace this phenomenon to archaic and Dionysian origins rooted in the mythologies of Magna Graecia. This is indeed their argument, which they pursue in a fashion that parallels the Griko activ-ists' attempt to disassociate the language from its negative past as a 'language of shame,' and to connect it to Ancient Greek. However, there is more to it; for De Giorgi (1999:51) tarantism is "a philosophy of rebirth and a *resource* for survival" (my stress). In reality, de Martino talks not only about the "aggression of the hidden past" taking place in tarantism, but also of "the dream of renewal ... in harmony with the season" (de Martino 1961:60). Local scholars seem to have privileged this renewed interpretation of tarantism, one that subverts its nega-tive stereotype and, most significantly, becomes the ideological basis for many of the claims of the current revival. Through the "dream of renewal," the shift from "the land of remorse" to the 'land of resource' is finalized.

If the local reappropriation of de Martino's work legitimized the revital-ization of tarantism in new terms, another book was to become influential for local politicians in their pursuit of cultural tourism. This is *Pensiero Meridiano* (Southern Thought), by the sociologist Franco Cassano (1996) from Bari (Apulia). In it, the diversity of the South is presented in opposition to the homologizing ideologies of globalization, and as the tool to redefine the meaning of modernity and identity. Cassano argues that the 'pathologies' of the South of Italy and of the world do not depend on its deficit of modernity; they are rather the symp-toms of what he defines as *turbocapitalismo* (turbo-capitalism): the forced race toward a type of modernity in which the rules are dictated always by 'others,' a race the 'Southerns' are bound to lose while becoming *naufraghi prostituiti del sistema* (prostituted castaways of the system). He instead proposes an alternative modernity evoking the value of 'slowness,' of traditions, and social networks, and invites readers to *riguardare i luoghi* of the South, which semantically means both 'to look at places again' and 'to look after them'; this way the South will restore its prior dignity as an autonomous subject of its own thought. Cassano's argument seems to be simultaneously a recognition and a challenge to Zeno's paradox—to the logic through which Achilles can never catch the tortoise, as it were. The South will never be able to reach the North, which has a head start, and is destined to get closer to it only by imitation. Cassano seems to suggest that Achilles stop racing, as it were, to keep moving at his own pace; he proposes the pursuit of a kind of development that depends upon local resources, that does not try to simulate the North.[11]

At the hands of local politicians, Cassano's book has led "from the Southern thought to the Southern action" (Pizza 2002:46). It turned out that slowing the 'pace' was not the only issue; there also remained the issue of the destination of the journey. As we have seen, however, paradoxically (or maybe not) the process of the current revival has led to the commodification of the local cultural heritage. Caroli (2010:9) writes,

> the alternative modernity pursued in Salento through the revitalization of traditions, building on Cassano's theories, is not as alternative as one may believe, taking into account that the process remains embedded in the commodification that would strive to fight, or in any case, it creates another [commodification]. (my translation from French)

To be sure, local politicians do not try to deny it; Sergio Blasi admits that the identity portrayed by the UCGS is "an identity to live and to sell,"[12] in other words an identity that serves the needs of a touristic market in search of bucolic landscapes and essentialized identities. Elsewhere he argued that "[We do not] consider tradition as a sweet-box to be kept in the cupboard of our living-room with our best porcelain, but as an essential *instrument* to give sense and meaning to a potential growth and development of our territory" (my emphasis).[13]

In a critical reading of the impact of Cassano's book on cultural politics, Berardino Palumbo defines it as a 'political pamphlet' replete with rhetorical strategies and metaphors, and he warns about the risk that such stereotypical models may be manipulated politically (2001:124). Cassano's reference to Greece and to the Mediterranean culture as the origin of the "*pensiero meridiano*," Palumbo argues, reproduce the very essentialized, stereotypical, and imaginary identities typical of modernity, which were constructed between the mid-eighteenth and mid-nineteenth century by the very economic and political

---

[11] Caroli (2009) ascribes this book in the current of 'neo-meridionalism' and building on Amselle (2008), more specifically of sudalternismo (South-alternism).

[12] In Santoro and Torsello 2002.

[13] From the introduction to *La tela infinita* (Mina and Torsello 2005).

powers that Cassano sets out to criticize. The complicity of self-ascribing to the ideology of Mediterraneanism, however—as Herzfeld argues in relation to both Italy and Greece—needs to be read in wider neoliberal and geopolitical context, with respect to the struggle over what he defines as the "global hierarchy of value" part and parcel of the globalization process, and which affects local economies and lives (Herzfeld 2004:3–11). Crucially, not only does such a struggle affect them, it also interacts with pre-existing local issues. It cannot be ignored that in the case at hand, this process is simultaneously embedded in Italy's longstanding Southern Question—the presumed political and socio-cultural 'backwardness' of the South in relation to the North. From the perspective of local politicians, it seems that even this accommodation of the dominant logic of commodification tastes of redemption. Even the more recent and critical reading of the 'orientalizing discourse' on the South (see Schneider 1998) has been turned into a strategically portrayed self-orientalization. What remains interesting is the subversion of the persistent negative stereotypes into positive ones—and this was part of Cassano's ideological and political project.

The cultural revival would seem to have achieved the aims that animated the activists of the middle revival: the past and its indexical manifestations (among which are Griko and pizzica) are now redeemed and turned into a route to a new future, simultaneously thanks to, and notwithstanding, their commod-ification. Playing with words we could say that the old categories of 'honor' and 'shame' applied by anthropologists to the first strands of Mediterranean studies have been replaced locally by one of 'honor after shame.' The current revival, however, have brought back to the fore and intensified debates about authen-ticity and authority, which were already latent in the 'middle revival,' creating ambiguities and contradictions *within* the community. Every local is in fact immersed in the dynamics of the revival; everyone is in what Hacking (1999:10) defines as "the matrix, within which an idea, a concept, or kind is formed," that is the setting within which the idea of a 'revived identity' is socially constructed. Crucially, in what follows will emerge a picture of Grecìa Salentina far from the 'homogenized' one portrayed to outsiders. I will also argue against an equally essentializing picture of the locals as passive recipients, or as unsophisticated consumers of an 'identity' which has been 'sold' to them as much as to outside audiences.

On the Eve of La Notte della Taranta

Massimo had invited me and a few other friends to a barbecue at his house in the countryside of Corigliano; he is a talented musician, and we often spend our summer nights singing, dancing, and of course, eating and drinking, while

Massimo plays the guitar, Francesco the *tamburello*, and Luca, sometimes, the accordion. The party is assured. That night there was also the rehearsal for the final concert of la Notte della Taranta in Melpignano; as Massimo's field is only two kilometers away from Melpignano we could hear the music and the songs rather well. As usual once the topic of *la taranta* emerged the discussion would take a long time, dividing the group between those who explicitly engage with the festival, playing in the concert or simply taking part in the party, and those who are more critical and who openly disassociate themselves from the dynamics it produces. That night the debate opened over the 'abuse' of external music influences in the concerts, which tend to alienate those more emotionally close to the traditional practices, so to speak; the hybridization of the Salentine music repertoire was indeed particularly contested locally in the first years of the folk festival. As the very term *contaminazione* (contamination) used locally attests, this debate is articulated around notions of pollution versus purity, setting those locals who were/are more critical toward the 'contaminating' influence, of different music genres against those who welcomed and welcome it.[14] Yet, even those more inclined toward the revival at times explode and say *E mo' basta cu sta pizzica* (Salentine: and now it is enough with pizzica). That night Sandro kept listening and then broke out, "Ok guys, the question is a different one. Are we happy when we now mention Salento and everybody knows where it is? Yes, we are. Are we not happy to be proud of our music? Yes we are. And are we also happy when we rent a room to tourists in our house? So let's keep listening to the rehearsal." Clearly no one was paying attention to the music in the background.

Francesca intervened and accused Sandro of missing the point. He in turn accused her of the same. She said, "Last year, my grandparents listened to the concert on TV, they told me they recognized only one song or two. They cannot recognize their own music anymore!" Indeed, the "rhetoric of purity" (Pizza 2004:271) transcends aesthetic judgments of authenticity versus innovation, and brings us to the issue of intellectual property and authority over cultural expressions.

The 'fight' that night was to be between Sandro and Francesca. He promptly replied, reminding her that her grandparents were among those who echo the catchy phrase, "The taranta may be dead, *Griko* may be dying. But they are helping us live." This kind of utilitarian comment is not uncommon either. Francesca tried once more to raise her voice: "But we are more than pizzica and tamburelli, and yet this is all we are known for! We have become a precooked

---

14   See Lüdtke (2009) for a discussion of the 'hybridization' of the local folk music repertoire and the fractures it generates.

meal for tourists! So, tomorrow your friends from England arrive, right Manu? Will they expect us to live with tarantulas and speak Griko to them?" Sandro left for a walk; I left for more wine. When I returned a few minutes later, Massimo had started playing the guitar; he usually honors our requests, so we started the usual repertoire of Italian songwriters and singers: De Andrè, Guccini, Bertoli, Gaber ... At a certain point Michela requested *Lu rusciu de lu mare*. Francesco picked up his tamburello, Luca followed him, and before we knew it, we were singing and dancing pizzica. When Sandro returned from his reflexive walk, he found us carried away by the music; he was not going to add anything. He simply smiled at Francesca, who smiled back while she kept dancing.

Caroli (2009), among others, has warned of the danger of commodification embedded in this process; she quotes Goffredo Fofi, who argues that "Salento is trendy now and Salentines enjoy this moment and do not seem to realize the dangers to themselves and to their land that this success brings along" (Fofi 2003, cited in Caroli 2009:13). Yet, the conversation between Francesca and Sandro is common in our nights at Massimo's; I have witnessed similar conversations across the community that argue against an uncritical embrace of the revival or a blind acceptance of its consequences by the population at large. The contact with and the interest shown by outsiders has certainly enhanced self-reflection—locals become aware of what distinguishes them, they discover themselves, as it were—which in turn may promote a process of self-redefinition. 'Pizzica' has reentered—albeit in a renewed form—the experiential reality of the locals, who hear, sing, play, perform, and dance it. What I recorded ultimately shows the variety of reactions, which include a sense of empowerment and pride in the rediscovered value given to the local cultural heritage (music and language included). A sort of discursive pride—what has been defined as 'Salentinite' —is an effect of the revival, although at times it is bittersweet.

My friends here allude in fact to the 'expectations' about Salento that tourists have seemingly been fed, as when I was ironically asked whether my friends from England would expect to find us living with tarantulas and speaking Griko to them; they therefore lament and resist the essentialized identities often associated with Salento. Yet, they are aware that these 'exotic traits' are also strategically exploited by locals—including themselves! That a segment of the population has benefited from the current revival also in economic/occupational terms cannot be denied. This explains the sort of utilitarian comments such as "the Taranta may be dead, Griko may be dying, but they are helping us to live." But then again, even those who discursively complain about the instrumentalization of the revival, and those 'tired' of its politics, would sing pizzica and play tamburello while having a barbecue at their country homes and just throw in a Griko word at the convenient moment, pointing to an enactment of 'cultural intimacy' (Herzfeld:1997). It therefore becomes paramount to critically evaluate the processes of co-construction of such 'reified identities,' and to analyze how locals may deploy, exploit but also resist them.[15] What we see at play here is ultimately the tension emerging from the struggle to comply with outsiders' expectations while resisting being trapped in narrow and essentializing definitions. Portraying and reducing Salento to 'just pizzica and Griko' also means eclipsing other cultural expressions—musicians who do not deal with pizzica complain that they have a harder time establishing themselves professionally, for instance—and to divert attention from environmental issues that have increasingly been plaguing Salento.

The revival seems to have divided locals into colliding camps while they claim their own right to participate in the debate around it, revealing it in all its contradictions. Pizzica has begun to lose its appeal to the local public, both young and old. Young people start to get 'tired' of hearing 'just' pizzica everywhere; the elderly instead feel alienated as they do not recognize the very cultural practices they feel they have 'authority' over. Local politicians, marketers of the territory, and legislators are now the spokespeople, and are considered complicit in portraying an essentialized version of Salento, pizzica, and Griko, one that fails to grasp its complexity.

Criticizing the Revival: Does the Tarantula Speak Griko?

The cultural association Ghetonìa is located on a narrow road in the historical center of Calimera, not far from the house that belonged to the philhellenist Vito Domenico Palumbo. It is almost hidden behind a very discreet front gate, but once you enter it, the typical Salentine courtyard appears before your eyes. All but one of the rooms surrounding the courtyard host the *Casa-Museo della civiltà contadina e della cultura grika* (Italian: the House-Museum of Rural and Griko Culture), with its permanent exhibition of material culture, featuring detailed descriptions in Italian and Griko. Silvano is the president of the association. He already knew of my work since I had been carrying out archival research in the association's library, with its rich collection of newspaper articles dealing with Griko and Grecìa Salentina. He is, indeed, very proud of the library; he has been actively engaged in advancing the cause of Griko for over three decades. He regrets that he does not speak any Griko, although he is fluent in MG.

As usual, he was sitting at his desk in the small office, which also serves as the reception area for the association and museum. I asked him to tell me more specifically about what was involved in getting funding to promote Griko. My question effectively offered him the chance to voice cultural activists' general

---

[15] See Herzfeld 1992 on stereotypes.

sense of dissatisfaction with the work of the UCGS, and with the current revival. He summarized the situation: "For decades, cultural associations and individual scholars worked hard to sensitize the general public to the importance of our traditions and language. This revival started off thanks to the associations, and to the cultural activists; and people started being proud of their own heritage."

Silvano pointed out that in the first years after the establishment of the UCGS, there was a strong collaboration between institutions and local scholars and associations. It was an exciting moment: the programs of the UCGS proliferated with initiatives and a series of projects designed specifically for the promotion of the language and/or of the musical repertoire. Among them were a significant number of publications in or about Griko; a short-lived experience of a news broadcast in Griko; and a competition for newly composed songs with Griko lyrics and their promotion on local radio. Recalling his many years of cultural activity, he exclaimed, "I even wrote what I call the 'book of dreams' to give coherence to the various projects of cultural activists and associations across the territory. And that was in 1991! I was thrilled when it was adopted by the UCGS as a guideline for initiatives that are part of the European INTERREG II program Italy–Greece."

The issue arose when it became clear that his projects were being 'modified' to comply with the regulations of the UCGS and with other requirements of the funding institutions, Silvano explained. Referring for instance to the establishment of the Rooms of Memory (Italian: *Stanze della memoria*), he stressed that these were designed to serve as information points for tourists who visit the villages, and who would be provided with brochures, leaflets, and promotional material; crucially, these "rooms" were to host a library of all the publications available in Griko for tourists to consult. His idea was to create tourist services by renovating historical buildings and typical houses in the historical center of the villages using the funding provided by the INTERREG program.

"You know what they did instead? They created new buildings; in fact they designed one building and then replicated that project for each village— huge buildings! ... And now we are stuck with these 'cumbersome' and ugly monsters. Instead of being 'rooms of memory' they are mausoleums!" Silvano sighed and continued to lament the poor financial management of which the Rooms of Memory are the most obtrusive example.[16] "Local administrators started managing European funding and the funding of the 482 law like they manage administrative funding! Culture cannot be managed in the same way ... culture has now become [merely] an accessory of the revival," he concluded,

---

[16] It seems this occurred because the deadline to apply for the funding was approaching and there was not enough time to develop projects specific to each village.

very disappointed. The idyllic collaboration between cultural activists and the UCGS indeed had a short lifespan, and cultural activists soon started voicing their complaints about the UCGS's insensitivity to their requests. For instance, they lament that no resources are invested in research or valorization activities—which on paper is the aim of The Foundation of the Night of the Tarantula. As Pizza (2004:219) argues with regard to music, the politics of the revival is not always able to retain control over the spaces that it creates.

Cultural activists accuse the UCGS of not valorizing their current efforts, while capitalizing on the work they carried out in the past. In this way, they disassociate themselves from the dynamics of the current revival and criticize it loudly, claiming instead a cultural expertise gained through years of activism. They particularly denounce the marginality of Griko within the festival of the Night of the Tarantula, since it is realized also through the financial support of the UCGS, and since it takes place mostly in Griko-speaking villages. On the one hand, cultural activists expect the UCGS to give the Griko repertoire and heritage pride of place; on the other, mother-tongue speakers sanction the interpretation of the few songs in Griko always performed during the festival. "[The singers] do not know how to sing in Griko, because they don't know even what they are saying, they don't pronounce well," my parents' neighbor 'Nzino (born in 1938) lamented. He was speaking for many others.

The criticism one hears more frequently refers to the instrumentalization of Griko by local politicians as a catalyst for fundraising, and to its exploitation as an 'exotic identity' in order to promote the territory and increase its touristic appeal. As Caroli (2010:5) reports, Massimo Manera, ex-mayor of Sternatìa and ex-president of the UCGS, in fact defines Griko as "the raw material available to access a social, cultural, civic, but also economic development of the territory." Cultural activists therefore denounce the current revival as an instrumental and managerial-type approach to culture. Going to the heart of the issue, Silvano put it this way:

> Local politicians created the Night of the Tarantula, which works fine on a media level; but then they have been using all funding, everything, supranational, national, regional, everything. The Night of the Tarantula has cleaned out everything. Do you find it logical that a museum of popular traditions like the one Ghetonìa created does not get a penny from the municipality? We even [have to] pay the local property tax.

Indeed, what has been upsetting cultural activists is that the UCGS has invested its financial resources into the marketing and realization of the festival La

Notte della Taranta. They accuse the UCGS of having ignored their projects by privileging such a big event—which attracts floods of tourists—rather than supporting the smaller realities and initiatives promoted by cultural associations. Characteristically, investment by the UCGS in the Easter calendar of *I canti di Passione*—in which *The Passion of the Christ* is performed in Griko—has indeed been less consistent over the years. In this sense the *taranta* is 'cleaning out' the funds destined for Griko. What may seem to be a metaphor for corruption is instead an accusation of poor management of financial resources, as well as of lack of expertise regarding the cultural heritage.

We see how on the one hand cultural activists consider the current revival to be the well-deserved reward for their decades of work; they fight to be recognized for sparking the revival, wanting to lay claims to cultural ownership and the management of the Griko cause and activities. Yet on the other hand, they accuse the UCGS of lacking the required cultural expertise to best invest the money and of having exploited their initiatives, only to manipulate their original claims and aims. These debates ultimately hide activists' fears of losing control over cultural and linguistic ownership, and reveal tensions about the division of labor in the mechanism of the revival. There is in fact another element to take into account: cultural associations cannot apply directly for the funding provided by Law 482; the national law is earmarked specifically for schools and local authorities, and in the case of Griko, to UCGS; to access that funding, they had/have to submit a project proposal to the UCGS, which is then evaluated and may or may not be funded. Silvano told me that they were nostalgic for those past times in which cultural associations could apply directly to the European Union for funding via the European Bureau for Lesser-Used Languages or other funding bodies, without the bureaucratic mediation of the UCGS—part and parcel of the institutionalization of the revival—which they feel alienates them and deprives them of their own authority. Indeed, what appears to be a conflict over cultural ownership is also linked to access to resources.[17]

The interplay of language policies

Significantly, Griko activists complain that National Law 482 is not sensitive to the specificity of Griko as a "historical and cultural minority language." Their

---

[17] During one of our more recent encounters, however, Silvano was more optimistic about future collaborations with the UCGS, since in 2017 the UCGS selected a project proposed by cultural association Ghetonìa for the publications of three notebooks by Vito Domenico Palumbo. These contain popular songs, fairy tales, and the Griko dictionary, collected by Palumbo during the late nineteenth/early twentieth century, and transcribed into Greek characters, which he had sent to the Philological Circle of Constantinople in order to participate in several editions of the Competition of Greek Poetry and Literature.

argument is that the law was written with the 'ethnic minority languages' of the Italian Alps in mind, an area where there is 'perfect bilingualism'. There, the need for interpreters and translators of minority languages to Italian is legitimate in the context of public administration and services, but in the case of Griko, the UCGS wasted that money, the argument goes—these are not the habitual domains of use of the language. Indeed, National Law 482 provides for concrete measures to be adopted in the fields of education, public administration, services, and media, without taking into account the historical specificities of each case, as well as the processes of language erosion and shift. Interestingly, the Italian Constitution (1948) itself does not neglect the subject of linguistic minorities. Article 3 affirms citizens' equality regardless of their language, and Article 6 states that the Republic safeguards linguistic minorities with appropriate norms. Since National Law 482 emerged half a century after the constitution's adoption, its effectiveness was in jeopardy, as during this period profound transformations affected the conditions of Italy's minority-language speakers (see Chapter 2).

School teachers and cultural and language activists alike stressed to me the need for a regional law that would more specifically promote Griko's documentation and preservation. In 2012 their request was met, when Regional Law 5, *Norme per la promozione e la tutela delle lingue minoritarie* (Italian) in Puglia passed. In addition to Griko, the "norms for the promotion and the safeguard of the linguistic minorities in Puglia" refers to the Franco-Provençal minority (in the province of Foggia), and the Arbëreshë minority (in the Foggia and Taranto provinces).[18] The regional law partly replicates the aims of National Law 482, effectively substituting it in the school domain; the major and crucial difference is that it provides funding directly to cultural associations—in addition to municipalities and schools—without the bureaucratic mediation of the UCGS. But in the application of the regional law other issues arose too, among them the lack of coordination among the various projects financed and realized in the various villages, and the lack of long-term planning. Since these projects' sustainability depends on budgets that change every year, even the most successful of them is doomed to remain fragile, cultural activists lament. Nino from the cultural association La Bottega voiced his concern this way:

---

[18] The regional law is the result of the lobbying of Sergio Blasi, the ex-mayor of Melpignano and regional councilman for the Democratic Party (PD) at the time of writing. Local authorities, individual municipalities, cultural associations, and schools can apply for and benefit from the funding provided annually by the law for initiatives related to: (a) the safeguarding, recovery, preservation, and valorization of the respective minority languages and related historical cultural heritage through research activities in history and linguistics, publication, and/or dissemination of related studies; (b) the teaching of minority languages in schools; and (c) TV, radio, and the press.

You know what happens? The region funds all projects in a sort of democratic distribution, without even evaluating them for their real contribution to the valorization of Griko. This way, all cultural associations, all municipalities of the villages get some of the funding. But this is the problem. This means that you apply with your project, but then the Region funds not even half of what you put in the budget. And you are still expected to realize the same project with half the money! You are bound to realize a mediocre project this way, and this is a waste of money.

Both legal provisions have also sparked complaints among Griko experts, who also highlight the limits of their application. School principals have their own complaints, and refer mainly to the unfair allocation of resources provided by National Law 482, since schools have on average received less than ten percent of what the UCGS received from the national law funds. The discrepancy is clear enough, and this leads school principals to argue that schools have been discriminated against by the very law that was meant to 'protect' the language, and thus its transmission. The issue of the funding protocol comes back to the fore; because of the bureaucratic procedures, each school may end up receiving the funding destined for Griko teachers as late as February—and the school year ends in early June. This may also mean (as has in fact happened) that Griko is taught for only twelve hours per year, effectively neutralizing the efforts of the teachers. Together with school principals, teachers also lamented the continuing reductions in financial resources provided by Law 482. Sandra, a Griko teacher from Corigliano, pointed out that the national funding was cut altogether for a couple of years, but she added, "Fortunately as soon as schools stopped receiving funding from National Law 482, the regional law passed and we [the school] started applying for and receiving funds through it. The thing is that the regional law funds a maximum of 10,000 euros per project, which means that schools are not motivated to apply collectively as a web of schools as they have done in the past." As Sandra and members of cultural associations alike point out, the regional law does not favor collaboration and integration of activities within the villages of Grecìa Salentina.

Legal instruments, together with financial resources, were/are indeed necessary for the articulation of claims, but as Cowan argues (Cowan et al. 2001b:1), the rights model "has had complex and contradictory implications for individuals and groups whose claims must be articulated within its terms." Indeed, if legitimation and recognition were supposed to give back to locals the control over their fate or to enhance self-determination, the unexpected consequence of these processes, and of the institutionalization of the revival, have been the reverse: the initial feeling of empowerment soon transformed into a feeling of loss of control over cultural ownership.

The multitude of voices I have presented in this chapter reveal how the management of the local cultural heritage produce tensions and no clear consensus among the locals. It ultimately shows the effects on the ground of the meeting and the clash of local claims, immersed as they are in a global frame of representation. In the next chapter I continue to treat such tensions, focusing specifically on the current ideological debates about Griko in which locals engage, reshaping time and again their relationship with the past and cultural heritage in the light of current concerns and wider expectations.

5

Debating Griko

The Current Languagescape

IN 1992 the European Council adopted a European Charter for Regional or Minority Languages, which then came into force in 1998. The charter intends "to protect and promote regional or minority languages as a threatened aspect of Europe's cultural heritage" (European Charter Guidance 2004:3); being the first international instrument focused solely on language, its symbolic contribution cannot be underestimated. Indeed, Italian Law 482 is to be considered one of its important outcomes. Significantly, the Charter represents a shift from previous legal measures supporting linguistic tolerance and protection to linguistic promotion. Through this ideological shift, which sits in the context of burgeoning rights discourses, Europe's cultural wealth and linguistic diversity becomes "one of the main sources of the vitality, richness and originality of European civilisation" (Ó Riagáin 2001:36). Such celebration of the common European heritage would seem to provide a way to overcome the nineteenth-century linguistic and cultural nationalisms that formed the basis for the establishment of nation-states. Moreover, the emphasis on 'diversity' as a symbol of Europe's richness, and the discourse of 'unity in diversity,' have been further promoted by international agencies such as Unesco, and have permeated everyday discourses.

As Susan Gal (2006b:167) notes, however, the emphasis on linguistic diversity is deceptive; the European Charter recognizes "named languages, with unified, codified norms of correctness embodied in literature and grammars"—that is, in order for minority languages to be recognized as languages in their own right, they have to go through a standardization process. Speakers of minority languages are therefore confronted with the expectation to reproduce the dominant ideologies that inform the construction of national languages—together with the attendant challenges—and also to conform to the old 'romantic/romanticized' expectations which rely on the same ideological tropes that match 'a language' to 'a people.' In the case of Griko, the lack of a standard generates multiple 'language ideological debates' (Blommaert 1999), which are more recurrent than the use of Griko itself. As typical of a metalinguistic community such as this, locals participate actively in them, and by discussing how to transcribe and teach Griko or how to enrich its limited vocabulary, they reveal their experiential perceptions and ideological projections of the role of Griko in the past-present-future.

By considering in depth locals' ideologies with respect to Griko's authenticity, I therefore fill out the cultural temporality of language through which perceptions of morality and aesthetics intermingle with affect, which poses constant challenges to language standardization, change, and to sporadic attempts at renewal. My claim is that for many locals Griko has ultimately become a metalanguage to talk about that past in order to position themselves in the present; moreover, according to the criteria through which locals evaluate the authenticity of language, they also determine who can claim authority over it—and vice versa. The analysis of the current languagescape reveals the repercussions of these debates on community dynamics, and the power struggles that have intensified through the current revival.

The (Non-)Standardization of Griko

According to Bakhtin (1981) language standardization goes against the natural tendency toward diversification; it becomes an ideology in itself. Moreover, as in the case of national languages, the standardization of minority languages leads to the stigmatization of certain forms, as certain other forms are valued more and elevated to the status of standard (Gal 2006b:171). This process creates heterogeneity and hierarchy rather than the expected uniformity, Gal continues, and this may lead speakers to question or reject the authenticity of the form chosen as the standard, or to consider their own linguistic forms less adequate and even less authentic by comparison.[1]

Griko does not have a standard; moreover, Law 482 does not distinguish it from Calabrian Greek. Despite considerable differences, Griko and Greko are nevertheless joined under the label of 'the Greek linguistic minority' on Italian soil. Griko itself is, in fact, characterized by internal lexical and phonetic variation among the villages of GS—what in technical terms is called diatopic variation, and which applies also to Calabrian Greek. This means that several variants of the same word may exist, or that the same variant may be pronounced—and

---

[1]   See McDonald 1989 and Timm 2001, who highlight these issues for the case of Breton, as well as Roseman 1995 and Jaffe 1999 for the case of Corsican.

thus become written—differently while remaining, by and large, mutually intelligible. When in the late 1970s the linguist Alberto Sobrero investigated the diachronic transformation of Griko by comparing his data with those provided by Morosi in 1870, not surprisingly he noted the influence of the Romance variety and Italian at the lexical level. More interestingly, he pointed out that words reported by Morosi as being used in only one village were then also used in other villages (*gruni*, 'pork,' was used only in Corigliano and now also in Castrignano and Calimera). Moreover, what Morosi had indicated as a characteristic form of a specific village was no longer to be attested there, but elsewhere: *magrà*, 'far,' was used in Sternatia and *larga* elsewhere, whereas in the late 1970s the latter form prevailed in every village except Soleto. These linguistic shifts do/did not depend on the influence of the Romance variety or Italian; rather, Sobrero argued, they attest to the erosion of the linguistic system due to the fact that each village reacted differently and at different times to its isolation from the Greek spoken around Greece (Sobrero 1979). If the absence of a hegemonic center explains historically the absence of a 'standard' Griko, today, locals' resistance to the standardization of Griko assumes a new significance, as I move to discuss.

* * *

It was a rather chilly Wednesday afternoon in early November. Adriana and I had arranged to meet at her place to then go for a walk through the village, but because of the *tramontana*—the northern wind—the temperature had dropped considerably. We decided instead to stay in. Adriana from Corigliano was one of my first informants who soon turned into a friend. She is in her early 50s, and unusually, given her age, a mother-tongue Griko speaker—she had grown up in a Griko-speaking environment and would always hear her mother communicating in Griko with their neighbors. To her, in contrast, her mother would speak Griko only in specific contexts and for specific reasons. "She would use it when she didn't want us to understand and always when she had to reproach me and my sisters. And that often happened ... It worked with us, so I use my mom's methods with my nephews too to transmit the language" (see Chapter 2), she explained on another occasion with a laugh. At the beginning of our frequentations, we would switch between Italian and Salentine; as I improved my Griko, she used it with me more and more often.

As she handed me a cup of coffee she had just made, I thanked her saying, "*Kalì sorta*"—literally "Have a good destiny"—*sorta* being a borrowing from Salentine (Italian: *sorte*). "That's how you say it?", she asked me, "I hear it here too sometimes, or people may just say 'Grazie' [Italian]. When I go to the gas station, I always thank the guy saying, '*Na stasì kalò*' [literally 'May you be well']."

The conversation about the different ways to say 'thank you' kept us busy for the next ten minutes. *Kalì sorta* apparently was meant to be used only by someone older to thank someone younger; in some villages, such as Sternatia, people tend to use *Charistò*. I commented that I found it hard at times to memorize the lexical differences characteristic of the various villages, and the preferred the choices of the villagers; that's when she suddenly exclaimed, "This is a language which has been transmitted orally. Its variation is its richness; is there anything nicer than this? I am going to find the script of *Loja Americana* [American Words], and you will see what I mean."

A few years earlier Adriana had gotten involved in the performance of this hilarious play, which builds on a number of misunderstandings arising from the use of a couple of English loanwords. It was by Prof. Tommasi—a retired teacher and one of the most respected local Griko scholars—in an alternation of Griko, Salentine, and Italian. I could guess what she meant before she went on to explain, as I had already viewed the tape of the performance: in it, every actor used their own language variety, effectively creating a polyphonic performance. I had also met with Renato from Calimera, who directed it; he was very enthusiastic about his accomplishment, and proud of having involved amateur actors from various villages in Grecìa Salentina: "I think it is right to respect the local variants; it is more popular and democratic. So, I say *Kecci* [small], but you say *minciò*? Say *minciò* then!", he had remarked.

"Playing in *Loja Americana* was real fun, Manu!" Adriana said, giving up looking for the script, "I will find it though, and you can photocopy it" (and she did, a few weeks later). Her mobile phone rang; it was her sister, who asked Adriana to collect her son from his soccer training. As we were leaving the house to fetch her nephew we commented on how cold the weather had turned. So I said, "*Pao na piako t'asciài atti' màkina, kajo*"—"I'd better take the hat from my car." She immediately intervened in Salentine, "You say *kajo* [better]—that's right. Here we say *kàddhio*."

Like Adriana and Renato here, locals generally value the richness of Griko that comes from its internal variation and often comment upon those variations, at times at the expenses of the communication itself. The frequent interruptions to highlight and/or clarify differences often put a conversation in Griko on hold, turning Griko itself into the topic of the conversation, as I have argued elsewhere (Pellegrino 2016b).[2] Pronunciation is always noticed—as

---

[2]   To be sure, this phenomenon is not confined to Griko, but it is also relevant to the Salentine dialect, which varies, and at times considerably, as you move progressively outside of Grecìa Salentina. Interestingly, dialect speakers of the villages of Grecìa Salentina are readily recognized since they tend to use the simple past also in Salentine, following Griko, instead of the past perfect used in the nearby villages.

Adriana did a few times that afternoon too—since it indexes the village of origin: apart from the 'smaller detail' mentioned above (*kajo/kaddhio*) the major differences refer to the Greek ψ (ps) and ξ (ks); these are pronounced differently in the various villages (e.g., *fs, sc, ss, ts*); so, for instance, the Greek ψωμί, or *psomì*, (bread) is pronounced *sciomì* in Zollino and Castrignano, and *tsomì* in most of the other villages; similarly, the Standard Greek ξέρω (to know) is pronounced *scero* and *tsero*, etc. As I can attest first-hand coming from Zollino, the pronunciation used in this village is often a source of comment, and is occasionally the target of humorous remarks, indexing a minority within the minority, so to speak.[3] Speakers often recognize and may even use (jokingly or accommodatingly) a lexical or phonetic variant from another village, while making the point that 'that' variant is not 'theirs.'

Indeed, while we were getting in her car, Adriana recalled another project she was involved in that had been carried out in my home village; this was about the Easter tradition *I passiùna* (see Chapter 3). She found it hard to sing using Zollino pronunciation, she explained, and so she sang in 'her' Griko from Corigliano. She is not the only one, of course. "There is no way I can put something different in my head from what I've always said and heard. Never and never (Italian: *Mai e poi mai*)," she firmly concluded. Locals' attachment to their own variety, to a specific pronunciation and/or lexical choice, is indeed widespread, rendering 'language standardization' something of an off-limits topic. It could be argued that this stems from a form of 'linguistic campanilism,' with a village's *campanile* (bell tower) being emblematic of the smallest discrete unit of social/linguistic identification.[4] There is, however, more to it.

As she drove through the village she passed near the house of an elderly lady she was close to while growing up: "When I went to visit her she would always say, '*Na, irte o ijo-mu essu*' [The sun arrived in my house]," Adriana remembered, moved. Then she pointed out to me the neighborhood where she grew up, commenting that she has nice memories of her childhood, although her father had migrated to Switzerland and spent over twenty years there. "We used to live in a *casa a corte* (see previous chapter) also with Nunna 'Ndata. She was a widow; her husband died at war," she said, using the typical way of referring to older women one is close to as *nunna*, which conveys a sense of familiarity as well as respect. She then continued to recount details of this neighbor's life with particular accuracy; with the same attention to detail and

---

[3]   Although I am complimented for having learned Griko as an adult, some locals—Griko experts included—may lament that I come from Zollino because of its atypical pronunciation of ψ (ps) and ξ (ks).

[4]   For the notion of campanilism with reference to Corsica and Bergamasco, see Jaffe 1999; Cavanaugh 2009.

affection she also recalled how in the evenings, together with her sisters, she would sit by Nunna 'Ndata's door step: "The light was always off!", she emphasized as if she were trying to recreate that scene, "and she would tell us stories [Salentine: *ci cuntava li fatti*] and often in Griko; she did not have TV and she didn't want one until she died."

As we were approaching the spot where her nephew was waiting for us, she shifted to comment on how well the heating system of her old car still worked. I agreed, and added that the *tramontana* wind had been giving me a headache all day. She teasingly asked me, "Do you have rheumatisms in your head?"—"*Echi reuma so kòkkalo?*" That led her to mention an anecdote about her grandfather, who once jokingly complained about his wife talking too much by saying, "*Eh 'Ntogna! Echi reuma ses anke, reuma sa chèria, reuma so kòkkalo, ce si' glossa 'e' sôrkete mai?*' (Griko)—"You have rheumatisms in your legs, hands, head and it never affects your tongue?" Adriana had inherited his sense of humor; we meanwhile collected her nephew and were heading back to my car.

As we see with Adriana here, specific words and expressions are not 'just words,' nor 'simple expressions,' but become images of and from the past, which are linked to locals' personal memories of language use. Each word chosen, each sound reproduced, is an echo of someone else or of a specific moment in time—Bakhtin (1981) indeed had it right a long time ago. Locals hang onto these, as they evoke the memory of others who had uttered them, connecting them across time and beyond phenomenological distance, mobilizing vivid emotions. This way the 'textures of Griko' become palpable; indeed, its materiality made up of both sounds and images reveals itself as it engages people in recalling a story linked to a specific word or expression, which in turn elicits an anecdote from their past. I have witnessed this countless times. Keeping *that* specific word, using *that* specific expression, and pronouncing a word in one particular way or another become therefore ways to keep the past alive, together with the memory of the people who inhabited it. If today Griko is no longer used primarily as a language of daily exchange, memories of language use are 'alive' and contribute to shaping its use up to the present, as I also show in the next chapter. In this sense, the material presence of Griko is all around through its sounds and forms. This may also explain, I contend, why no one village variety has so far prevailed over the others, and also why attempts to standardize Griko have always been challenged in the name of the local declination of 'unity in diversity.'

This applies also to the local language teachers—who are referred to as 'language experts' (Italian: *esperti di Griko*)—and to local Griko scholars. A few years later Adriana and I would get involved in a project called *Pos Màtome*

Griko (How We Learn Griko); it was financed by the European Commission, and aimed at the development of teaching materials for Griko as a way to address the lack of dedicated textbooks. Having taken part in the project I can attest that it was fraught by various challenges, to which I will return.[5] Tellingly, however, the possibility of creating a standard was briefly mentioned and soon collectively dismissed on the basis that "it would be detrimental to Griko's richness and historical development," to use Prof. Tommasi's words. He was involved in the project, together with Giorgio from Sternatia and Sandra from Corigliano, while Adriana acted as a consultant in her capacity as a mother-tongue speaker. Indeed, the outcome of this project differed from the original vision: each of us compiled the various CEFR competency levels (A1, A2, B1, B2, etc.) drawing on our own village variety. The resulting polyphonic structure may create difficulty for new learners and readers, as the critique goes.

Yet what prevails is the view that "No local Griko has, or should claim any superiority over the others. No Griko speaker can presume to teach Griko to another speaker," as Paolo from Martano phrased it. There are also pockets where it is still believed that "the Griko from Calimera is more correct" based on the misplaced assumption of its stronger affinity with the Greek spoken in Greece. Such comments also originate in the prestige associated with intellectuals' activities within the 'philhellenic circle of Calimera' (see Chapter 1). Largely, however, locals do not rank Griko's variation internally. By valuing it and Griko's 'unity in diversity,' locals ultimately resist language standardization, and will likely continue to resist it as long as experiential memories of language use persist. Yet, while the *Pos Màtome Griko* project received a mixed reception, it was appreciated that it involved local Griko teachers. One of my informants pointed out to me, "At least you avoided cold interventions from external language experts, linguists, or 'aficionados' [Italian: *appassionati*] of Griko who don't really know us and expect to come and teach us our own language." On the one hand this highlights how the latter are perceived as lacking the experiential, material and affective dimension of the lived use of the language, which is itself embedded in time and memory; on the other hand, it points to intellectual property issues and the power struggle over who retains authority over Griko and cultural heritage more broadly, which I introduced in the last chapter, and to which I will come back.

---

[5]   The four partners of the project were the British Hellenic College of Athens, the Istituto di Culture Mediterranee (Institute for Mediterranean Cultures) and Agenzia per il Patrimonio Culturale Euromediterraneo (the Euro-Mediterranean Cultural Heritage Agency), based in Lecce, and also the University of Cyprus. I was invited to take part in the project while writing up my PhD thesis by Mr. Karkania, whom I had interviewed while conducting fieldwork in Greece. He is a Griko aficionado, as well as the director of the British Hellenic College.

The Limits of 'Unity in Diversity':
The Teaching of Griko

The teaching of Griko in schools is a highly contested matter. It is also the language domain that faces the biggest challenges, and where the limits of the ideology of 'unity in diversity' reveal themselves. At a discursive level, Griko's unity in diversity would seem to find support in the school setting. This is how the then-schoolmaster of Castrignano, Professor Nucita, phrases it in one of her articles:

> We overcame the dilemma of the variants that our language shows ... We agreed that 'diversity' keeps enriching 'diversity,' as every community, through its specific language expresses its own social and evolutionary history. The phonetic and graphic diversity of the lexicon of every village is certainly linked to the evolutionary history of the specific territory ... We adopted a diversified method: to introduce children to the variants of other villages, comparing them to the variant of their own village.[6]

However, in practice, the limits of applying these views soon emerged. Prof. Greco from Sternatia indeed complained openly that, at the moment, the reality is rather different than the theory: If for the current academic year a teacher from Calimera is appointed, she would teach the Griko of Calimera; the following year, however, a teacher from Corigliano might be appointed, and she would teach the Griko of Corigliano. "Children therefore find enormous difficulties" in learning the language, Prof. Greco said. Indeed, the teacher's variety of the language almost inevitably becomes the default standard for each classroom, at times provoking reactions from parents, while teachers are not necessarily nor equally competent in every village variety, and their mobility from one village to another according to the school year complicates things further.[7]

In order to grasp these intricacies, I undertook participant observation of weekly Griko classes at primary schools, rotating through the villages of Grecìa Salentina over a two-month period. What immediately became evident was that Griko was not taught in the old normative scholastic way. Giovanna, for instance, would resort to teaching her own poems—which were beautiful, I might add—in her classrooms. Sandra and Maria would translate contemporary

---

[6]   http://win.associazioneitaloellenica.org/forum/article_read.asp?id=109.
[7]   See Jaffe 1999 for Corsican. Meek 2009 describes the same dynamic for the case of teaching Kaska, a Northern Athapascan language, where students were taught the dialect of their teacher, and this caused some parents to complain to the administration.

songs into Griko, such as 'YMCA.' Ivana would use Pantaleo—a rabbit she would create on the spot from a handkerchief, as grandparents used to do—who would then interact with the children in Griko. Giorgio, instead, experimented with teaching Griko and Modern Greek comparatively in collaboration with the MG teacher sent by the Greek Ministry of Education; at times he would use articles written in Griko from the local journal *Spitta*.

When I first interviewed Griko teachers they constantly mentioned the lack of a standardized Griko orthography, and of dedicated teaching material (at the time) as the biggest issues they had been encountering. Interestingly, however, even after the publication of *Pos Màtome Griko*, this has not been adopted as a textbook by all Griko experts, and even Giorgio and Sandra make partial use of it. Indeed, Griko teachers often privilege teaching schoolchildren poems, songs, and popular rhymes in Griko, while the wider repertoire of popular culture and the importance of the language, its history, its traditions tend to be presented discursively in Italian. At the end of the school year, each school often organizes initiatives such as theatrical or musical performances, in which the children are the protagonists, and 'perform' using the knowledge of Griko they acquired during the classes. In other words, the teaching of Griko in school is not aimed at the production of new speakers but rather at conveying and replicating past cultural and linguistic artifacts. Figure 22 below is a good example to this effect, and is taken from the teaching material provided by Sandra.

Figure 22. Teaching material

The text provided here alternates between Griko and Salentine. It makes reference to the goblin of popular tradition—the Sciakùddhi—who, in order to adjust to modern times, migrates from living in the fireplace to living inside a can of Coke. Griko experts therefore continue to draw on the wider repertoire of popular culture (see Chapter 3), but they purposively 'adapt' it to contemporary life, trying out innovative ways of presenting Griko—in dialogue with the past, but recontextualized in the present. This was indeed Sandra's aim, she said.

Sandra has been teaching Griko since 2002, and when I asked her to tell me which of the projects carried at school she considered most successful, without hesitation she mentioned the *Orchestra Sparagnina* (Italian). The Sparagnina Orchestra involved about thirty schoolchildren—now young adults—from the school of Corigliano, who, over the course of ten years, learned to play instruments such as accordion, tambourine, guitar, and percussion, and to sing the traditional repertoire of songs in Griko, learning fragments of the language along the way. We see here the relevance of music in the transmission of language—however partial—and how they are mutually supportive: playing/singing the Griko repertoire enhances language learning, and is also fun; by learning, Griko students can fully appreciate its musical/performative expressions. Sandra has successfully dragged her entire family into singing and playing Griko at cultural events dedicated to Griko, and she is proud that she managed to transmit to her eldest daughter a passion for the language. Sandra's daughter Tina now teaches Griko to children as part of a project funded through the regional law. "As long as we pass on the love for the language, we fulfill our task. Anyone who teaches knows that the results come with time; some of these kids may get involved with Griko in a few years, when you least expect it," Sandra added.

As for the popular reception to the teaching of Griko, if we compare the finding of the Lecce Group in the late 1970s with a recent sociolinguistic survey by Alberto Sobrero and Annarita Miglietta (2010) and Miglietta (2009), we read that 45 percent of the sample in Sternatia and 42 percent in Corigliano consider it an effective way to preserve the language. However, there have been instances in which parents rejected the teaching of Griko, as happened in Soleto in 2005; indeed, Article 4 of Law 482 states clearly that the teaching of minority languages depends "also on the basis of the request of the children's parents." According to the schoolmaster, this instance might be singled out, since Soleto (together with Melpignano) is a village where the language shift away from Griko happened toward the end of the nineteenth century; parents' cold reception toward teaching Griko could be linked to a lower sensitivity to the topic, he argued. Percentages and villages aside, there is certainly a wide divide, as there are parents who show personal attachment to Griko and welcome its transmission—albeit through the teaching of its cultural heritage. At the opposite end, there are parents who instead lament that Griko takes up time that could be more fruitfully spent teaching children English. Indeed, the teaching of Griko in school would seem to confer the minority language the same symbolic capital as Italian—or English, for that matter. However, by striving to reproduce the dominant language ideology, Griko may keep losing out and being perceived as a 'recreational' subject, depriving it therefore of the 'seriousness' of other languages and subjects. It seems that Griko does not mix well with the normative monolingualism historically dominant in such an institution, and that locals at large do not challenge that assumption. Rocco phrases it differently: "The death of a language is the school. When you impose a language in the school, it means that it is dead. No one learns a language at school."

The 'politics of orthographic representations'

Although Griko lacks a 'standard,' in recent years it has interestingly been enjoying a renewed life in its written form, thanks to the activity/contribution of local scholars and laypeople alike. The journal *Spitta* (Spark), written in Griko and published since the end of 2006, is a typical example. Giuseppe from Martano, a retired schoolteacher, is one of the editors and a passionate activist for Griko. As is often the case among those belonging to the 'in-between generation,' he is a 'semi-speaker' who was not taught Griko as his mother tongue, and who has been increasingly engaging with the Griko cause. For over a decade he has also tenaciously been compiling and curating a website which includes grammatical tables, as well as recordings of elderly speakers, their transcriptions and translations into Italian.

Commenting on this initiative he pointed out that how to transcribe Griko was one of the first and largest issues *Spitta* encountered. This shift from the traditional oral use of Griko to its current and predominantly written use poses its own challenges. Indeed, if until the fifteenth century the Greek alphabet was utilized (see Chapter 1, especially the activity of the Monastery of Casole), since contact between Salento and Greece receded, Griko survived predominantly as an oral language; this was the case until the end of the nineteenth century, when the exponents of the circle of Calimera started writing again, mostly utilizing a transliteration in Latin characters (see Chapter 1). A proposal to go back to using the Greek alphabet has been put forward, but so far it has not found many advocates on the grounds that this would alienate the speakers themselves, becoming a language only for experts and aficionados. Not surprisingly, there is still no local consensus on how to transcribe it, while, interestingly, all activists claim they aim to 'facilitate' the reading of Griko; this is the principle on which they base their choice of the orthographic conventions adopted—however different they may be.[8]

Indeed, Giuseppe knows that one of the strongest criticisms raised against *Spitta* relates to orthography, as the articles published do not conform to the same conventions and present a wide variation. As seen in Figure 23 (below), on the right-hand side, the sound of the Greek 'χ' is represented as 'ch' (as in *chrono*), mirroring the most commonly used transliteration of Greek. The language reference here is Standard Modern Greek. On the left-hand side, it is instead represented as 'h' (as in *eho*), whereas 'ch' stands for 'k' (as in *checci*),

---

[8]   The movement from an 'oral' text to a 'written' one is never a neutral process, but rather an ideological one, which may highlight connections between orthography, sociolinguistic identity and power (Jaffe and Walton 2000), aesthetics, and linguistic inequality (Jaffe 2000; see also Bucholtz 2000; Ochs 1979).

taking as reference the Italian language. Significantly, the very choice to refer to the Italian or Greek alphabet to write Griko reveals different ideological alignments and projections; it ultimately indicates how writers have in mind a different set of final readers: the Italian or Greek audience—or people who know or have studied Greek. While in the first case Griko speaks for locality, in the second case it is projected as one of the languages of Hellenism in the world, so to speak. Apart from the ideological and political implications of these choices, the reader is put into distress.

Figure 23. The Journal *Spitta*

Daniele from Calimera is one of the most refined connoisseurs of Griko, and feels strongly about these issues: "It seems absurd to me to write in the Greek alphabet; we shouldn't do it because we have a whole series of palatal, semi-consonants and one cacuminal sound that you can't reproduce with it. Language is a protocol." Because of its hybridity, Griko requires a phonetic transcription for which both the Greek and Italian alphabets are insufficient or inadequate, Daniele argues. Advocating coherency and simplicity, he has proposed a writing system that addresses the multiple local pronunciations by opting to use the Latin *psi* and *xi* to reproduce the equivalent ψ (ps) and ξ (ks) of the Greek alphabet, going back the origin of the words that contain them. For instance, the Greek ξέρω (to know) is written *xero* instead of *scero/tsero/ssero*; the Greek word ψωμί (bread) is written *psomì* instead of *sciomì/tsomì/ssomì*. This would provide a standardized approach "which overcomes localisms and aims to write Salentine-Greek in a way in which everyone can recognize themselves, including the Greeks" (Palma 2018:109).[9]

This debate is not confined to *cultori del griko*, or language activists and experts; it permeates and reaches literate Griko speakers, becoming a topic of concern and dispute leading them to passionately participate in conversations and in online forums. "Everyone writes as he pleases," one informant told me, on the grounds of either simplicity or closeness to the oral form. "Everyone writes as he hears it, or as he can," he then added. The result is an appreciable range of orthographic variation among the written texts that circulate, also due to the fact that even the same individual may at times be inconsistent with his own criteria or change them over time. Meanwhile, as Alexandra Jaffe (2003:521) notes for Corsican, "in the absence of any kind of recognized language academy able to impose one official orthography, the orthography debate stands as a conventionalized public discourse used by people to express their views about the nature or the state of the language."

Giuseppe humbly acknowledges the limitations of the journal *Spitta*: for those who write, the stumbling block is indeed the orthographic representation. As for the reading audience, there are two issues, he says: "Elderly Griko speakers often cannot even read; if they can, they find huge difficulties in reading Griko. Those who can read but do not master Griko have difficulties

---

[9]   He argues therefore that a writing system similar to the one adopted for MG is not adequate, since it had to deal with different and more recent influences from Slavic languages, Turkish, and Venetian, while "Griko has kept more faithfully characteristics that go back two, three millennia" (Palma 2018:119–121). Since 2010 he has been giving Griko classes in his own house; his 'school of Salentine Greek' is attended by a group of about ten semi-speakers over the age of sixty who come from various villages of GS (Calimera, Sternatia, Castrignano, Corigliano). Interestingly in his lessons Daniele follows the Rocci dictionary of Modern Greek in alphabetical order as a starting point for a discussion on the etymology of Griko words— mainly in Italian.

too." Certainly, elderly literate Griko speakers struggle to read this journal. This may be in part linked to their limited exposure to the practice of reading in general; or the difficulty may lie in the very practice of 'visualizing' what they have only 'said or heard.' Add to this issue that reading is not an interactional practice that presupposes a human encounter, as they are used to: the result is that elderly literate Griko speakers may find reading *Spitta* a lonely enterprise, alienating and frustrating at times, leading some of them to argue that "This is not Griko."

Ideological debates about Griko

The Kaliglossa (Good Language) cultural association from Calimera is particularly linked to the Griko–Hellenic Festival, an annual initiative that first took place in 2007 and went on for a few years; the inaugural festival, as well as that of the following year, centered on a poetry, music, and theater contest in Griko, while an Ancient and Modern Greek language contest was incorporated from year three onward. The following is excerpted from the association's website:

> [The association] is aware of the difficulty of proposing the Griko of today as a language of common use and communication. Yet it tries to foster its knowledge through adequate acquisition strategies and through the circulation of written texts. In this regard, it strives to stimulate and encourage the writing of new texts (poetry, music and theatre) with the aim of enriching the already *notable literary repertoire* in this language. (my emphasis)

The contest's regulations, interestingly, make it clear from the outset that,

> The jury will select those compositions which follow the spirit of an *authentic kaliglossa* [good language] and will take into account how the authors use the lexical repertoire of each language, limiting to the minimum the recourse to foreign words. It is furthermore requested an accurate and coherent phonetic transcription of Griko. (my emphasis)

These words reveal clearly that the association's activism is not aimed at language revitalization as such, which would upgrade Griko and render it again a language of common use and communication, as it were. The association instead fosters its knowledge by promoting the written production of an 'authentic *kaliglossa*,' aiming more at language restoration. Language shift has indeed led to further linguistic erosion and to the impoverishment of Griko's vocabulary, as speakers have 'forgotten' words and replaced them with borrowings from Salentine and Italian, although grammatically adapting them to Griko.

As Grazio from Sternatia characteristically put it, *"To griko ka kuntème àrtena? Durante sti strada fikamo tossa loja ka 'e tàchume pròbbiu stennù plèo'"* (Griko)—"The Griko we speak today? Along the way we abandoned so many words and we don't remember them any more." These dynamics have not surprisingly led to the emergence of a personalized and 'intimate' vocabulary unique to the speaker—what in linguistics is labeled idiolect.

The linguistic recovery of forgotten forms therefore becomes one of the issues debated locally; it regularly emerges in my encounters with Daniele, who used to be a member of the Kaliglossa association. This is how he addressed it: "The Griko we speak in Calimera lacks a word for 'feast' for example, so we use *festa* [Italian/Salentine loanword]. In Sternatia, however, they use *jortì*, which coincidentally corresponds to MG too. Well, in such cases, I propose to use the Greek-deriving word if this is present in neighboring villages." These constitute, he argued, instances of linguistic recovery. Similarly, Gianni De Santis from Sternatia purposely used, in his songs, Griko words that had fallen into disuse, but which he learned from his grandmother, thus enacting instances of linguistic recovery. How far back in time to go to restore Griko and retrieve words of Greek origin is another matter altogether; when the topic arose it initiated debates about whether to resort to oral memory—as Gianni did—or whether to use the written material starting from the nineteenth century onward. This would effectively mean resorting to the pioneering work of the linguist Morosi, and to the collection of oral tradition provided by early *cultori del griko* at the turn of the twentieth century—which in turn opens up discussions about the kind of sources to use and their scientific reliability.[10]

The Griko–Hellenic Festival contest's regulations interestingly embed an explicit invitation to authors to avoid resorting to foreign words in the name of an authentic *kaliglossa*. Daniele often reiterates, "The authenticity of Griko is my obsession, to use a language as pure as possible and as purified as possible from dialect and Italian." More than once he poignantly commented, "Let's keep at least what we had!" For instance, once he heard me using the expression *'kàngesce o kosmo,'* as I do quoting my elderly friends (see Chapter 2). He reacted by saying I should use the Griko verb *"addhàsso,"* mostly fallen into disuse, instead of *"kangèo,"* which is an adaptation from the Salentine *"cangiare"*—and thus to say *"èddhasse o kosmo."* Linguistic recovery is hence also a way to 'purify' Griko. Not incidentally, Daniele used this very verb; this indicates how he rests on and reproduces the language ideology promoted by the philhellenic circle of Calimera (see Chapter 1). The use of adaptations and/or borrowings from

---

[10] The meticulous works of linguists such as Rohlfs and Karanastasis are considered among the most reliable sources, even if the methodology of linguistic collection is at times put into question.

the Romance variety or Italian to compensate for forgotten terms, and/or to implement Griko's restricted vocabulary, therefore should be/is scrupulously avoided.

In such instances we see at play the legacy of the old-fashioned ideology of the past, which saw Griko as a 'bastard language,' as a 'contaminated language,' because of the presence of Salentine borrowings or adaptations. Metalinguistic practices such as these highlight an underlying 'puristic language ideology' that considers Salentine as an agent of contamination of the perceived original 'purity' of the language pre-contact. Here authenticity is defined on a temporal scale; the further back in time you go, as it were, the less contaminated, thus the more authentic, Griko you will find. The 'authentic' Griko is therefore defined based on its distance from Salentine/Italian interferences.

The internalization of this ideology is indeed nothing new; what is new is that speakers, activists, and *cultori del griko* are now metalinguistically aware of it. They police, as it were, the linguistic boundary with Salentine/Italian, and tend to highlight and sanction each and every word in Griko, which they readily recognize as adapted from them—again at the expense of the conversation itself. This folk appropriation of the ideology of 'purity,' has led to what Deborah Cameron (1995) has defined as 'verbal hygiene,' leading some speakers to even apologize when using words borrowed or grammatically adapted from Salentine or Italian; they feel uncomfortable when they cannot meet the expectations to speak a 'pure' Griko. This discomfort can also happen in interaction with Greek tourists visiting Salento, or with linguists conducting research in Grecìa. This phenomenon has, in fact, interested mainly those speakers who have followed and participated in the revival mechanism more closely. My informants from Sternatia, for instance, are very self-conscious about this ideology, partly because they attend Modern Greek classes at the Chora-Ma association and have been learning some MG, partly because Sternatia is the village most visited by Greek tourists. These dynamics, in turn, have important implications for the future envisaged for the language and the community's self-representation.

Another language ideological debate that engages activists and speakers is whether and how to implement a language that lacks a 'vocabulary of modernity.' This is often the case with minority languages whose communicative functions have diminished over time due to language erosion and shift. Since the severing of contacts with Greece, Griko was progressively excluded from various linguistic domains and came to be increasingly associated with the rural world, while speakers have kept creatively incorporating Salentine and Italian resources to fill its gaps. Daniele told me that there had been internal discussions among the members of the Kaliglossa association about the proposal to replace borrowed or adapted Romance words with standard Greek words, but that no agreement had been reached. He pointed out his personal doubts that recourse to Greek would be a good solution: "I fear Greek could kill Griko, but not everyone agrees with me," he added (to be sure, scholars such as Rohlfs and Karanastasis argued against the use of Modern Greek, which would de-historicize the language, a view that is still common among Greek linguists). Instead, Daniele was very pleased to point out that one of the editions of the Festival contest was won by an entrant from Sternatia who had inserted in his poem the term *jinekosìni*, a neologism that contains the word *jinèka* (woman) and the suffix *sìni* (the quality of); that is, 'femininity.' Neologisms of this kind, he argues, respect Griko without altering it.

Daniele ultimately argued that in order to preserve the authenticity of Griko, any MG term should be avoided; introducing them, he explained, would be "an artificial intervention." Renato from Kaliglossa equally pointed out that they make the effort to use the existing terms in Griko as much as possible, but he added, "If Griko does not have a word for something, you cannot invent it." Referring to such a practice, he concluded emphatically, "This way they create a fake Griko because when Griko lacks a word, they insert it from MG. It's not right! It's like when you restore a painting; if a piece of it has disappeared and you paint over it, you are creating a fake. Instead you should leave a blank spot there, that's all." Tellingly, Silvia from Calimera, rather uncomfortably confessed to me, "I sometimes use Modern Greek, especially when returning from Greece I end up getting confused for a while, but I feel I betray Griko this way." Her metalinguistic comment about "betraying" Griko when/if using MG borrowings or adaptations reveals an implicit moral judgment.

Indeed, we see how what is considered 'authentic' and 'fake' becomes a matter of what is 'right' and 'wrong', highlighting the moral dimension into which debates about Griko are embedded. MG ironically might end up reclaiming the unfortunate definition of 'agent of corruption,' of 'contamination' of Griko, just like Salentine, and it is morally sanctioned for potentially 'killing Griko.' Just like with Salentine, the linguistic boundaries between Standard Greek and Griko are indeed watched over; also those cases in which the confusion with/interference of Greek is momentary are promptly noticed and commented upon, and often sanctioned, thus calling into question the competence and also the authority of the speaker. I personally witnessed a Griko speaker from Zollino, who also knows Modern Greek, being harshly criticized for having 'mistakenly' used the standard Greek term *paraskevì* (Friday) instead of the Griko equivalent *parassekuì/parasseguì*. I was also personally reproached for getting confused and using the standard *proì* (morning) instead of the Griko *pornò*.

To be sure, conscious attempts to integrate Griko with Modern Greek have occurred in the past. One example is Cesarino De Santis's literary production in the 1970s, in which some poems make extensive use of it; or Domenicano Tondi from Zollino, who in the 1930s wrote a Griko grammar heavily influenced by MG, with the aim of creating a Griko *koinè*. Both of them are criticized for creating an 'abstract' language. Prof. Sicuro, instead, did not share fears about the impact of MG on Griko. He insisted on the importance of MG, and would summarize effectively his position by saying that, "Griko has no future. The future of Griko is Modern Greek." Griko on its own, he argued, would bring only isolation; his wish was therefore to project Griko as a language which could enable global connections. Indeed those who share an ideological fascination with 'all things Greek' look at MG as a reference, considering it not only as a source of prestige but also an agent of the renewal of Griko and hence a source of inspiration to create neologisms by resorting to Greek calques. Antonio from Zollino exemplifies this position. He has been attending MG classes at Chora-Ma for the last ten years and vehemently supports his proposal to introduce into Griko the MG term *àniksi* (spring) due to the presence in Griko of the verb *anìo* (open). This reasoning provokes the reaction of Mimmo, who does not agree with the introduction/creation of terms such as spring and autumn, since this would go beyond "the Griko temporal rhythm," as he put it, which was characteristically set by only two seasons (winter and summer, *to scimòna, to kalocèri*). Antonio is also among those who advocate the use in Griko of the term *biblio* for 'book' instead of *libro*, a term that speakers borrow from Italian and adapt grammatically to Griko; he further supports this choice by referring to the fact that, even in Italian, we use the word *biblioteca* for library. In this respect, the intensification of contact with Greece, the availability of MG courses provided by the Greek Ministry of Education, and the interest shown by Greek aficionados of Griko who have visited the area since the 1990s have all contributed to this. These contributions have indeed impacted the language ideologies and practices of those who have been involved more closely in the dynamics of Griko's revival, further influencing their language choices and 'tastes.'

Interestingly, Griko mother-tongue speakers from Sternatia who have attended Modern Greek classes also tend to resort to Modern Greek, particularly when meeting Greek tourists. Here, however, the use of MG is conscious and not due to extemporaneous confusion, as was the case of Silvia from Calimera above: it simultaneously becomes a way to 'show off' their knowledge of MG and a way to facilitate conversation with Greek visitors—here what takes precedence is the value of language as medium of communication (see also Chapter 7); in contrast, they do not resort to MG when speaking among themselves, or to other Griko speakers from nearby villages.

The constant search for the Greek flavor of Griko may also create funny examples (see Figure 24). *Panetteria* is the Italian word for 'bakery,' while

Figure 24. The sign of a bakery
shop, Martano

artopoieío in MG means literally 'the place where bread is baked.' The story goes that the owner of this bakery in Martano wanted to use Griko in his shop's sign, and asked Prof. Sicuro for help. As Griko lacks such a word, Prof. Sicuro suggested the word *artopoleío*, an MG word that means 'the place where bread is sold.' He pointed out, however, that this term would not be understood by Griko speakers—and, I will add, they would not be able to read it, as it is written using the Greek alphabet. What Prof. Sicuro probably ignored is that the word *artopoleío* is seldom found on shop signs in Greece. The common term is, rather, *artopoieío*, or *praktorío ártou* or *furno*, the final one curiously being borrowed and adapted from Italian!

Between the Past and the Future:
Stuck in the Present

In one of my first encounters with Giuseppe, he defended the initiative of the journal written in Griko by stating that, "*Spitta* represents the only testimony of the real Griko—of today's Griko, I mean. Although there are many publications of poems in Griko, in these instances the language is sought and refined; in a word, it is artificial, hence not the spontaneous spoken language." By stressing that *Spitta* exemplifies the 'real Griko,' he accuses of 'artificiality' those initiatives that privilege and foster the 'poetic' written modality, such as that proposed by the Griko–Hellenic Festival, although he did not specifically refer to it. What these initiatives have so far shared is the view that integrating Griko's vocabulary with MG terms "would contaminate and denaturalize our language," as one of *Spitta*'s founding members stated.

Giuseppe in fact follows a sort of fieldwork strategy in writing his articles, recording elderly mother-tongue speakers narrating an event, then reporting the narrations faithfully. "Whichever its limitations, *Spitta* is a snapshot of Griko!", Giuseppe emphasized. He therefore defines Griko's 'authenticity' not by the 'notable written production' of scholars, but by its closeness to the contemporary language, proposing it in a prose modality. This presents hybrid linguistic forms, mixing Griko with Salentine (and Italian), but such a hybridity is perceived as a form of continuity with past practices, and this is what renders the language 'authentic' in its own right. The attempt of the *Spitta* initiative is backed up theoretically, as linguistic compromise and the acceptance of hybrid forms enhances the language's survival chances.[11] This has indeed contributed to the 'survival' of Griko up to the present; in fact, Griko speakers from Sternatia—which is popularly held as the village with the highest percentage of Griko speakers—characteristically rely more heavily than nearby villages on hybrid forms and borrowings from Salentine/Italian; this allows them to speak fluently also about the themes of the present. By contrast, as linguist Nancy Dorian argues, puristic attitudes may "create problems for efforts to support minority languages" (1994:480).

In the linguistic continuum from more puristic toward more accommodating language ideologies, Giuseppe and the contributors to the journal are among those who are more acceptive of hybrid forms, neologisms and calques, as *Spitta's* articles show. The journal's aim, as the title itself declares, is to make Griko 'sparkle' instead of linking it to and segregating it from an ideal and/or pre-contact past. Indeed, he is proud that the journal engages with contemporary topics, in this way embracing a language ideology that links Griko to the 'present' and thus projects it into the future. Giuseppe's personal aspiration is to act as a connector among generations and inspire young people to learn and speak Griko, also providing them the tools to do so. Those enthusiastic about this initiative proudly claim that *Spitta* is proof that Griko is 'alive,' expressing their animosity toward those who did not believe it would 'survive,' including the scholars who had predicted its death and the politicians who had long not invested in it. Popular reception of this journal, however, ranges from enthusiasm to open criticism, revealing the multiplicity of language ideologies in interaction and the deriving tension stemming from the polysemic local understandings of what 'authentic' Griko stands for. Giuseppe has grown increasingly disappointed, and feels lonely in this enterprise since his extemporaneous attempts or 'timid' actions toward language renewal/revitalization often soon die out of lack of generalized local consensus. Commenting on the *Spitta* initiative, Rocco from Sternatia, told me:

> Certainly it is a praiseworthy experiment; however, they want to write about modern topics, therefore their writing becomes unyielding, elementary, and inevitably they must resort to Italian or Salentine.

---

[11]   See Dorian 1994; Jaffe 1999; and Woolard 1989, among others.

The traditional texts from the past such as songs, proverbs, poems, are highly poetic instead.

Luigi from Martano is harsher: "This experiment is odious. Griko is a language to use for poetry, for songs; otherwise it is nothing." Roberto from Calimera makes a similar point: "Griko is the expression of nostalgia, it is surely not something modern." Prof. Tommasi echoes them:

> I like the idea, but they stretch the language by trying to write about current events; every ten words, five or six are not Griko words. The same goes for the news in Griko on TV: no one could understand anything. Griko was a folk language [*lingua popolare*]; so, either you use its own words, or you make no sense at all.[12]

Prof. Tommasi has always stated explicitly that he does not foresee for Griko any future as a spoken language, but rather as a *testimonianza*, as 'proof,' of the cultural heritage to leave for posterity in the written form. Interestingly, while compiling the textbook *Pos Màtome Griko* (How We Learn Griko) that I mentioned above, he actually disagreed more tenaciously on the communicative situations to choose and describe in the various units of the book—among them, going to the airport, to the bank, going to school, etc.—arguing that there was no point in dealing with topics where Griko's vocabulary lacks linguistic resources such as those above; his position was broadly shared. The creation of neologisms and/or the linguistic recovery of forgotten terms/verbs were not explicitly addressed, in fact, and thus not systematically covered in the book. The agreement reached was that we should use existing texts from the folklore collection of songs, poems, sayings, but also from recent publications or texts.[13]

The level A1 units for children covered basic and thus relatively uncontested topics such as greetings, the family, the weather, etc., but also physical descriptions of people, food, and leisure activities. Interestingly, as the level of proficiency increases to B1 and B2, the topics covered increasingly relate to the past: songs of Grecìa Salentina, fairytales, popular beliefs, traditional crafts and

---

[12] Prof. Tommasi has been extensively writing and publishing grammar books, plays, and books in Griko; his personal website, moreover, ranges from grammatical notions to popular poems, songs, proverbs in Griko, to his own articles about Griko. He has also been teaching Griko over the years, mainly as part of initiatives promoted by two different cultural associations based in Calimera.

[13] The project prides itself on being the first to apply to minority languages the Common European Framework of Reference for Languages (CEFR) according to six levels of proficiency; this was, however, also part of the very issue, since such choice underestimated/misrecognized the dynamics involved in cases of language shift and erosion, and the consequent challenges it posed.

customs, traditional recipes, etc. The very content of the units was heavily based on descriptions of the past; also the more recent texts documented traditional Griko life, as it were, building on the description of locals' memories. Indeed, the past was ever present.[14]

The prevailing argument is, in fact, that Griko vocabulary is restricted to covering mainly the domains of the peasant world—and of family—and that this renders the language inadequate for the communicative domains of the 'present,' of the contemporary and modern world. For this reason the Spitta initiative receives a mixed reception, and this is also why an early initiative of broadcasting news in Griko on local TV—which goes back to 2005, and to which Prof. Tommasi refers above—was widely criticized. Griko's linguistic resources are considered instead more apt to be used in songs and poems, so the argument goes, and this is indeed reflected in locals resorting to Griko for performative purposes. This practice, as I show in the next chapter, has been increasing over time.

What emerges from my ethnography is how Griko is largely perceived as 'a language of the past,' which while being temporally close, points to a world and an experiential reality that do not exist as remembered despite being described by it. Griko, however, remains in context *in that* local chronotope; this way it is indexical of 'that' inevitable historicity, connecting it with 'that' past. When people look back at the past emotionally, with nostalgia, Griko becomes its representation, its expression, as Roberto stated above; it becomes an object of contemplation.

On the contrary, de-contextualizing Griko by 'bending' and 'stretching' it in order to write (or speak) about contemporary topics is largely considered as fake, even folkloristic—and attempts to this end are often silenced or marginalized. The majority of the locals seem indeed to be more concerned about Griko's authenticity (however defined) than they are about its 'death' as a language of daily communication. Indeed, even when they 'could' speak Griko, they often do not; they tend to resist attempts to continue a conversation in the language

---

[14] The book *Katalisti o kosmo* (Griko)—*tra passato e presente. Lingua, tradizione e folklore nella Grecìa Salentina* (Italian) by Prof. Tommasi includes twenty dialogues that he re-elaborated, building on the material collected during a Griko seminar held in 1995–1996, and attended by Griko speakers and activists. As the title itself suggests—*The World Turned Upside Down—between the Past and the Present. Language, Tradition and Folklore in Grecìa Salentina*—the book provides through these dialogues "values, beliefs, models of social relations that characterized the life of our community until the first decades of the twentieth century, a period which can be indicated as 'the past' to which we refer while narrating" (Tommasi 1996:6; my translation from Italian). Five of these dialogues were used in levels B1 and B2 of the textbook *Pos Matòme Griko*. Indeed, what is striking about them is the continuous expression of dialogue between the past and the present, which shifts from memories of the past to moral evaluations of the present.

beyond the 'usual' topics, switching to Salentine and/or Italian, and remarking it does not come 'naturally' to them—it is out of context, so to speak—or else that 'that Griko' is not the same language as the elderly would speak. While locals often metalinguistically comment with regret on Griko's limitations in expressing the needs of the present, they ultimately resist language change and/or renewal, equating it to 'decay.' Similarly, they consider that leaving to posterity—in writing—an incorrect version of Griko would show a lack of respect toward both the language and the people who speak it. Characteristically, Gianni from Sternatia poignantly argued, "It is best to let Griko die with dignity than to humiliate it." In other words, the prevailing view at present is that Griko should be kept 'as it is.'

These dynamics, however, extend beyond concerns about language competence, accuracy, purism or compromise; it shows, I argue, how authenticity ultimately builds on locals' perceptions of morality and aesthetics, which feed into each other. Locals, therefore, may rest on their own memories of the past, as discussed above, directing their preferences and attachments to a specific lexical choice, expression, and pronunciation, and thus linking Griko to a local chronotope. In such instances morality and aesthetics converge with affect. Being socially distributed, locals' language ideologies may intermingle with projections of a temporally distant but glorious past, yet a past which connects contemporary Southern Italy and Greece; this in turn equally influences language choices and tastes, projecting Griko as a language which enables global connections—as one of the languages of Hellenism in the world. Hence, the moral drive to 'keep Griko as it is' translates into 'purifying' it aesthetically of Salentine/Italian borrowings, which would not be comprehensible beyond locality and would confine Griko to it.

By *debating Griko*, locals have certainly endured interest in the language; more to the point, the analysis of these multiple debates shows how they are not about language per se; often framed as debates over what counts as 'authentic' Griko, they are rather disputes about competing language ideologies, which are linked to different historicities. They ultimately unravel what I call the cultural temporality of language by revealing locals' views and perceptions, about the role of Griko in the past-present-future. By celebrating Griko's internal variation as richness and resisting standardization, by debating linguistic recovery and renewal, by contending the form in which it ought to be transmitted to posterity, locals express their moral alignments to the past as well as their projections to the future, which build on and recursively affect language ideology and practice. Such ideological debates ultimately lead to a power struggle over who holds the 'knowledge' to determine what is 'right' or 'wrong' for Griko, and so determine its future—whether mother-tongue speakers, *cultori del griko*, or language experts—and what defines it, whether embodied knowledge or philological expertise. This is what I turn to discuss.

From Authenticity to Authority: The Older the Better?

One November night, I was hanging out with Uccio (in his late eighties) and Cosimino (in his mid-seventies), both fluent Griko speakers from Sternatia. We had just attended a Modern Greek class at Chora-Ma in Sternatia. Giorgio was passing by and stopped to say hi. We were chatting in Griko, and I was asking Cosimino and Uccio to clarify the use of the form "we speak Griko." Mine was a genuine question, as I kept hearing locals using multiple forms, so it was a matter of grammar that was not totally clear to me at the time.

Uccio immediately invited Giorgio to answer, and with a hint of irony said, "Eh, Gio! You, how would you say what we are trying to say?" Giorgio replied promptly that the correct form is *milùme is Grika*. His reply overlapped with Cosimino's, who instigated the controversy and suggested that 'maybe' both *milùme to Griko* and *milùme is Grika* are correct. Then Giorgio explained— switching to Salentine—that the correct forms are: *milùme Grika* and *milùme is Grika*, clarifying that here *Grika* is an adverb; *milùme to Griko* is also correct, but in this case Griko is a noun. His 'grammatical' explanation seemed to upset Uccio, who intervened and, addressing Cosimino, said, "We [who are] without pen, we say it as it comes. But these who have taken up the pen, these who write there ..." Giorgio tried to reply, but Uccio interrupted him. After having invited him to answer my question, as he represented the 'authority' as a Griko expert/ teacher, Uccio did not let him speak, continuously fighting to hold the floor and raising his voice to speak over Giorgio.

The hint of irony with which Uccio invited Giorgio to answer is part of the troubled relationship he seems to have with the authoritative voice of Giorgio as both an educated man and a Griko teacher. Uccio concluded, "Our language, it is not as if there is something written by anyone. But now, *these people*, now they are writing the grammar" (emphasis in original). Uccio's remark to Cosimino, "We [who are] without a pen" indicates the authority that elderly people project onto educated people, an authority they feel they lack as the majority of them had limited access to education. Yet the power relation changes totally when it comes to Griko. Uccio had learned Griko as his mother tongue, whereas Giorgio is not perceived as having this same fluency. This is due to his younger age; he simply has not lived *that* past. Nevertheless, he is highly competent and respected as an expert.

Uccio's heated reaction has to do with the sudden proliferation of 'Griko experts' who are part and parcel of the revival. This has had the unexpected effect of isolating elderly Griko speakers, who became rather skeptical and suspicious toward the newcomers. They feel their own 'expertise' is being supplanted by non–mother-tongue speakers. This contextualizes Uccio's simultaneously defensive and aggressive attitude toward 'people with a pen.' He is reclaiming his legitimate authority over Griko, as it were: Griko is a language of oral tradition, and fluent speakers use it "as it comes" (organically). Moreover, speaking Griko is not a reflexive practice. It is linked to speakers' experiential past and present; they therefore do not need to look for rules. By contrast, "*they*" look for rules—meaning language experts, grammar writers, Griko scholars, and me! He twice stresses the word 'now,' nodding to the ongoing revival.[15]

Elderly Griko speakers in fact rarely engage in these folk linguistic exercises unless they are prompted by 'semi-speakers' or researchers. Adriana bluntly made the same point: "I *think* in Griko, all these experts of Griko do not! They need to think about what they are saying. A language is *really* yours only if you think and dream in it" (emphasis in original), she concluded, emphatically reclaiming her own legitimacy as a mother-tongue speaker, and thus her authority over Griko, challenging the authority of those who do not 'think' and 'dream' in the language). Comments such as this insist on the "moral significance of 'mother tongue' as the first and, therefore *real* language of a speaker" (Woolard 1998:18, emphasis in original). This ideology leads to a constant monitoring of how people speak Griko, which in turns disinclines less fluent speakers—and potential new speakers for that matter—from using the language and causes them to engage in a continuous self-monitoring to avoid failing to meet expectations.

It is indeed true that Griko speakers and local Griko scholars often question the competence of Griko teachers, some more openly than others; I have heard them do so repeatedly. Among the recurrent debates, they refer to the quality of the training offered to Griko teachers. There is a strong consensus that the Master's program was a failure, since several subjects were being taught (musicology, archeology, history, popular traditions, Modern Greek, Greek history, and tourism), but lessons specifically dedicated to the Griko language were insufficient to train new Griko teachers.[16] Giorgio from Sternatia was very clear about his views; he argued that those who attended the Masters, but who did not already know Griko, certainly did not learn it from the course. Tonia

---

[15] For a remarkable similarity, see McDonald (1989:288), who reports her informants as saying, "we don't know la grammaire for Breton, but it exists in books chez ces gens-là." See also Nevins (2004) and Meek (2009) on the issue of the authority of the elderly.

[16] This training was part of two major initiatives. The first goes back to 2000 and was attended by the majority of today's Griko teachers. The second took place in 2005–2006: a yearly Master's degree course on "the language, history and culture of GS," financed by Law 428 with the collaboration of the University of Salento.

from Zollino, who attended it, pointed out that most of those who can speak Griko could not attend the Masters, as they do not hold a university degree; they are therefore not qualified to teach it. Meanwhile, those with the appropriate qualifications lack competence in the language, and so on.

However, generalizations are misleading. When I interviewed Griko teachers, their assessment of their own linguistic competence varied considerably from case to case: those who are older have had more exposure to Griko than the younger teachers; some of them also know Modern Greek or Ancient Greek, some of them do not; some are more passionate about Griko than others; and some of them have lost their zeal for Griko in the process of trying to teach it. Having undertaken participant observation during Griko classes, I can attest to the goodwill of the teachers and the effort they put into teaching. As a result, I found the criticisms rather harsh; these teachers work in the face of many challenges locally, and they are constantly vulnerable to annual funding issues at the national and regional level, which is dependent on their total number of teaching hours per year (see Chapter 4).

From their perspective, Griko teachers feel they are looked upon as second-tier teachers, which is reflected also into their underpayment compared to 'fully appointed' teachers. Indeed, according to Article 4 of National Law 482, the use of the minority language is envisaged alongside the use of Italian: this means that Griko teachers are expected to teach only in the presence of a 'fully appointed' teacher, who may or may not come from a Griko-speaking village (most of the time not). This renders their task even more difficult. When, in the early 2000s, Griko experts were trained to teach the language they were young locals in their late twenties—the new hope for the future of Griko, as it were. Yet, they often feel their linguistic competence being scrutinized and the relevance of their role being questioned, and so complain about the general resistance to specialist control. In another conversation Giorgio let his dissatisfaction slip when he told me, "Everyone feels entitled to judge. When we talk about medicine, the experts are the doctors, right? If we talk about veterinary medicine, the experts are the vets, right? When it comes to Griko, however, everyone sees himself as a 'Griko expert.' Everyone is an 'expert'!"

Who Knows What for Whom?
Power Struggles over Griko

It all started with a rather simple question. Michele, born in 1975, and, unusually for his age, a mother-tongue Griko speaker from Sternatia, asked the members of the WhatsApp group *I glossa grika* (the Griko language) I had set up, "How do we say 'river' in Griko?" The group is composed of speakers and/or activists, as well as Griko scholars and aficionados. The first to reply was Paolo, a Griko speaker and activist, who suggested that the word might have been 'lost'—probably due to the scarcity of water in the area—and proposed using *potàmi*, incidentally the MG word for river; he justified his choice by saying that we keep the root in the verb 'to pot' (to *potìsi*).

Tonia, a Griko teacher, asked about the Calabrian Greek word for "*fiume*" (*potamò*). Alfredo supported Paolo's choice, and referenced the Italian word *hippopotamo*, which would make it possible to avoid adapting the Salentine/Italian *fiùmo*. This is when Raffaele, another Griko teacher, texted at length, pointing out firmly that *fiùmo* is the Griko word to use because it was attested in Vito Domenico Palumbo's tales, and also by the linguist Morosi, and there was no need 'to go to the trouble' (Italian: *scomodare*) of using Calabrian Greek, or building off 'hippopotamus.' He added, "Let's keep the language the way it has been transmitted to us—by the way there are still elderly speakers who speak correctly and we can ask them how they say things without 'turning everything upside down' (Italian: *stravolgere*). We see here again the moral imperative to 'keep' Griko as it has been transmitted, and to 'respect' those who still speak it.

The WhatsApp debate went on, and others intervened with varying views: "A language is not something to fix and transmit, but a living organism which changes over time, so if Griko speakers find it useful to add a neologism, I do not see anything strange about it. I'd go for *potàmi*," Silvio—a speaker and *cultore del griko*—added, trying to divert from the general tendency to keep Griko 'unchanged.' The chat was abruptly interrupted by this message sent by Raffaele: "Everyone is free to do all linguistic recoveries he pleases; in any case the elderly, who are the true speakers, will keep speaking like they have always done, ignoring these recoveries and neologisms. By the way these are matters for linguists."

As is often the case, the Griko teacher's last message 'silenced' the proposal for language change/renewal, in this instance by pointing out that generating neologisms or 'recovering' forgotten terms are not a matter of individual will; rather, there is the element of whether other Griko speakers accept such changes—and elderly speakers, Raffaele argued, would not. Indeed, languages evolve over time when they are widely used, and when changes are embraced by others. When they are not, the outcome is an idiolect, a personalized and intimate vocabulary that allows communication only among those who share it, but that excludes others. Ironically Griko's internal richness is partly due to the fact that it 'survived' through idiolects, but now that it is no longer a language predominately used to exchange information, any change to it is instead matter of representation, which creates tensions among speakers.

Significantly, the Griko teacher's last message also reveals, once again, how smooth the shift is from defining the 'authentic' Griko word to defining who can claim authority over the language. He first ascribes it to past speakers ("*Fiùmo* is the Griko word to use because it was attested in Vito Domenico Palumbo's tales, and also by the linguist Morosi" in nineteenth-century sources); this reveals a language ideology that privileges "the authoritative word" of distant ancestors (Bakhtin 1981) whose influence is still felt. Then he shifts authority over Griko to present-day elderly speakers, who are *true* speakers (my emphasis) because it was their mother tongue. Here competence is largely associated with age ("There are still elderly speakers who speak correctly and we can ask them"). His last message, however, also refers to linguists, as operations/interventions such as linguistic recovery and the formation of neologisms fall under philological/linguistic expertise.

What we see at play here is the semiotic process of fractal recursivity, defined by Judith Irvine and Susan Gal as "the projection of an opposition, salient at some level of relationship, onto some other level" (2000:37). We have seen how the ideologically constructed opposition at the temporal level—pre-contact past/recent past—is projected onto the linguistic level, becoming an opposition along the purism and compromise continuum. This opposition is then further projected onto the social level, onto community members shifting from Griko speakers to experts, present and past. One of the characteristics of fractal recursivity is that this opposition can be reproduced repeatedly and be projected onto narrower and broader comparisons (Gal 2005).

By debating what authentic Griko stands for—a debate which intermingles issues of morality and aesthetics, as discussed above—locals simultaneously define who can and cannot claim authority over it; this ultimately highlights the power struggles intensified by the current revival. Indeed, at times embodied knowledge prevails over philological expertise in the definition of authority; at times it does not. Speakers of the past may be—and usually are—perceived as more authoritative than today's speakers, while today's speakers tend to remain more authoritative than language experts. In the meantime, experts, *cultori del griko*, and activists who have long engaged with the language may claim more authority over Griko than those who have approached it more recently, and so forth. This process continuously creates separations, "in a series of interconnected layers that are necessarily embedded in the original construction, which is what makes it recursive" (Razfar 2012:66).

What is revealing is how all these activists and *cultori del griko* motivate their engagement with Griko by referring to the duty to preserve it; they express a sense of moral responsibility toward the language itself but articulate it in different ways: to systematically record and document Griko, to transmit it in writing, to use as a performative resource—as we will see in the next chapter—and only a minority among the minority, to promote its use as a spoken language for daily use. This dynamic at times produces a bond among those who share the same language ideologies and visions of Griko's past and future; such 'intergroup intimacies' then become the humus for social encounters, for building interpersonal relations, and for creating synergies and collaborations among activists, speakers, and *cultori del griko*. The opposite dynamic, however, equally takes place, when divergent language ideologies serve to produce not only interpersonal but also 'intragroup estrangements'; these generate tensions and lead activists and *cultori del griko* to carry out independent activities and Griko courses that further fracture the languagescape. Even those who agree to promote Griko as a spoken language end up disagreeing on whether and how to implement it; those who agree to transmit it in writing may not—and often do not—agree on how to transcribe it and so on, while they tend to complain when their positions and proposals are not shared or followed. Many among the Griko speakers, activists and scholars mentioned above have sometimes fallen out with one another at different moments in time, because of their different positions on issues such as orthographic transcription and linguistic renewal and/or the future envisaged for Griko.

Significantly, what is morally right and emotionally sound for Griko is not only fueled by their concerns about the fate of Griko, but is also linked to their personal investments in Griko, as each of them claim in the process their competence, expertise, and long-lasting engagement with Griko (in other words, their own authority over it). *Cultori del griko* and activists who have engaged with Griko for decades now enjoy the prestige associated with knowing the language and the social recognition and visibility achieved as experts in the field, both in Grecìa Salentina and in Greece, where they equally cultivate relationships; they may consequently fear being overshadowed, so to speak, by those who only recently 'joined in.' This dynamic once again highlights a growing sense of uneasiness about losing control over their own spaces of action.[17]

Following the argument by Michel Foucault, such power struggles exemplify "a politics of knowledge" and the relations of power, which pass via knowledge (1982). In a vibrant metalinguistic community such as this, where competence in and knowledge of Griko are supposedly diffuse—where 'everyone is an expert' of Griko—the struggle starts from the need to define and assert the kind of knowledge that confirms authority and confers power; this means to establish a

---

[17] See Pizza, 2004 for a similar observation with regard to music. He noted a growing sense of weariness among local musicians who refuse to be 'taught' by anthropologists or journalists what it means to play a tamburello or to dance pizzica, as they fear losing control over their own spaces of action as this becomes simply a 'phenomenon' to be exploited (2004:219).

hierarchy which elevates one kind of knowledge/expertise over another. This is, however, constantly contested, negotiated, and only provisionally achieved; it keeps fluctuating from experiential knowledge and embodied linguistic competence (mother-tongue speakers) to philological expertise (language experts and scholars of Griko), passing though active engagement (Griko activists). This ultimately leads to a struggle over who gets access to the material, as well as symbolic means of re-presentation—a dynamic which expands to the management of cultural heritage more broadly, as I discussed in the previous chapter.

My ethnography has, however, revealed not only how these multiple social actors constantly and simultaneously attempt to validate their own knowledge and exert authority, but crucially their need and desire to draw recognition *from* others and *over* others. This is ultimately what confers social prestige and hence power at the local level, allowing those who hold it to proclaim what is 'right or wrong' for Griko—which orthographic conventions will prevail, whether Griko eventually will or will not be 'updated' to express modern needs, and so on—ultimately the right to present and re-present Griko, and to determine the route to its future. Indeed, one of the salient traits defining a relationship of power is that it is "a mode of action which does not act directly and immediately on others. Instead, it acts upon their actions: an action upon an action, on existing actions or on those which may arise in the present or the future" (Foucault 1982:789).

All the language ideological debates discussed in this chapter are, however, deeply embedded in the demands of the present. Processes of minority languages standardization, renewal, and/or revitalization remain entangled in globally shared political and economic dynamics. This ethnography, on the other hand, shows that ultimately, neither can such processes be disentangled from the historical specificities of each minority language, from the prevailing local sensibilities of its speakers, or from the social dynamics they generate on the ground. The current languagescape ultimately shows that the role that locals envisage for Griko on its path to the future remains vigorously contested. Yet, Griko has re-entered the experiential reality of locals in multiple forms that go beyond such debates, and beyond the 'vitality' of Griko as a medium of daily communication, as I move to discuss in the next chapter.

6

"Certain Things Never Change and Those Sound Better in Griko"
Living with the Language

WHILE surfing the internet one December morning, I came across an article in the Italian online newspaper *La Repubblica* about five commercials aired by RAI—the Italian state-owned public service broadcaster. It was 2010 and the advertising campaign for the renewal of the license fee was dedicated to the 150th anniversary of the Unification of Italy. Each of the five commercials had the same format: it presented three scenes in which contemporary characters spoke their local dialect and were not understood by their interlocutors. There was a basketball coach who explained his game plans in 'Neapolitan' to the players who did not understand him; a school teacher taught mathematics in 'Salentine' to his students, who could not follow him; a priest officiated a wedding in 'Piedmontese' before the eyes of the incredulous bride and groom; a politician spoke in 'Ligurian' to a journalist who stared back at him, astonished. The commercials ended with the Italian flag waving, while the Italian hymn *Fratelli d'Italia* played in the background; the commentator concluded by saying, "If Italians were those of 150 years ago, they would probably still communicate this way. Since then, we made a very important journey and RAI has always been with us." Each one of the characters closed the commercial with a positive comment in Italian (such as "How marvelous," "How lovely," "Fantastic," "Isn't it beautiful?" and "Simple, isn't it?"[1]).

The commercial's text emphasized that dialects are not mutually intelligible, while implying that they are not spoken today since doing so would divide an otherwise linguistically united Italy. Italian regional and local 'dialects,' together with minority languages, had indeed been the targets of what De Mauro (1979) defined as 'dialect-phobia,' the State intolerance toward them,

---

[1] *"Se gli italiani fossero quelli di 150 anni fa probabilmente comunicherebbero ancora così. Da allora abbiamo fatto un cammino molto importante e la Rai è sempre stata con noi."* https://www.youtube.com/watch?v=GhwTc0FM9zg

which was based on a deep-rooted aesthetic and moral prejudice that equates them with backwardness. Italian television presented instead the journey from Babel to modernity, as it were, by celebrating its utility in standardizing and diffusing Italian (see Chapter 2).

The commercials motivated a Facebook protest, "Facebook against the RAI commercial 2010 on 'dialects': shame, they are living languages." In less than two weeks, three thousand people had joined the protest, and several blog posts appeared that criticized the commercials' underlying negative stance toward dialects. In mid-December I read an article that triumphantly announced that RAI would replace them, so when I traveled back to Italy to spend Christmas with my family, I was struck by the new commercial. It showed the same actors from the previous one—the priest, the politician, the schoolteacher—each of whom used their dialects to offer seasonal best wishes. The voiceover said, "In the Italy of regional identities and cultures there are many ways to give wishes." Once again, the RAI logo appeared superimposed on the Italian flag, followed by the message "RAI: 150 years of such wishes" accompanied by the Italian national anthem.[2]

The protests against these commercials reflect the missions of Unesco and other European bodies that seek to protect language diversity. As with minority languages, the revitalization of dialects is part of a wider valorization process, but the vignette above also illustrates how this global discourse of 'unity in diversity' finds particularly fertile ground among Italians. By drawing on phraseology such as "intangible heritage" and Italy "as the outcome of the unity of diverse identities," the protests reproduce its underlying language ideology, which led the RAI to do the same in the replacement commercial. As a matter of fact, Italy is characterized by a multilingualism that far exceeds the twelve minority languages recognized by Law 482, since Italy's so-called regional 'dialects'—which are in fact unofficial languages that developed from Latin (Tosi 2004:248)—are not protected by Law 482. This in turn has opened up debates about the need to equally safeguard Romance dialects; significantly, in the very title of the Facebook group, dialects are referred to as "languages," challenging the official distinction between the two. In reality, there is nothing intrinsically linguistic to differentiate them. As Gal and Irvine (1995) highlight, the distinction is rendered by social forces that are external to the linguistic practices themselves; what distinguishes them is ultimately the political power assigned to national languages.[3]

---

2 "*Nell'Italia delle identità e delle culture regionali ci sono molti modi per farsi gli auguri ... RAI, 150 anni di questi auguri.*" https://www.youtube.com/watch?v=GhwTc0FM9zg

3 National Law 482 provokes criticisms as it then becomes difficult to justify and to understand why Sardinian or Friulan are recognized as languages while Bergamasco and Venetian are not. At the same time, however, the lobbying for the legal recognition of these other local varieties by

Interestingly, almost ten years later the Facebook protest group against the RAI commercial is still very active, and followers now post and comment articles about linguistic topics, displaying their attachment to the values of local dialects. Against the moral panic about their disappearance not only has the use of dialects persisted, but since the 1990s they have enjoyed a renewed vitality or renaissance. Salentine has increasingly been employed in domains other than the traditional oral one: in local TV commercials, in comics, and in local newspapers and computer mediated communication. The dialect is also used by the nationally famous music group SudSoundsystem, who have helped pioneer this trend by composing songs in Salentine, or alternating Salentine with Italian, a trend that has been followed by new local singers ever since.[4] We also find it in the movies, directed by the local director Edoardo Winspeare. Moreover, typical Salentine expressions and proverbs have entered the everyday visual space, appearing on t-shirts and various types of paraphernalia (keychains, backpacks, gadgets, etc.). The vignette above, however, also shows the continuous tension between the 'new' (European) and the 'old' (nation-state) language ideology, a tension within which Griko is caught.

The People with Two Languages

Quiddhu ca volia an sonnu me venia! (Salentine)	I dream what I want
Ci'ppi telo ivò assinnu to torò! (Griko)	I dream what I want
Quello che vorrei appar nei sogni miei (Italian)	I dream what I want

Quiddhu ca volia, Lyrics by Rocco De Santis, Avléddha

In their sociolinguistic survey investigating "the vitality of Griko," linguists Alberto Sobrero and Annarita Miglietta (2010) remark that locals' linguistic repertoire is now dominated by Salentine, as only twenty-two percent of the sample is able to complete a conversational turn started in Griko without switching to the Romance variety; this led them to conclude that only one person from Sternatia out of five people has a 'good' conversational competence

---

the national law is contrasted by the minorities already protected, since their recognition would also mean a redistribution of the financial support, and thus a reduction in the funding provided to each minority.

4 See Grimaldi 2006, 2010; Scholz 2004, for the use of Salentine and the alternation of Italian and Salentine in songs; for the renaissance of dialects, see Berruto 2006.

161

in Griko, and therefore that "the overall competence is rather modest" (Sobrero and Miglietta 2010:129, 133). In the same article the authors call into question the Unesco Language Vitality Index, designed to determine languages' degree of vitality or endangerment according to six main factors (intergenerational transmission, number and proportion of speakers, shift in domains of language use, response to new domains and media, material for language education, and literacy); highlighting the methodological issues arising from these classifications, Sobrero and Miglietta define such instruments as contradictory, misleading, and insufficient to describe the local linguistic reality, which may therefore lead to equally misleading and contradictory results (2010:133–136).

Linguists have indeed criticized the unreliability of such instruments in assessing languages' vitality; it is telling, however, that notwithstanding their own critical reading of the Unesco chart, Sobrero and Miglietta (2010) define the overall vitality of Griko in Sternatia as 'modest' based on the prevalence of code switches to Salentine. This reveals, I argue, the pervasiveness of what Alexandra Jaffe defines an approach to 'language-as-code,' which prevails in academic and policymaking spheres, and which delegitimizes the mixed codes and practices deriving from language contact and shift (Jaffe 2007:61–67)—and with them the resulting hybrid linguistic identities.[5]

If we look back at the lyrics of the song *Quiddhu ca Vulia* (by the Griko singer and songwriter Rocco De Santis) above, we can easily see how he uses Griko, Salentine, and Italian, alternating them, providing a characteristic example of the specificity of the case at hand, which needs to be taken into account. The coexistence of Griko, Salentine, and Italian renders this a highly heteroglossic languagescape where the boundaries between Griko and the Romance variety have long been flexible (Chapters 1 and 2); indeed, the alternation of Griko/Salentine is very common, while, as we have seen, the acceptance of mixed forms has contributed to the very persistence of Griko to the present day. Moreover, the use of Salentine is a widespread and accepted practice that interests all ages, with no distinction in social class or gender. As for Salentine/Italian, Sobrero argued that we can talk 'simply of alternation' between the two codes (1992:27–28).

As for Griko, the title of one of the De Santis brothers' CDs is telling: it is called *Ofidèa*, which means 'snake.' I remind the reader of the 'offensive' expression

---

[5]   Code-switching (CS)—the use of two or more languages in the same conversation or utterance—is a widespread phenomenon in situations of language shift or multilingualism. Blom and Gumperz (1972) made the distinction between situational and conversational code-switching: the first refers to language switches that coincide with a change of interlocutor, setting, or topic, whereas conversational code-switching is motivated by factors within the conversation itself. A third type of CS identified by Gumperz is 'metaphorical code-switching,' which occurs where a switch carries a particular evocative purpose deriving from the speakers' conscious transgression of the 'typical' language boundaries.

"people with two languages/tongues, people with two faces" (Chapter 2). Here the De Santis brothers, Rocco and Gianni, reappropriate this image to elevate its meaning, and to transfer it to the language itself. Yes, Griko the language—rather than its speakers—becomes the snake:

> [One could] identify Griko with the snake: its so-called two-pronged tongue brings us ideally to Griko bilingualism; the nature of Ofidèa is bilingual, as bilingual was the Byzantine culture from which we descend and it is expressed in the Romance dialect and in Griko.
>
> Rocco De Santis (liner notes)

Griko, like a snake, has two tongues, but this is no reason for self-deprecation. In their songs the De Santis brothers alternate between both languages, just as Griko speakers do. To resort to Salentine while speaking Griko, or to alternate both codes, had become a 'natural' practice—blurring the linguistic boundaries. This is reflected in traditional songs that alternate strophes in Griko and Salentine. In light of such a heteroglossic and dynamic languagescape it is therefore hardly surprising that locals draw on all linguistic resources available to them, together with their symbolic weight. Yet, guidelines such as those provided by Unesco to assess languages' vitality/endangerment transcend academic discussions, carrying important implications for the community. As Hacking argued, those belonging to a specific classification—the minority language speakers in this case—may be affected by it, and their experiences of themselves may be changed by being so classified (Hacking 1999:11).

Similarly, the academic insistence on describing Griko as always on the verge of disappearing can in fact be understood as the enactment of the semiotic process of erasure, which renders invisible those patterns of speaking that do not fit the prescriptive scholarly ideology (Gal and Irvine 1995). Defining *tout court* the alternate use of Griko/Romance or any instances of code-switching as an intrinsic "lack of competence" implies the objectification of language-as-code. I argue instead that, in order to fully appreciate what is happening on the ground, we need to move beyond the search for "unadulterated and authentic speech" (Gal 1989:316), a tradition in which studies of language 'death' have been long embedded. In order to grasp the nuanced ways in which linguistic identities emerge, it becomes essential to pay equal attention to those creative uses of minority languages that are often disregarded or considered marginal.

In this chapter I address Sobrero and Miglietta's (2010) call for a study of actual linguistic behavior, but my aim here is not to assess Griko's vitality, or speakers' competence. Following Alexandra Jaffe I apply, instead, an approach to 'language-as-practice' (Jaffe 1999, 2007) wherein multiple forms of language practice become socially and culturally meaningful for locals beyond the boundaries of 'full competence' or full communicative use of the language. I therefore show how non-Griko speakers and those with a passive competence creatively resort to Griko, making the best of the limited linguistic resources available to them. Rather than focusing on their lack of competence, I stress the sociocultural relevance of such instances of language use, however limited or partial, and their implications for personal and community self-representation. After all, linguistic practice is also always metadiscursive (Jaffe 1999:14).

Griko is indeed part of the texture of locals' everyday life in multiform ways; it has reentered the experiential reality of the larger community and is increasingly being used in domains other than the traditional ones. I therefore analyze the many ways in which locals *live with Griko* and engage with it other than by speaking it, and I foreground the various modalities in which the language finds space for expression—writing, singing, reciting poems, storytelling, etc. As we will see, the performative/artistic dimension in which Griko is embedded dominates such events, with locals continually drawing on the Griko linguistic-cultural tradition. Through this process, they reenact old practices, revealing their relationship with the past and the emotional and moral values it evokes, exhibiting further instances of the power of the cultural temporality of language in shaping language practices.

The Younger Generation's Repertoire in Griko

When, as in this case, the shift takes more than one generation and takes place through a restriction in the language's functions, the result is a pool of speakers with varying degrees of competence. This is mainly a generationally dependent variation; competence is often partial and sometimes only passive, as is the case for the 'in-between generation,' born in the years following WWII, who were not taught Griko as their mother tongue. Those belonging to the younger generation—that is those born in the 1970s and after—are bilingual Italian/Salentine speakers, and largely cannot be defined as Griko speakers. Clearly 'age in a vacuum' is not a marker in itself, as exposure to Griko depends on the specific biography of each speaker, and to the time spent with grandparents and elderly people in general. Take Donatello (born in 1970), whose parents are Griko speakers who often used Griko at home and with extended family; since we were young adults he would speak Griko—often repeating his mother's words—and he keeps using it when meeting his friends from Sternatia. Mattia (born in 1980) inherited the 'passion for Griko' from his father; his maternal grandfather was Greek, so he is also fluent in MG. Or take Enrico (born in 1982) who made a conscious effort to learn the language from his grandfather, and who is now fluent in Griko. Since those who have actively engaged in either improving their limited competence or in acquiring the language remain the minority inside the minority, these 'exceptions' tell a lot about the individual.

Exceptions aside, the competence in Griko of the young generation, if any, varies considerably, moving from knowing just a handful of words, to knowing a handful of sentences, to knowing a number of formulaic expressions. Indeed, the small repertoire the young generation skillfully makes convenient use of consists mainly of such formulaic expressions. Among them we find greetings such as greetings: *Pos pame? Pos istèi? Pame kalà; istèo kalò/kalì* (How are you doing? How are you? I am well); salutations: *Kalinnìtta, stasu kalò/kalì* (goodnight, goodbye); exclamations: *Pame? Tela 'ttù. Anòise? Anòisa. Ìpa ivò* (Shall we go? Come here; did you understand? I understood. I said); insults/swear words: *Amo ce piatti sto' kkolo; Ti kazzo lei armènu?* (Go to hell! What the fuck are you saying?). This repertoire is constituted by formulae that the younger generation can imitate and reproduce more easily. At times more competent speakers may (inadvertently or not) trigger the insecurity of those younger speakers who 'make an effort' to speak the language.

For example, consider Alessandro, a man in his early forties; sipping coffee with him and his father Giovanni, born in 1951—a fluent speaker—we were talking about his family history in relation to Griko. At a certain point, Giovanni expressed regret for not having taught it to his children, but immediately clarified that his eldest son, Alessandro, does speak it: "'*O mea to kuntei, olo to kuntèi, 'o minciò to anoà*" (Griko)—"The eldest [son] speaks it; the small [son] understands it." This is when Alessandro intervened in Griko to explain to me that he learned the language with his grandfather and father because they would speak it covertly (see Chapter 2); hesitating, he said, "*Me to' ciuri, me to' nonno, jai cini kuntèane atse skuso*" (Griko)—"With my father, with my grandad, because they would speak it covertly." Alessandro's use of the Salentine "*skuso*" for "covertly," however, immediately triggered Giovanni's reaction, who sanctioned it and used instead the Griko "*krifà*." I sat with them drinking coffee for another half an hour, but Alessandro did not intervene in Griko again; as his competence had been sharply scrutinized and corrected by his father, he switched to the Romance variety for the rest of the conversation, while Giovanni and I kept alternating between Griko and the Romance variety.[6]

---

6   This dynamic is, however, more widespread, as similarly elderly mother-tongue Griko speakers tend to put into question the competence of those belonging to the 'in-between generation': Antimino, for instance, often comments on his nephew Vito's mistakes, pointing out that he only recently started using Griko; this way he reinforces the perception of Griko as a language that belongs to the realm of the elderly, thus claiming his own authority.

It is, however, not unusual to hear what in prescriptive terms are non-Griko speakers resort to Griko occasionally. This confirms, I argue, the relevance of the practice of retrieving and creatively putting into use the available linguistic repertoire in Griko—however little this may be. These instances of language use fall under what, building on sociolinguist Ben Rampton (1995, 2009), I call 'generational crossing': the practice of using Griko by citing and reappropriating words or entire expressions from the stock of memory, and of recontextualizing them in the present.

The Younger Generation's 'Crossing'

As I often do, that afternoon I invited my friend Annu to come over for coffee. She is one of my closest friends; born in 1984, she works in a call center and is full of resources: she is very creative in manufacturing woolen things and repurposing materials, and she signs her handmade creations with the Griko label *maddhì* (wool). Her father passed away recently; he was a Griko speaker who worked in the fields all his life, a tiny and shy man with sparkling blue eyes and a beautiful and attuned voice that both Annu and her brother have inherited. Annu has been a lead singer of *The Passion of the Christ* since 2005; Antimino—the father of this tradition, as it were—often compliments her for her mimicry abilities; indeed, she faithfully reproduces his gestures when interpreting the work. Since 2016, the Bottega del Teatro has been organizing a workshop to keep transmitting this tradition to school children, ages seven to nine, who then perform it during the Easter week—among them my own niece Carola.

Annu's Griko is mainly restricted to the vocabulary covered by the text of *The Passion* and to her memories of her grandmother and father speaking Griko; however, she often resourcefully drags the right word out of it and uses it in the right context, always surprised at her own capabilities; this demonstrates the relevance of traditional practices such as this in transmitting fragments of the language. Equally central is the affective dimension in which Annu's memories of language use are embedded, as they are strictly linked to her closest loved ones; once I asked her to try to describe in Griko what the language means to her; she thought about it for a few seconds, took a piece of paper and slowly and very thoughtfully wrote and then read, "*Ivò agapò to Griko jatì ene i glossa ti' manamu, tu ciuriumu ce ti' nonna Teodòssia*"—"I love Griko because it is the language of my mother, of my father, and of my grandmother Teodossia."

That afternoon she was intent on showing me the pictures of her little niece Lara, the daughter of her brother Loreto, who also played and sang *The Passion*.

The night before she had dinner with them and she reported, very amused, Loreto's words to Lara: "So, I turn around and I hear Loreto saying to Lara, '*Prai ittù*' (Come here), and indeed she went!" Annu exclaimed, laughing. While we were trying Annu's homemade biscuits, she added all of a sudden, "You know, just on my way back from work there was this guy in the car who didn't know how to drive, so I told him, almost swearing, '*Ise 'na spirì fessa, isù, de?*' (You're a bit stupid, aren't you?)."

Like Annu and Loreto, those who belong to the younger generation may use expressions they heard in the house, and may resort to Griko from time to time "just for fun" (*'na lô is sfottò*); to be sure, this may also mean their use of jokingly intimidating expressions their grandparents would occasionally use when the kids misbehaved (among them: *arte su sirno 'nan ascla* or *arte su sirno 'na korpo*, both meaning "I am going to slap you now"). These expressions are now cited and reproduced in conversation to create a 'funny' effect; for instance, often when someone is too loud or difficult, Annu particularly likes to say *Ti ise àscimo kecci. Fonazzi sa' krio*—"How bad you are, child. You shout/scream like a ram"; apparently Annu was not an easy child.

As Sobrero and Miglietta (2010:126) note, from Weinreich onwards the playful as well as the cryptic functions of a language have been considered as residual functions of a moribund language. Yet, such instances of language use demonstrate how also for the younger generation words and/or small sentences in Griko are 'images of/from the past' linked to their emotional memory, their childhood memories, when they used to spend time with their grandparents and the elderly. From the stock of their memory they retrieve the image and thus the word or the expression linked to it; indeed, in our conversations, when someone said something in Griko, very often a story followed that recalled the situation in which they had heard that word or sentence and the people who used it. This would evoke emotions together with memories of language use.

Interestingly, however, in these instances meaning-making may not be their first goal, and they may also create pseudo-communications with the help of a few words or expressions. A characteristic example of this occurred a few years ago on Christmas Eve; we were enjoying our food and wine, when my friend Massimo told me, "*Manu, tela 'ttu na su po 'na prama*"—"Come here I need to tell you something." Before I could react, my friend Antonio joined in: "*Teli krasì?*"—"Do you want some wine?" Gabriele intervened, "*Fèremu mia rèccia*"—"Bring me a *reccia* [a type of dry bread]." Antonio added, "*O kecci! Techùddhi! Pame na plònnume*"—"The little boy! Poor baby! Let's go and sleep." Maurizio, who comes from a nearby non–Griko-speaking village, exclaimed, addressing his brother in Italian, "You see, I told you they are really indigenous!" We all laughed and kept drinking.[7]

This example shows again the 'playful function' of Griko in the younger non-Griko-speaking generation. In this case the speakers come from Zollino and Corigliano, where the younger generation shows an even lower competence in Griko as compared to Sternatia's speakers of the same age range.[8] They have no regular communication in Griko and their respective knowledge of Griko varies: following Dorian's terminology (1982), Massimo would belong to the category of a 'low-proficiency semi-speaker'; he certainly has a good passive knowledge—he is able to understand it—and has the ability to manipulate words in sentences. Antonio and Gabriele have been exposed to Griko only occasionally and they have basically 'stored' random words and sentences; they would therefore belong to what Dorian (1982:26) calls "semi-passive bilinguals, who are rarely able to manipulate words in sentences and whose verbal input is mainly short phrases and single-word utterances." However, what seemed to be a meaningful conversation, in reality was not. Massimo did not need to tell me anything; there was no dry bread on the table and there was no little boy around. They creatively threw a few sentences into the conversation, this time in such a way that it made some sort of sense; at other times, they do not even make the effort to make sense and simply rehearse in turn their knowledge of words or sentences, by listing them, creating an Ionesco-type of scene.

Such instances of 'generational crossing,' in which those in the younger generation resort to Griko, therefore acquire a particular relevance. As defined by Rampton (2005, 2009), 'crossing' refers to those situations in which a language that does not belong to a speaker is used in order to cross ethnic boundaries; he discusses this through the case of British, Asian, and Caribbean adolescents who borrow and mix codes. In my application of this notion, however, language crossing involves a movement across 'generations' rather than social or ethnic boundaries. Indeed, Griko is not a language considered to 'belong' to the younger generation; it is rather perceived as the language of the 'elderly' and of their experiential world, which the younger generation has not inhabited, but a distant world they have heard being described by their grandparents,

---

[7] Robert Moore (1988:463) refers to a similar scenario in the case of speakers of Wasco, a Native American language. "For contemporary Wasco speakers and semi[-]speakers, 'words' have taken on certain objectual qualities, and 'language,' is seen as a collection of words"; these are however disconnected from grammatical knowledge.

[8] As noted, Sternatia was the last village that shifted away from Griko; in practice this means that in Sternatia speakers are generally more competent than speakers in the same age range from other villages. This applies also to younger speakers; among those who were born in the 1970s there are also fluent speakers who interact in Griko with the immediate family of origin (parents, relatives at large).

and upon which they also reflect. Through an act of emulative performance those belonging to the younger generation therefore imitate the elderly and report their speech acts, in this way crossing the generational boundary that divides them from their phenomenological experience of Griko. The joking and self-ironic effect they consciously may produce through this language use is linked to their own 'alterity'; however, by evoking that specific chronotope, they use the language as a tool to connect with the elderly, and with the cultural repertoire.

This means that Annu, Massimo, Antonio, and Gabriele do not use Griko because of their 'Griko-ness'; rather, by crossing the temporal distance, they identify with and perform their 'Griko-ness' by using Griko, at times to the exclusion of bystanders. This tacit dynamic is shared by the inner-group, and in its inward articulation works as a 'we code'; it is, however externally oriented too, and plays with the audience's non-competence. In fact, in the case above, Maurizio and those friends from non–Griko-speaking villages believed my friends were having a proper conversation. In this external orientation, Griko becomes a symbolic resource used by young speakers to perform a rediscovered self-understanding and cultural identification. Interestingly, although this practice was not totally absent before, it has been intensifying considerably in the last few years. Crossing can therefore be considered one of the effects of the current revival.

If Rampton's notion of 'crossing' helps describe the act of bridging the generational gap, Jeffrey Shandler's (2004) notion of 'postvernacular Yiddish' is crucial to address the nature of this use of Griko. With this term, Shandler refers to the contemporary use of Yiddish in the post-WWII United States. Following the decline of vernacular Yiddish after the Holocaust, Yiddish has in fact acquired a new significance, one which transcends communicative purposes, becoming a form of cultural communication. Shandler writes, "In postvernacular Yiddish the very fact that something is said (or written or sung) in Yiddish is at least as meaningful as the meaning of the words being uttered, if not more so" (2006:22). As in the vignette presented above, meaning-making is not what matters the most: what prevails instead—as Shandler argues for Yiddish—is the deliberateness with which Griko is used, when used, and the performative aura in which the language is enveloped. As we will see, this has become a dominant feature of the contemporary use of Griko.

One could argue that the instances described above do not prove the 'vitality' of Griko, that they will not 'save' Griko's 'life'; that they might be 'isolated' cases with no statistical relevance. Indeed, the number of those who use Griko as a medium to exchange information in daily life keeps falling, as elderly mother-tongue and fluent speakers die. Griko remains a language for a minority, and a niche language for experts, as the revival has not had tangible effects in terms of raising the number of speakers. Those belonging to the younger generation, and who largely are non–Griko-speakers, may take discursive pride in Griko and its cultural heritage, without feeling the urge to learn the language. Here language ideology does not translate in practice; indeed, if young speakers are an exception, more of an exception are young people who want to learn the language. Those who had limited exposure to Griko—thus a weaker emotional attachment to it—and those who show little engagement with the topic of cultural heritage, do not invest much energy, if any, in 'performing Griko.'

Yet, I consider all these 'traces of language' revealing, and I argue that disregarding the communicative practices discussed above would lead to only a partial snapshot of the current languagescape. Beyond its limitations, the revival has enhanced self-awareness and restored prestige to the language. Indeed, and similar to what Shandler (2004) argues for Yiddish, if Annu and Mattia sing in Griko, if Donatello uses it to reconnect with old friends, if Enrico decided to learn it, if Antonio recites Griko poems to his child, it is because they deliberately choose to do so, not because they are 'naturally' expected to do so.

The Alternative 'Lives' of a 'Dying Language'

Griko has also reentered the experiential reality of the locals in a renewed form, acquiring a 'visual' dimension. One *sees* Griko more often than one hears it (Pellegrino 2016a). This is attested by the spread of the use of Griko for the names of restaurants, taverns, bars, B&Bs, associations, projects, etc., which started in the late 2000s and intensified throughout the 2010s. It has most recently been chosen as brand names for local products (such as beer), or even as the name of parties for local elections. Griko becomes, this way, symbolic of a recent reappropriation and reassessment of its value in various domains—including as a marketing tool, since it adds a distinctive and exotic flavor.

However, if we were to refer to Factor 5 of the Unesco Index, the vitality of endangered languages is determined by the number and type of domains in which they are used; these are subsystems of a community, such as the family, the economy, the church, and so on (Fishman 1965). Therefore, not only do old domains need to be maintained, but new ones—such as the media, broadcast outlets, and the Internet—need to emerge in line with the times. Text messaging in Griko can be accounted among these. Interestingly, this also seems to help semi-speakers' linguistic production. Among these is my friend Monica (born in 1971), whose father and mother were Griko speakers who characteristically did not teach it to their children, but who kept using it among themselves as a secret code when they did not want to be understood by their children (see

Chapter 2). Equally characteristically, Monica has a good passive knowledge—she understands it all—but she states that she cannot put a sentence together; when I returned to the village in 2008 to start my fieldwork, she proudly gave me a copy of *Spitta* that she had translated word by word into Italian. In reality, she underestimates her own understanding of Griko; if it is true that she does have difficulties speaking it, she easily writes in Griko: "It is easier, I take time to think and remember how my father would have said ..." That is, Monica relies of her memories of language use within the family to construct her own sentences. Here is a sample, taken from her text messages:

sozzo erti sesena sti Grecia? prin se filò depoi se mbrazzèo	Can I come to [see] you in Greece? First I kiss you and then I hug you
puru ka stei larga isù mu stei panta ambrò st' ammàddia	Although you are far away, I see you always before my eyes
su arizzo na pakko asce friseddhe? su ndiazete, de?	Shall I send you some 'dry bread'? You need it, right?

Regardless of their language competence, Griko aficionados or experts have increasingly used Griko in our WhatsApp group *I glossa grika*. Equally important to note is the case of people resorting to Griko for email. My seven-month online ethnography (January to July 2007) of the mailing list of the *Magna Grecia* newsletter showed that fifty percent of the emails written exclusively in Griko were Easter wishes; in the remainder of messages recourse to Griko was restricted to greetings and salutations. One exception was the email I have transcribed below, in which the author clearly looked for rhymes and produced a semi-poetic message to share his joy for having received the journal *Spitta* at his house "far from Calimera" (from other email exchanges it was revealed that he lives in the north of Italy).

ettase feonta, sa spitta fse lumera, ettase puru 'sse	[the journal] arrived, like sparkle from fire
mena ti steo macrea poddhì atti Calimera. sas xeretò	It reached me far away from Calimera
poddhi aderfia grica, nzigno na meletiso, kuntento,	I send you all my regards Griko brothers I start
sia ti steo sto paraiso.	reading Happy, as if I was in heaven

Besides the relevance of the use of endangered languages in these new domains, and beyond the type of new domains "accepted by the endangered language" (Brenzinger et al. 2003:11)—to use the wording of the Unesco Index—what I find equally crucial is the impact and potential effects of such expansion of domains in terms of community power relations, self-understanding, and representation. With regard to the domain of the internet, for instance, computer-mediated communication has become a powerful tool for minority languages, and for the circulation of language ideologies. Indeed, since the 2010s the use of Griko on the internet has intensified—also through Facebook where groups focus on dialects or minority languages in general, and where Griko aficionados or speakers also comment and contribute in Griko. They follow with particular interest pages dedicated to Calabrian Greek, as well as other Greek varieties around the world. On these Facebook pages, linguistic kinship—the affinities among Greek variants—becomes itself a language to articulate global belonging; this discourse bears significant implications for the creation of transnational/global 'imagined' communities (Anderson 1991), 'imagined worlds' (Appadurai 1996), which can only be fully appreciated over time.[9]

As for the domain of occupation, a handful of Griko-speaking musicians have found through the language occupational relief by performing both in Grecìa Salentina and in Greece, where they are regularly invited; there is also a renewed interest by singers who are not Griko speakers to sing songs of the Griko repertoire, and more recently to even cowrite lyrics in Griko. Griko has also officially entered the educational system through National Law 482/99, and with this entry came Griko experts/teachers. However, we have seen how this extension of domains generates internal power dynamics and clashing claims as to who retains authority over Griko and the right to represent the community at large (Chapter 5); this goes beyond the 'vitality' of the language itself.

What I want to emphasize here, however, is the broader shift from the traditional oral use of Griko to a written and performed mode. I have already talked about the promotion of writing Griko through initiatives by *Spitta* and Griko-Hellenic festivals; these are in a way driven efforts; more to the point they only

---

[9] An interesting avenue for future research would be the development of an initiative promoted by a young philologist from a village just at the outskirts of Grecìa Salentina, who out of his personal passion for languages got involved with Griko, and he is learning it. Motivated by a summer school for Calabrian Greek organized by the Calabrian cultural association Jalò tu Vua and their dedicated Facebook page, he intends to promote analogous initiatives in Grecìa Salentina. His aim is therefore to gather young people—from within and outside today's Griko-speaking villages—and infuse into them interest in acquiring Griko specifically as a spoken language, also accessing dedicated European venues for sustaining minority languages. Language ideologies keep traveling, so to speak, and through the visibility offered by Internet, travel much further and faster.

represent the tip of the iceberg. My ethnography shows what—playing with Stewart's (2003:492) terminology—I call 'an epidemic of writing' among elderly mother-tongue speakers and 'semi-speakers' alike (Pellegrino 2016a). I consider this emergent abundance of writing activity in Griko and its 'contagiousness' to be one of the more interesting outcomes of the revival.[10]

Take Annamaria as a characteristic example of those belonging to the 'in-between generation': born in 1958, she would fall under Dorian's (1982:26) definition of a semi-speaker, "an individual who has failed to develop full fluency and normal adult proficiency." She used to speak Griko with her parents, who were both Griko mother-tongue speakers, and since they died she has become even more engaged in keeping the language alive; she therefore looks for occasions and people to speak it with. She frequently goes across her field to find Paolo, a Griko mother-tongue speaker in his early eighties. She often talks of her gratitude to the De Santis brothers: *"Arte enna ringrazième ton de Santis, ka kanni ta travùdia is Grika. Ola ta travùdia pu èkame, ivo ta tsero"*—"We have to thank De Santis, who writes songs in Griko. I know all of his songs, they inspire me." The following is one of her poems, which her then-teenaged son, Fabrizio, set music in 2000 and performed with his band Athànatos (Immortal).

'En ìtela na fiko mai i chora	I would not ever want to leave
pu jenìttimo	the village where I was born
'en ìtela na fiko na pao a'tto spiti	I would not want to leave the house
pu ìstika mi' mànamu	Where I lived with my mother
'en itela na fiko patèra	I would not want to leave the priest
stin anglisìa	nor the church
'en ìtela na fiko i kiaterèddha mia	I would not want to leave my daughter
ma, iso choma ene agrikò,	But, this land is bitter
ce 'na prikò sciomì	and bitter is the bread
'nghizzi na pao pleon ambrò.	I need to keep going
ma fitisòmme isu ce prakalìse ton Kristò	But help me and pray Christ
ja ivò 'en ìtela na fiko tinò	Because I would not want to leave anyone

---

[10] With 'epidemic of dreaming' Stewart (2003) refers to an outbreak of dreams among schoolchildren on the Greek island of Naxos in the 1930s; this continued a tradition of dreaming of buried icons, which had begun a century earlier, at the time of Greek independence. See also Stewart 2012. My creative paraphrasing of Stewart's expression intends strictly to refer to the 'contagiousness' of the writing activity in Griko.

Translating into Griko is yet another activity in which the 'in-between genera-tion' increasingly engages. Antonio (born in 1950) enjoys translating Greek poems or songs, and he is very careful to reproduce the same metric. Since his retirement a couple of years ago, he has been dedicating himself wholeheart-edly to improving his Griko; this is indeed common among the 'in-between-generation,' and clearly the free time that comes with retirement facilitates this process. It also suggests that the 'passion for Griko' grows as one grows older, as it were, taking on an almost ontological dimension that often reflects people's nostalgia about their past, which is then articulated through language. Rather than speaking it, Antonio privileges writing it, and he has a whole list of MG poems and songs that he intends to put into Griko, also to show its affinities with MG, he argues, with which he is equally fascinated.

Interestingly, writing is an activity that also engages the elderly. When I met Giglio from Sternatia, he invited me to join him and his neighbors whenever I wanted, so that I could improve my Griko. I would join them during the long and hot summer nights, as they sat on straw-bottomed chairs in front of the doorstep of their house. They gather and simply talk or recite poems they have written; theirs is "the street of the poets," as I like calling it (see Figure 25). The group usually consisted of two old couples and two widows in their eighties, two men in their fifties, and a young couple in their late thirties; occasionally also a young lady with her toddler would join. Elderly speakers in Sternatia continue to speak it among themselves, within the household, with neighbors, and in the village square or market, for daily communication. Because of my presence, Giglio often chaired the conversation, prompting them one by one, to say a poem or a story in Griko. Some of these were popular poems or stories, either in Griko or dialect.

Figure 25. Giglio and I, Sternatia

In one of these encounters, Uccia (see Chapter 2) was enjoying herself thoroughly and congratulating herself after having recited one of the poems she had written—*Spitàcimu palèo* (Griko: My Little Old House), which she dedicated to her neighbors when she moved to her new house around the corner, just two hundred meters away. She then moved to recite another of her poems. When I went to visit her on another occasion, she proudly showed me the folder where she collects all her poems—ten at the time—whose topic range considerably. One was about her eldest son who lives in the North of Italy, and a few were spiritual compositions.

Posso mu fènete òrrio o spiti o protinò	How nice my first home seems to me
Apò motte jùrise mapàle is se mena	Since when it came back to me
Iciumpì echi o jeno pu agapò	There are the people I love
Ce pao panta na tus vriko oli mera	And I always go to visit them
Icherèome na kanonìso cittes kambarèddhe	I feel happy to see those small rooms
ka ine paleè kundu 'se mena	Which are old like I am
Môrkete stennù motte ìmosto chlorèddhe	I remember when they were young
Ka ikantàlizza nitta ce mera	And I would sing day and night

(Griko from Sternatia)

Giglio told me that he compiled and edited a small book (2003) financed by the municipality that was a collection of poems written or composed by elderly people of Sternatia. On the occasion of the yearly *Festa degli anziani* (Celebration of the Elderly), the authors would then recite their own creations. He also introduced me to Vincenzo, 'the poet,' who lived on the same street; he was a cheerful man who died at age 96, whose poems were published by a Greek schoolteacher from Corinth. A similar anthology collects poems composed mainly by elderly people from Corigliano—again, the result of a collaboration between local and Greek aficionados of Griko.[11]

I find particularly telling the very engagement with writing Griko by the literate elderly. We have seen how some elderly people had difficulties reading *Spitta*; likewise these are people who have not engaged with writing in general, who attended school for a few years and who never 'needed' to improve their written competence. Most of them, like Uccia, have composed poems in the past, but transcribed or had them transcribed recently. Their engagement with the written form and/or their desire to have their own poems transcribed thus takes on significance. Through

---

[11] *Jeno kalò a'ti' xora* (The People from Sternatia) (2008, Chrístos Tártaris, C., and Greco, C. eds.). See also *La Poesia grica: una realtà da scoprire e valorizzare* (Griko Poetry: A Reality to Discover and Valorize) (1998, Anchora, A. ed).

this epidemic of writing and the shift from an oral to a written mode of communication in Griko the elderly seem to ideologically reclaim a place of authority. Simultaneously, by reproducing the dominant language ideology they have long internalized—a language becomes such when it is written, as it were—theirs is an ideological claim for the recognition of Griko as a language.

Moreover, the practice of composing poems in Griko is widespread, attesting to the popular productivity of Griko in this genre; apart from the well-known contemporary poets—Cesarino De Santis from Sternatia, Cici Cafaro and Ernesto Corlianò from Calimera, among others—almost every village prides itself on the presence of a poet.[12] Interestingly, while investigating this topic, I kept encountering more and more people who write poems—regardless of their competence in the language; moreover, locals would recite to me poems composed by their own parents, other relatives, or acquaintances, suggesting that this is an established practice that locals have found productive through time. This is also when I found out that the following poem, which my mother often recites, was not composed by her as I thought, but by her mother—my grandmother Luce Aprile (1898–1979)—in the mid-1940s; it describes her pain as her eldest son never returned from the battlefield during WWII. We recently discovered that he died on the Greek island of Rhodes in 1944.

Pu enna chasùne i studi môla ta chartìa,	Where do all studies and paper have to disappear
mu piakane 'a pedì senza kamìa amilìa	they took my child without saying a word
ce to vrai pu tàrasse mu màvrise i kardìa	and the night he left my heart turned dark
kundu i nitta skotinì	like the dark night
mana, mana, ti mu ponì	mother, mother, it hurts
na pensèsso citto pedì	to think to that child
mu to pirane sti tàlassa	who was taken to the sea
ce 'e jùrise mai ampì	and he never came back
ce pesèno me ti toja	and I will die feeling the pain
ka 'e torò pleo itto pedì	of never seeing my child again.

---

[12] Franco Corlianò was a railway employee and an artist. He is the author of: *The Griko Italian, Italian-Griko Dictionary* (2010); *Three Owls on the Dresser: The World of Childhood in the Salentine Greek Tradition* (2010), a collection of games and toys, lullabies, riddles, and nursery rhymes; and *Salentine Greek Proverbs: History, Culture and Tradition* (2010). He is best known as the composer of the song *Klama* (Tears), more widely known as *Àndramu pai* (My Husband Leaves), a song about migration, which became famous in Greece thanks to its performance by the Greek singer Maria Faranduri. Cici Cafaro from Calimera is a happy and boisterous young man in his early nineties; he keeps writing poems, and he has rendered his courtyard a sort of museum of traditional local artifacts.

A common feature of these poems is the search for rhymes (which the previous poem demonstrates)—thus there is an alignment to a specific aesthetics, which in its simplicity gives value to the form as much as to the content. As we have seen, the journal *Spitta* is often criticized on the grounds that its prose does not suit Griko; indeed, Griko is most often portrayed as the 'the language of the past,' which supposedly lacks the linguistic resources to describe modernity without borrowings or adaptations. By the same token, I argue that locals' engagement with poetry reflects an equally dominant language ideology, which instead confers to Griko the value of expressing timeless emotions and feelings such as love, pain, sorrow, joy. "Certain things never change," Antonio explained, "and those sound better in Griko," he added. To be sure, here I look at poetry as the means and not as the object of inquiry, to emphasize how throughout time locals have kept 'composing in Griko'; by 'putting them (i.e. their compositions) into writing,' they have followed the tradition initiated by V. D. Palumbo and the circle of Calimera, who collected poems, songs, and proverbs of the oral tradition, providing a material legacy on which locals could continue to draw (Chapter 1). Like these scholars, locals continue to contribute to this material legacy and enrich it with their own productions of poems, translations, and writings, thereby contributing to the preservation of Griko (Pellegrino 2016a).[13]

Poetry in particular continues to serve a performative function, in multiple ways, since both poems of the popular tradition and also poems by Palumbo have been set to music by the band Ghetonìa. This is telling, since it reproduces a traditional practice which blurs the boundaries between poetry and music (Banti and Giannattasio 2004:290). We have indeed seen how, since the 1990s, Rocco and Gianni De Santis have been composing songs in Griko, setting to music some of their father's and siblings' Griko poems (Chapter 4). You have also met Luigi, who recently released his CD of poems/songs in Griko to "make the language re-sound in its simplicity," as he explained to me. Crucially, this practice also has metapragmatic effects, since it has allowed for the circulation of the poems and songs of the traditional repertoire, as well as new poems/songs. We have heard Annamaria's comments above about how through them she improved her Griko and found inspiration herself, and we have also seen the relevance of music in teaching Griko (Chapter 5). Indeed, over time, 'composing in Griko'—both poems

---

[13] Azzaroni and Casari highlight instead the social function of Griko poetry by the so-called *poeti contadini* (Italian: peasant poets) such as Cesarino De Santis and Cici Cafaro, who served a specific function of protest, denouncing social injustices or claiming cultural belonging (Azzaroni and Casari 2015:265). On his site *Ciùri ce pedì*, Prof. Tommasi includes two sections dedicated to poetry, making a distinction between folk/popular poetry and the more recent *Poesia colta*. See Montinaro (1994), who presents a collection of poetry of oral tradition comparing it with ancient Greek poetry, focusing particularly on *moroloja*, funeral laments (the Griko equivalent of what Greeks call *miroloja*; see also Giannachi 2012).

and songs—has remained the preferred modality of expression for locals, which has also contributed to the transmission of 'fragments' of the language and of traditional practices. Writing poems, singing, playing, reciting poems, and story-telling in Griko: it is through its performative tradition that the language has reached the present, despite not being a medium of daily communication.

Nostalgia and Beyond: Griko Cultural Events

The majority of the projects submitted by municipalities, schools, and cultural associations in Grecìa Salentina to apply for annual funding through Regional Law 5/2012 tend to be metalinguistic in nature; that is, they valorize knowledge of Griko linguistic-cultural traditions over the promotion of Griko as a language of daily communication. They may focus on local intellectuals of the past, on some aspect of local history, or on the traditional repertoire of songs and poems in Griko. Among the most recent examples falls the project *Loja ce Lisària. Itinerario poetico in Griko* (2017—'Words and Stones, Poetic Itinerary in Griko'). This project was submitted by the Pro-loco of Corigliano, and resulted in the installation of twelve information posters at significant places in the village. The posters featured the likes of a traditional poem, a saying, or a song from the Griko repertoire, including the New Year and Easter traditional songs (*Le strine* and *I passiùna*). Through the QR-code included on the posters, people can access videos, and watch and hear locals old and young, perform the works.

Figure 26. Attraversando il Griko, Maria and Sandra performing, Calimera

A similar project by the title *Sti' ffenèstra: Versi di griko in arte* (By the Window: Verses in Griko through Art) was promoted by the municipality of Calimera and the cultural association Ghetonìa. This project was put into place through the installation around the village of thirteen works by local painters, which were associated with verses in Griko by local poets and authors of the past; it is effectively an art gallery on the streets that simultaneously aimed to embellish thirteen blank windows. Once again, we see how this project extensively draws on the material legacy of poems in Griko, which combined with paintings, here fulfills an aesthetic function. Importantly, through these installations around the villages, Griko keeps entering the visual landscape. It is also revealing that these two projects were conceived not only for internal use but also for touristic fruition, as attested by the English translations provided. This points to an emerging trend and a venue for future investigation.[14]

Figure 27. Attraversando il Griko, the crowd following the event, Calimera

As for cultural events dedicated to Griko, some have become established appointments for Griko activists and aficionados; the Grikanti Festival, for instance, has been held since 2010 in the *masseria* of a Griko speaker and

---

[14] I remind the reader that the funding provided by the regional law is earmarked for municipalities, schools, and cultural associations of Grecìa Salentina; these submit a project to the regional government, which is then evaluated and may or may not be financed (see Chapter 4). In 2017 the total number of projects submitted and financed was twenty-four, out of which three were intended for schools, nine for municipalities, and twelve for cultural associations. Only two were purposely aimed at teaching Griko: *Pos Màtome Griko* (How We Learn Griko) and *Meletò, grafo ce milò Grika* (I Read, Write, and Speak Griko). Among the projects submitted in the past and funded by the law, I find *Evò ce Esù* (Festival of Minority Languages Cinema) of particular relevance. Parco turistico Palmieri, based in Martignano, is the association which promotes and organizes the festival.

activist, and it is dominated by music in Griko and Salentine, as well as dance. Attraversando il Griko, which literally means 'going through Griko,' is linked to the cultural association Ghetonìa from Calimera (see Figures 26 and 27, above). It first took place in 2008, and the very choice of the location for the event is telling: participants literally follow the activists through the narrow streets of the village historical center and enter the courtyard of typical local houses—the Griko *avlì*. These locations reveal the activists' desire to bring Griko back to the very places where it used to 'live,' as it were, as the natural background for the performance of songs, poems, dances, and traditional music.

At these cultural events Griko often fills the aural landscape without being used as a primary language. Participants usually alternate with each other, singing songs in Griko and Salentine—among them *Àremu rindinèd-dhamu* (I Wonder, My Swallow), *Kalinìtta* (Goodnight), and *Lu rusciu de lu mare* (The Whispering of the Sea). They recite poems of the oral tradition, as well as their own poems, or their translations into Griko of Greek or Italian poems, thoroughly enjoying themselves in doing so. Locals recollect their memories by telling stories, and through them they evoke more memories of similar performances in the past. Here we see emerging again the centrality of poetry as a social and performative activity, which, together with storytelling, is linked to past practices.

These encounters link those who attend them to past experiences and/ or nostalgic representations of that past; the Griko courtyard is indeed often evoked. To use the words of Sandra, whom you met in the previous chapter, the courtyard was "a living space to share and the very heart of community life: everything happened in the courtyard and everyone used to share what they had, even if it was just some bread and they would help each other caring [for] children or the elderly; *avlì* and *ghetonìa* (neighborhood) go hand in hand. It was not just a space, but a way of living." A discursive nostalgia for the Griko-speaking community of the past may emerge; Griko becomes therefore indexical of that *ghetonìa*, which exemplifies the community of the past; it is, however, not the past itself to be nostalgically longed for, it is rather the social organization based on reciprocity and solidarity to be sentimentally reconstructed and evoked, in sharp contrast to contemporary individualism.[15]

---

[15] See Avineri 2012 for the concept of 'nostalgia socialization' in the case of Yiddish. See also Cavanaugh 2009.

Nostalgia is indeed a sentiment as much as a metacomment on the present: *"Passon mia ikrìvete sto villino-tti jiatì èchume ole tin villa arte, de?"*—"Each of us hides inside their little house, because now we all have a house, right?" My friend and life teacher, Splendora, would always emphasize how the changing post-WWII environment had improved locals' living conditions, but had also transformed the living space, the spatial setting, the very habits linked to the place (see Chapter 2). Through this temporal dialogue the present and the past are continuously compared and contrasted; stressing the hardship of the past serves the double purpose of putting into light the comfort of the present, but also its dubious morality, as it were, in sharp contrast to the portrayal of the past. This then leads to expressions such as 'life was better when it was worse.' Nostalgia becomes a discursive strategy through which locals express their affective attachment to a 'time past,' and morally evaluate the present.

Performing Griko, Evoking the Past

A keen north wind was blowing that night—a relief in the hot Salentine summer. Maria and Ninfa, both from Calimera, were getting ready. Ninfa sat, firmly holding her notes in one hand and her violin in the other; a local singer and musician, she looked almost nervously at Maria one last time, awaiting confirmation that she could start. Maria—a schoolteacher as well as a Griko semi-speaker and activist—was standing next to her. She then turned around, giving her back to the audience; that must have been the agreed signal; indeed Ninfa started almost whispering in Griko:[16]

Ninfa:

Nitta, nitta atse fengo	Night, night of moonlight
pano sti' tàlassa	above the sea
Pedìmmu, pedìmmu,	my child, my child
tsunna na su po	wake up, I need to tell you something
Enna su po	I need to tell you something

Then Maria started reciting in Italian, her voice alternating and at times overlapping Ninfa's reciting in Griko.

---

[16]   https://www.youtube.com/watch?v=zFlmMVwxWK4

Maria:	**Ninfa:**	
Luna, luna che faccia	*Fengo, fengo, ja muso*	Moon moon as face
luna focaccia	*fengo, mia focaccia*	moon as focaccia
luna allo specchio	*fengo, jail*	moon, mirror
sussurro all'orecchio	*krifizzi att'aftì*	whisper in my ear
luna sul mare	*pano sti tàlassa*	moon over the sea
mi devo svegliare	*Tsunna, tsunna*	I need to wake up
(Italian)	(Griko)	

The audience was immediately carried away by this start and attentively followed Maria's narration.

Maria:

Che anno è? Il '43, o il '44 (Italian)	What year is it? It is 1943, or 1944
e iu stau aqquai (Salentine)	and here I am, I stay here
ettù steo, (Griko)	I stay here
Echo ettà chronu	I am seven years old
sette anni tengo (Italian)	I am seven
umme, e' cerò atse guerra	yes, it is a time of war
c' evò ìsteo ettù (Griko)	and I stay here
sto con I nonni miei (Italian)	with my grandparents
o tàtamu stei stin guerra (Griko)	my father is at war
papà mio sta alla guerra (Italian)	my father is at war
prima all'Albania così mi hanno detto (Italian)	he first went to Albania, so I was told
ma però sono 3 anni (Italian)	but three years have passed
che non sappiamo più niente di lui (Italian)	since we last heard from him

Maria then continued alternating between Griko, Salentine, and Italian to recount a series of stories and anecdotes involving people from Calimera, but representative of the time in which she sets her performance: *"ene cerò atse guerra"*—"it is a time of war," she says, referring to WWII. Ninfa at times intervened, playing the violin in the background; between one story/anecdote and the next she would sing songs of the popular tradition both in Salentine and Griko. She is now an internationally known singer thanks to her participation in the concerts of the Notte della Taranta, where she also sings in Salentine and Griko. The entire performance was rhythmically choreographed by Ninfa's and Maria's overlapping voices as they repeated the inception of the performance as a sort of refrain before Maria proceeded to tell the subsequent stories.

At the end of the performance, Maria explained—in Italian—that those were stories she had collected from her own father and uncle; she stressed how she had heard them recounted time and again, albeit with a few changes "because memories change," she pointed out, before adding, "but probably most of you have the same memories, or similar ones."

Through the years Attraversando il Griko became an established event, increasingly attracting people from neighboring villages, as well as the curiosity of tourists. In the last few years it was organized in collaboration with associations from other villages, effectively becoming a touring cultural event centered around performances, poetry, and the music of the Griko repertoire. Through time, the performative aura with which Griko cultural events are imbued has become dominant; indeed, Griko activists such as Maria started to rehearse for the event, and to curate their contribution/performance more systematically. Significantly, and with a very few exceptions, Griko is not the primary language used in such events. Characteristically, Maria's and Ninfa's use of Griko throughout the performance is limited: Maria, who wrote the script of the performance, selectively inserted a few words and sentences, but if pieced together they provide a condensed version of her story. Equally characteristically, in this performance they reproduce the blended local languagescape, using Griko, Italian, and Salentine: this is also a functional and inclusive choice since it allows non-Griko speakers to follow/appreciate the performance. However, this choice is not necessarily linked to the performers' or audience's competence/lack of competence in Griko—Maria admits she has difficulties speaking it, although she understands it.

What prevails in these contexts is the use of Griko to express cultural distinctiveness; similar to what Shandler argues for Yiddish, it is Griko's exceptional nature that is to be prized here, and not its use of a tool for routine communication. Echoing him, rather than considering this shift as a failure, I find it more enlightening to treat it as "a distinctive cultural enterprise in its own right" (Shandler 2004:38). By doing so, we are also able to appreciate the multiple ways in which locals have responded to the moral panic about Griko's death and the sense of cultural loss associated with it. This leads me to argue that while the use of Griko as a vehicle to convey information has progressively faded out, its performative and artistic use has increased (Pellegrino 2016a). Locals contribute to building the materiality of Griko with their own productions and performances, showing continuity with past practices and recontextualizing them in light of the present.

The choice to resort to Griko even if simply inserting a word or a short sentence here and there reveals an aesthetic taste that has been intensifying over time; but Griko is not simply used for performative purposes; it is precisely through locals' conscious and intentional use that their linguistic identity takes shape and manifests itself. This indicates, I contend, that the more Griko is dying, the more it is being 'resurrected' performatively in a dialectic process—indeed a 'dying' language may also have 'alternative lives'; or rather, it means to acknowledge that *people live with languages*, engaging with them in multiform ways that often escape rigid classifications aimed at assessing language vitality and endangerment, whose underlying stance tends to delegitimize hybrid linguistic practices and/or ignore the cultural and semiotic functions and uses of languages. Living with Griko means speaking it, alternating it with Salentine, resorting to it for fun or as a symbolic resource to perform cultural identification—it means to write poems in Griko, to sing its songs, to perform it, to translate into it. Griko often resounds through affective echoes: it may spark intellectual curiosity, and at times also the desire to rediscover a sense of cultural belonging. For those who are part of the 'in-between generation,' engaging with Griko is often a way to keep redeeming it from the stigma long associated with it.

The analysis of these practices ultimately reveals the power of the cultural temporality of language highlighting the relationship to the past that individuals establish through language. Indeed, in these instances and through these performances, Griko becomes a tool for members of the community to establish a connection to the past—their own experiential past and/or that of previous generations; in other words, to connect with older members of the community. In the performance analyzed here Maria, for instance, effectively interpreted her own father, who was only seven years old at the time of WWII, while his own father was in the battlefield. Younger members of the community like Maria clearly did not experience firsthand the hardship of that past, but they are frequently socialized into it; indeed, the elderly rarely miss the chance to highlight the experiential distance between the past and the present, evoking 'the hardship of the past,' the harsh living conditions, the scarcity of food, the lack of comfort. Formulaic expressions such as *'Toà en' ìane kundu àrtena'* (Griko: 'Back then things were not like today, 'or 'Back then we all lived in one room, we all ate from the same plate') are some of the door openers to the past and its story world. Through this discursive practice, the younger generations have been socialized into the phenomenology of the past, as it were. By the same token, by using traditional cultural models—such as storytelling, singing, etc.—they reformulate claims to the past and 'reenact' it; importantly, they refer to the past in order to evaluate the present, and in light of the present, they keep negotiating the meanings and values to attach to it, effectively re-storying it and Griko. Indeed, in Maria's performance referenced above, the past with its memories became the raw material on which she built a story whose message transcends the temporal divide between the past and the present; in this case recalling the wounds of the war years becomes also a plea for peace.

Engaging with Griko may equally entail evoking Hellenic belonging—a language ideology nourished also through personal relations that locals have cultivated through time with Greek aficionados of Griko. The activists of Calimera, for instance, have long-standing relationships with Greek aficionados of Griko, who have often collaborated in Attraversando il Griko. It is also not unusual to find Greek tourists who are attending Griko cultural events to be fascinated by Griko and its history, who contribute to the circulation of a language ideology that celebrates Griko as a living monument of Hellenism. "Griko smells of antiquity," Antonio from Calimera proudly says. Griko activists advance in this way multiple claims to the past, and at times simultaneously: to a local, more recent and redeemed past, as well as to a distant but glorious Hellenic past, following the footsteps left by local philhellenists. Lastly, among Griko activists there are also those particularly eager to reestablish contact with the Greeks claiming a common cultural heritage. In the next chapter I present my ethnography in Greece and introduce you to Greek aficionados of Griko; the investigation of the dominant Greek language ideologies of Griko will complement the understanding of the dynamics of the current revival.[17]

---

[17]   See also Pipyrou (2016:54) for a similar argument about the Grecanico associations of Calabria, who make a case for belonging not only to Ancient but also Modern Greece.

7

The View from Apénandi
Greece's Gaze on Grecìa Salentina

"MANU, we've arrived in Ioannina," my then-partner Thodoris exclaimed relieved, awakening me from my nap. He had driven most of the way from Athens and was rather tired, although we had improvised a picnic on the way. Still half asleep, from the car I stared at the lake and its island, which had looked as pretty from afar as it proved to be close up, and all of a sudden the memories of my one-month stay in Ioannina three years earlier flooded back. "Turn here, the hotel must be around here," I told him. To his and my own surprise—I always get hopelessly lost!—I still remembered the way to the hotel, where Niko, the manager, awaited us. Our picnic had delayed our arrival; at the hotel reception desk, we were told that he had just left, then as we were being shown our room we were informed that we would be his guests for the night. As Thodoris looked at me puzzled, I explained to him that there was no point in insisting to pay, and that we would find another way to thank Niko. "He is a big man with a big heart," I began, recalling how generously he had treated me when, a few years earlier, I had attended an intensive MG summer course at the University of Ioannina. At that time, it was Antonio from Corigliano, a close friend of Niko's and likewise engaged in the Griko cause, who had given me his contact information.

Niko is in fact not only the manager of the hotel, which serves as the *simeio anaforús* (reference point) for people arriving from Grecìa Salentina and Salento as a whole; he is also the president of the Politistikós Sìllogós Fili tis Gretsía Salentina. The cultural association Friends of Grecìa Salentina was established in 1993 in Ioannina, but counts among its members people from all over the Epiro area. Its mission is "to contribute to the preservation and promotion of Griko and its traditions and customs, as well as those of other hellenophonic areas," Niko had told me, switching between MG and Italian flavored with French, in which he is also fluent.

Niko is what I call 'an aficionado' of Griko, and like the rest of the Greek aficionados of Griko that I met and will introduce to you, he travels often to

Grecìa Salentina and has personal relationships with people on the other shore. When I saw him for the first time in Ioannina he welcomed me with open arms—literally—and was evidently thrilled to meet me, knowing I come from Grecìa Salentina. At that time, he helped me to find a flat to share for the month, a flat just around the corner from the hotel. Thodoris listened to me patiently go on and on about Niko's kindness as I continued to recount how he had taken the time to show me Ioannina, and to drive me around the area, to Metsovo and Meteora. Finally Thodoris cut short my flow of memories by asking, more puzzled, *"Nai nai ... jatì omos?"*—"Yes yes ... But why?" When I, feeling overwhelmed by Niko's immediate availability, affection, and generosity, had asked Niko a similar question years earlier, he replied without hesitation, *"Jatì? Jatì ise apò ekì. Mas arési polí na échoume schési me tous filous mas apénandi. Pame apénandi kathe chrono"*—"Because you come from there. We like very much to have relations with our nearby friends. We go across every year." Luckily, Thodoris was too tired to keep inquiring and let it go. I, on the other hand, had taken a fair amount of time and effort to appreciate fully Niko's reply and the view of other aficionados of Griko.

The view from *apénandi*—Greece's gaze on Griko, Grecìa Salentina and its people—is the central theme of this chapter. *Apénandi* can be translated as 'opposite,' 'facing,' 'across from,' or 'in front of.' I often heard my Greek friends and acquaintances use this expression in Ioannina, Patra, and Corinth to refer to Grecìa Salentina. *Apénandi* suggests proximity, something within your gaze; first and foremost, it has a spatial connotation. Not incidentally, all three towns have ports. What divides Greece from Grecìa Salentina is the sea, which interestingly enough Italians refer to as the Adriatic and Greeks as the Ionian Sea. Yet this expression is not confined to the spatial sphere; at a metaphorical level it suggests closeness and familiarity.

In presenting this picture of Griko drawn by my Greek interlocutors and aficionados of Griko, I build on the ethnography I carried out in Greece as part of my doctoral studies, and during my subsequent stays in Athens and on the island of Ikaria. However, observations deriving from my encounters with Greeks visiting Grecìa Salentina, and from Greek–Griko encounters on both shores are equally part of the data from which I draw my analysis. For instance, I also met Niko in Grecìa Salentina on various occasions; only one year before my fieldwork he had organized an *ekdromì*—a trip to Grecìa Salentina and had contacted the cultural association Chora-Ma of Sternatia. The collaborations between Greek and Griko cultural associations, which had begun to intensify in the 1990s, continued to strengthen. We saw in the previous chapters how the teaching of MG provided by the Greek Ministry of Education since 1994 had played a role in the local languagescape.

I was therefore drawn to carry out fieldwork in Greece, as I wanted to follow the network of cultural collaborations with and ties to Greece, and to better understand the effects of both the institutional and popular measures being undertaken in support of Griko. I was particularly attentive to local discourses/metadiscourses about Griko and Grecìa Salentina, as I planned to assess how they contribute to the reproduction and circulation in Grecìa Salentina of a language ideology that highlights the Hellenic cultural heritage and celebrates Griko as a 'living monument of Hellenism' (MG: *ena zondanó mnimeío tou Ellinismoú*). In Greece, I soon realized that the very fact that I come 'from over there' granted me a very warm welcome; it was not a total surprise and I cannot deny that it was wonderful to be so warmly embraced, although at times this caused me some embarrassment. More than anything, I felt puzzled by it. What is their gaze on Grecìa Salentina, Griko, and its speakers? The more I listened to my Greek friends and aficionados of Griko talking about this topic, the more I heard them talking about themselves: Griko emerged from their narratives as a "spiritual extension of Greece" (Triandaphyllídis 1952, cited in Stewart 2006:74), as it were.

In order to contextualize my ethnography and findings, as usual I need to begin in the past—in this case the past of Greece—to trace the dominant attitude of the Greek State toward Greekness/Hellenism within and outside its own borders. What strikes me about the case of Griko and of its speakers is that it represents a case of "matter out of place" (Douglas 1966:39) with respect to the historical categories of *chaméni patrída* (lost homeland) and of *omogéneia* (roughly translated as 'people of the same descent') that the Greek State developed soon after its inception. Although inapplicable to the case of Griko (and Greko), the rootedness of these categories has guided the Greek State in the policy it has implemented in Grecìa Salentina (and also Calabria), namely, the teaching of MG.[1] Likewise my ethnographic exploration of Greek popular perceptions of Griko offers an interesting avenue to assess how the inscribed 'cultural ideology of Hellenism' and its historical continuity has been internalized by my Greek interlocutors, and how their views of Griko are filtered through it.

Greece: The State and Its Nation

Apénandi ultimately indexes a notion of cultural proximity, the historical product of relations between Greece and Southern Italy that have spanned millennia. History continued to run its course, and by the time the Greek War of

---

[1]   I remind the reader that the term *Greko* refers to the variety spoken in Calabria; I use the terms Greko and Calabrian Greek interchangeably.

Independence broke out in 1821 the links between the two places had been long severed. The very existence of these linguistic enclaves in Southern Italy had been forgotten for centuries; it was rather ironic, then, that it was in precisely this same year that German philologist Witte 'rediscovered' them. By that time the Griko speakers were a small unit living in rural areas; they were Catholics following the Roman rite, and were to be ruled by the Bourbons until the Unification of Italy in 1861. The history which then unfolded is immersed in the dynamics of the *La questione meridionale* (Italian: The Southern Question), which developed soon after the Unification of Italy: a dynamic concerning the economic, political, and cultural/social relationships between the North and the 'backward' South. This dynamic had and still has its own legacy in terms of struggles over local community self-understanding and representation, in which the place itself has long defined a sense of belonging.

On the other shore, since its very establishment the Greek State has defined belonging by resorting to notions of ethnic origins, Orthodoxy, and the cultural heritage of Hellenism (Venturas 2009:125–140) including language, although the meaning and entailment of these notions and to what end they were/are deployed have been shifted over time. During the four hundred years of the Ottoman Empire, religion was the adopted criterion through which populations were defined, and through which sense of belonging was described. Therefore, Greek-speaking Orthodox Christians belonged to the same *millet* as Albanian, Bulgarian, Vlach, and Serbian-speaking Orthodox Christians—*millet* being translated into Greek variously as *génos* or *éthnos*, and denoting 'group, community.' In fact, the revolution was declared on behalf of those who "believe[d] in Christ" (Stewart 2006:64); gradually, however, Greek 'nationals' became defined not only by their affiliation with the Orthodox Church, but also by speaking the Greek language and by proof of their descent from Greek ancestors. This is reflected in the policies that defined Greek citizenship in the nineteenth century.[2]

As Stewart (2006:65) argues, the meaning of *génos* or *éthnos* began to lose its previous polyglot sense during the period of early Greek nationalism, paving the way for the modern connotation of the terms ethnic and ethnicity. Likewise, the corresponding notion of *omogéneia* over time came to identify those ethnic Greeks living in the Ottoman Empire and those diasporic

---

[2]   See Tsitselikis (2006). The First Provisional Government (1822) attributed citizenship to all native Christian inhabitants of the regions in revolt; in 1823, the second National Assembly added speaking Greek as a mother tongue as a criterion, whereas it extended citizenship also to nonnative Christians living in the regions of the revolt. In 1827, the third constitution of revolutionary Greece was drafted, and the criterion for enlistment of all Greeks-by-descent in the service of their reborn homeland was added (Vogli 2009:101–102).

populations who had migrated to Europe during the Ottoman period (Stewart 2006). What goes by the label of the 'Great Idea' (*Megáli idéa*), a notion established in 1844, is indeed a political vision of an extended Greece that would incorporate the 'unredeemed' coethnics—*omogeneís*. Behind this political irredentism was the expansionist ambition of the Kingdom; the Greek gaze was directed to the East and to those lands of the Byzantine Empire that had been lost to the Ottomans. The Greek nation-state effectively emerged as an 'island' whose borders expanded through repeated annexations of territory; in 1832, it embraced only three quarters of a million of the more than two million Greek-speaking Christians under Ottoman rule; on the eve of World War I, its territory had increased by nearly seventy percent, but Greece achieved its present configuration only after WWII (Clogg 1979). Up until 1922, the Greek State looked for support for its irredentist policy by addressing itself to the communities of the merchant diaspora who had contributed to the rise of the Greek national movement (Venturas 2009; see also Calotychos 2003; Herzfeld 1982). The Great Idea was to come to an end only with the Asia Minor Catastrophe—the war initiated by the Greeks against the Turks in order to annex Smyrna—and with the compulsory population exchange between Greece and Turkey in 1923, in which the criterion of religion prevailed over the ability to speak Greek.[3] After that, the Greek State continued to address the many Greek emigrants to the United States, Canada, and Australia.

Southern Italy was outside of that particular chapter of Greek history. Its people were not living in a 'lost homeland' (*chaméni patrída*) belonging to the Ottoman Empire, nor did they belong to the Greek merchant or elite diaspora (or to a distant non-Eastern Mediterranean diaspora). In other words, these linguistic enclaves in Southern Italy were not on the political or ideological map of the emergent Greek nation-state. By the same token, on the other shore, Griko speakers did not see themselves as a people whose motherland had just been liberated. The story of Griko I am recounting in this book in fact began in the late nineteenth century, when relations between Greece and Grecìa Salentina resumed thanks to the activity of intellectuals/folklorists from both shores. It started with the 'first language ideological revival' of Griko, promoted by the philhellenic circle of Calimera, although—as we saw in Chapter 1—its intellectualist efforts to link Griko to Hellenism failed to reach Griko speakers at large: they could not identity with that discourse because their lived reality of the language linked them to a different past and to local dynamics.

---

[3] Over a million Christian Orthodox, many of whom spoke no language other than Turkish, had to leave Turkey for Greece, and about 400,000 Muslims who were established in Greece had to leave for Turkey. The Muslims of Western Thrace and the Orthodox of Constantinople remained *in situ*.

Hellenism and Romanticism

At the time of the War of Independence and afterwards, 'Greece' had to deal with its own dynamics. Its very emergence as a nation-state was notably supported by Western European philhellenism, which had developed in France, Germany, and England in the nineteenth century. Philhellenists were admirers of the Greek classical aesthetic and philosophy, and they evoked the notion of cultural Hellenism, giving Greece the ideological foundations of its raison d'être and its justification for realizing the national project in political terms (Calotychos 2003). Hellas was chosen as the name for the newborn country, revealing the extent of philhellenists' romantic fascination with classical culture and their implicit claim of cultural continuity. This Romantic ideal would link the Greeks of that time to a civilization that had disappeared almost two millennia earlier, a civilization that would have resisted any important cultural influence of other peoples (Most 2008; Stewart 1994). Whether on the eve of independence ordinary Greek speakers of today's Greece had any developed notion of their Greek/Hellenic ancestors remains questionable; yet they were romantically expected, as it were, to have preserved knowledge or memory of their classical past (Herzfeld 1982; Stewart 1994). From its very inception, the Greek State has therefore invested in crafting a national culture to match the expectations of the philhellenic dream, as it were. In order to prove the continuity of the Greek identity in all its manifestations and expressions, disciplines such as historiography, archaeology, philology, and folklore notably engaged in the construction of a continuous past linking modern to ancient Greece (see Herzfeld 1982). Greek history was to be Hellenized along a coherent temporal narrative in which Macedonian domination, the Hellenistic and Roman periods, the Byzantine era, and the Ottoman Empire had to be synthesized as phases of a continuous Hellenism (Liakos 2008; Livanios 2008; Plantzos 2008). Likewise Christian 'Greeks,' who had called themselves 'Romaioi' throughout the Byzantine and Ottoman periods, were conflated with the 'Éllines' of Ancient Greece to become 'Helleno-Christian.'

Language, as the tenet of nationalism and of many nation-state building processes in Europe, was soon elevated to be the purest trait of the national identity; yet 'Greek' was not the language of all Orthodox Christians, and for that reason it was also the most vulnerable tenet of the Greek national project. In Athens alone, half of the people spoke Albanian at the outbreak of the Greek War of Independence in 1821 (Herzfeld 1997). In the newborn Greece, Slavic, Albanian, and a variety of local Greek dialects were spoken, while varieties such as those spoken in Cappadocia, Epirus, Crete, and Pontus, were barely mutually intelligible (Stewart 2006). Particularly telling is the case of Solomos from

Zakynthos, whose language of education was Italian, and who wrote a 'Hymn to Liberty' (1823), which subsequently became the Greek national anthem.[4] In Italy the languagescape was equally internally heterogeneous, with only two percent of Italians speaking the national language at the time of the Unification of Italy in 1861. Indeed, although modern nation-states are usually depicted as the natural repository of national languages—the expression of the spirit of the people, as it were—in many nation-state building processes in Europe language has been the very means through which a sense of community was created and reinforced (see Anderson 1991, among others). Greece likewise required a national Greek standard, and in response to philhellenic ideals, *katharévousa* was crafted, a language that adopted the morphology of ancient Greek; once this was 'purified' of foreign loanwords (including from Turkish, Italian, Slavic, and Albanian), it could then be considered "the quintessential index of Greek continuity" (Calotychos 2008:237)—and thus the very means by which to 're-Hellenize' the Orthodox peasant populations under Ottoman rule, including the Turkish-speaking Greeks (Horrocks 1997; Clogg 2002). The vernacular *dimotikí*,[5] which had meanwhile become associated with low-status domains in a classic example of diglossia, became the national language only after the restoration of democracy in 1974.

The memory of the 'language question' (*glossikó zítima*) and its implications had long been alive among the majority of Greeks (Herzfeld 1997). Equally alive is the legacy of the 'Hellenization' of Greece in modern times, "one of the most successful efforts of restoring a remote past through nationalism" (Liakos 2008:236). Greeks seem to embody those ideologies of history and of language upon which the Greek State was constructed.[6] My ethnography in Greece contributes to this argument, showing how these ideologies have helped to shape both the Greek gaze with respect to Griko and Grecìa Salentina, and how they are further reproduced.

The Greek Ministry of Education and the Teaching of Modern Greek in Southern Italy

The teaching of MG in the South of Italy is part of a bilateral agreement between the Italian and Greek Ministries of Education. As part of my fieldwork in Greece, I decided to investigate this further, as I was interested in finding out the legal framework within which this agreement came into existence and whether it was

[4]   See Van Dyck (2009) for the role played by diasporic Greeks in the Greek 'language question.'
[5]   '*Roméika*' was what 'Greeks' called their language until independence (see Herzfeld 1986; Liakos 2008).
[6]   I am drawing here from Stewart (2003, 2008) in my use of 'ideology of history.'

part of the overall policy aimed at 'Greeks abroad.' I called the Greek Ministry countless times in order to identify the person in charge of the program. I sent a letter with five questions[7] to a number of different departments (International Educational Affairs, Education for Greeks Abroad, and Intercultural Education and Education for Greeks Abroad[8]), but received no reply. I visited the Ministry on three separate occasions before and after the elections in October 2009 that resulted in a change of political party. Like a package, I was sent from one person to another, shuttled from phone call to phone call. This proved to be one of the most difficult parts of the research in Greece, a task at which I failed miserably, since all my would-be interlocutors refused me any information. This could have been a reaction that Herzfeld (1983:143) identifies as *Efthinofovia* or "fear of responsibility," that is, "the stereotypical unwillingness to take any initiative in even the most marginally anomalous [bureaucratic] situations." Although regrettable, as my requests went unanswered I am left to make inferences about the involvement of Greece at the institutional level without benefitting from the 'official' perspective.

When talking to my Greek friends, and to aficionados of Griko, they often expressed to me their disappointment with the absence of support by the Greek State regarding the Griko- and Greko-speaking communities of Southern Italy, and argued that this was due to its fear of being accused of intervening in internal Italian affairs. Others pointed out that the biggest difference between Hellenophonic communities of Southern Italy and Pontic Greeks or Greek-Albanians is religion. We have seen that Orthodox Christianity has been a key factor of Greek identity since the inception of the Greek nation-state. According to historian Charles Frazee (2002:39–43), despite the long-shared history between Catholicism and Orthodoxy, many Greeks regard Catholics with suspicion. He suggests this might be motivated by a concern that the Catholic Church may attempt conversions, and also by their historical association with the West—specifically, that they have benefited from foreign protection and financial support. They are consequently considered 'foreigners.' Frazee points out that, despite being one the largest religious minorities in Greece (Latin-rite Catholics are mainly

---

[7] This is the list of questions: 1) When did the Ministry of Education first send teachers of Modern Greek to the Griko-speaking villages of Apulia? 2) What are the reasons that brought the Greek State to activate this program? What is its overall goal? 3) Is this policy part of the program sponsored by the Greek Ministry of Education for Greek citizens abroad (*Apódimos Ellinismós*)? If not, what legal framework defines the program? 4) What exactly does this program entail? 5) What is the general stance of the Greek Ministry of Education toward the Hellenophonic minorities of Italy (Apulia, Calabria)?

[8] Diéfthinsi Diethnón Ekpedeftikón Schéseon, Diéfthinsi Pedías Omogenón kai diapolitismikís ekpédefsis, and Diapolitismikís Ekpedefsís respectively.

located on the Cycladic islands of Tinos and Syros, and in the capital region) the Catholic Church remains without legal status in Greece; the right-wing party (*Nea Demokratia*) thus considers adherents "Greeks by law, but not by consciousness" (Frazee 2002:24–43). As some of my interlocutors suggested, the fact that Griko and Greko speakers of Southern Italy are Catholics who follow the Latin rite cannot 'officially' be overlooked by 'the State.'[9]

One might regard the involvement of the Greek state in Griko and Greko affairs as minimal; the measures taken are admittedly few, but I believe it is enlightening to explore the ideological basis of such an involvement, and to highlight the dynamics emerging from it. These linguistic enclaves in Southern Italy are a recent discovery, and they are indeed an unexpected new chapter in the history of Greece, as it were; this explains the lack of a consistent policy. It could be argued that since the Greek State lacks a suitable category for them, it has been forced to interpret them using the categories presently available, regardless of degree of applicability. As regards Calabria, "the relations that this state fosters with the communities affects conditions similar to those of a diaspora" (Pipyrou 2010:92, 2016). The teaching of MG is an example of this, as this is a policy usually restricted to diasporic communities, especially since language is the other key determinant of Greek identity.

If in the nineteenth century *katharévousa* was used as an instrument to 're-Hellenize' the Greeks, in the twentieth century MG similarly became the instrument with which to keep Hellenism alive. Fear that Greek migrants would assimilate in their host countries and hope that they would return to the homeland to revitalize it motivated the establishment of Greek schools in European countries since the early 1970s, and particularly after the restoration of democracy in 1974 (Venturas 2009). A crucial shift in these policies occurred, however, in 1996 when a new bill passed stipulating that Greek education abroad should no longer be reserved for the descendants of migrants in Western Europe, but should also be directed to the ethnic Greek populations in the countries of the former Soviet Union and Albania.[10] This reflected an ideological shift that aimed to retain the *omogeneís* in the diaspora, while serving the "national center from afar" (Venturas 2009:133).

This point is crucial, I believe, as the Griko and Greko enclaves of Southern Italy could find an easier fit with this revised ideology of Hellenism. It could

---

[9] See Frazee 2002 for a historical overview of the Catholic presence in today's Greece.

[10] In the 1990s, the state spent around sixty million euros per year for Greek language teaching abroad, and it appointed about two thousand teachers on second assignment to foreign countries (fifteen hundred to Western Europe) at a time when there were no more than 105,000 students worldwide taking various kinds of Greek-language courses (Kondyli 2002:224, cited in Venturas 2009).

also be speculated that they represented a preexisting model of practice for this policy shift, given that the teaching of MG in Southern Italy predates the 1996 bill by two years. This revised ideology of Hellenism provided the Greek State with a further way to deal with the 'anomalies' represented by these communities of Southern Italy. Douglas in fact argues, "Positively we can deliberately confront the anomaly and try to create a new pattern of reality in which it has a place" (1966:39). In this 'deterritorialized' and 'imaginary' nation, also the Griko- and Greko-speaking communities of Southern Italy could find a place; the limitations of the historical category of *omogéneia* could be overcome once this was extended to incorporate "ever more categories of populations of 'Greek descent' living outside the country into the nation in practical and in symbolic terms" (Venturas 2009:136). Through such a categorical extension, the 'anomalies' of each group would lose their relevance, as it were; each became the addressee of a deterritorialized version of the *Megáli idéa*.[11] However, as Venturas notes (2009:136), this relies on the same rhetoric and the ideological tropes that had proved successful in the previous version. In other words, as she stresses, it does not alter the paternalism of the State.

For the Greek State, as regards the Griko- and Greko-speaking communities of Southern Italy, this is a win-win outcome. As opposed to Pontic or Albanian Greeks, these communities do not constitute a political issue, as they represent neither a pool of potential returnees nor an enemy state. Lack of political animosity and lack of interest on their side in obtaining Greek citizenship in fact partly explains the Greek State's policies and reactions to these communities. Let us not forget that the Griko- and Greko-speaking communities of Southern Italy have never advanced separatist claims. Lack of Greek consciousness aside, Greece represents for them no political advantage, as their motivations to become Greek citizens are few. As members of the European Union, they are already entitled to settle in Greece with full rights to work. Therefore, they are in a much different political position compared to the Pontic peoples from the former Soviet countries and the ethnic Greek Albanians, for whom Greece represents a stronger economy and the availability of a European passport. On the other hand, for Greece, at a practical level, Southern Italy too represents a natural extension zone for Europe. When I interviewed a former mayor of one of the Griko-speaking villages on the Italian shore and discussed with him

---

[11] Some among the populations of Greek descent, such as Pontic Greeks and Greek Albanians, also presented some challenges with respect to the criteria of 'Greekness.' While they are Orthodox, language did not always prove to be a valid criterion. While, as Voutira (1991:313) notes, Pontians from the ex-Soviet countries "mostly speak the Pontian language, a form of Greek with many Homeric elements which can be understood with difficulty by the citizens of Greece," 'Greek Albanians' may speak very poor Greek (Triandafyllidou and Veikou 2002:199).

particular European INTERREG projects between Greece and Italy that had been stepped up in recent years, he told me that, "Greece has always looked to us as a bridge to Europe."[12] Moreover, at a symbolic level, the 'anomalies' and 'ambiguities' (Douglas 1966) of the Griko- and Greko-speaking communities, whether paradoxically or not, render them an unexpected 'gift' of Hellenism. Whereas Pontic and Albanian Greeks are expected to prove their 'Greekness,' in the case at hand, a language kept in remote areas of Southern Italy for millennia—or a millennium, according to the theories—without any investment from the Greek State, is turned into proof of the true value and durability of Hellenism. This is the discourse that appeals to the part of the Greek population sensitive to this type of national pride, which then further promotes it. Griko—as Calabrian Greek—becomes *ena zondanó mnimeío tou Ellinismoú*, a 'living monument of Hellenism.'

When 'Greeks Meet Griko': Greek Aficionados of Griko and Cultural Associations[13]

The Griko- and Greko-speaking enclaves of Southern Italy quickly became an object of interest to Greek philologists (see Chapter 1). But knowledge of these linguistic islands began to go beyond merely the scholarly field in the 1960s, mainly through publications by the philologist Angela Merianou,[14] which presented an idealized image of the topic. The existence of the *Ellinófona choriá tis kato Italías* (Hellenophone villages of Southern Italy) kept diffusing, and reached the Greek public at large through a series of documentaries called *I géfires tou Ioníou* (The Bridges of the Ionian Sea), aired in the early 1970s on State television, and through the 1983 release of a CD entitled *I Ellinikí musikí parádosi tis Kato Italías* (The Greek Musical Tradition of Southern Italy) by the Peloponnesian Folklore Foundation.[15]

---

[12] As we saw in Chapter 4, the availability of European-funded programs (such as INTERREG) aimed at stimulating interregional cooperation are beneficial for both Grecìa Salentina/Puglia and Greece. For instance, the INTERREG II program for Italy-Greece (Training in the Language of Grecìa Salentina; "*Katartisi stin glossa tis Gretsia Salentina*") took place in 2000 and involved the Università del Salento and three Greek universities—the University of Patras, the University of Ioannina, and the Ionian University—in "research about the cultural and linguistic identity of the Greek-speaking area of Salento." The research provides an in-depth analysis of the linguistic, historical, and archaeological aspects of Griko-speaking villages.

[13] Here I purposely draw from the title of an event in Greece at which people from Grecìa Salentina were hosted, called "The Greeks meet the Greeks"—*I Éllines sinandoún tous Éllines*—to which I will return.

[14] Merianou 1980, 1989. Also Prelorenzos 1978; Vranopoulos 1999.

[15] In Greek, the place is generally referred to as *Ta ellinófona choriá*, literally 'Greek-speaking villages' (both for Apulia and Calabria). Grecìa Salentina is also referred to as *Salentiní Ellada* and *Ellada tu Salentu*, literally 'Salentine Greece' and 'Greece of Salento'.

When I set off for Greece to do fieldwork, my plan was to focus on cultural associations as a means of exploring what motivated their members to engage with Griko; in other words, to 'explain to myself' their fascination with this language, with the *mistikó* (secret) of Griko, as Vasilis from Ioannina put it. Through my fieldwork in Grecìa Salentina, I had already identified the Greek associations that regularly collaborate with associations on the other shore.[16] They were established between the mid-1980s and early 1990s, and some are still active to different degrees. As they are located in various parts of Greece, I traveled to meet their leaders and members, had lengthy conversations with them, and participated in and observed the activities they promoted. The history of their establishment follows a common pattern; in most cases, it followed an independent trip to Grecìa Salentina by an individual or small group of people who took the case of Griko to heart and became eager to contribute to the preservation and promotion of the language, as well as of local traditions and customs. The range of activities promoted is typical of cultural associations. They include *ekdromés*, short trips to Grecìa Salentina through which Greek participants familiarize themselves with the place and its traditions. There are also exchange programs for people from Grecìa Salentina to spend time in Greece, and these are organized to the same effect. Finally, cultural and social events, ranging from music and theater performances to literary contests, are organized on both shores.

Once in the field, however, I had inevitably broadened the scope of my investigation, since the initiatives taken in support of Griko at the popular level led me to meet a variety of social actors who engage with the cause of Griko through a panoply of activities—activities that are not necessarily linked to an association. In what follows, I introduce you to some of them in order to highlight the variety of individuals and/or groups of people who show a genuine affection toward Grecìa Salentina and to its people, to whom they feel connected (*deméni*). These individuals and groups are an integral part of my ethnography. Among them, Kostas, a painter who grew to like Salentine music so much that he established a musical band called Encardía, made up of Greek musicians who sing and play (and write) songs in Griko. And there is Christos, a teacher who has compiled a small textbook in Griko and teaches it to schoolchildren in the Corinth area. I met both of them in Greece and subsequently in Italy. While living in Athens, I regularly

---

16 Friends of Grecìa Salentina (Ioannina); the Apollonian Academy (Corinth) and ODEG, and the Organization for the Internationalization of Greek language (Athens). Their original names in Greek are: Fili tis Gretsía Salentína, Apollónia Akadimía and Organismós gia tin Diádosi tis Ellinikís Glóssas, respectively. A fundamental role was also played by associations that no longer exist, among which is the Association of Friends of Greek-speakers Based Abroad (SFEE, Sindesmos Filon Ellinofonon, Athens), founded in 1973.

spent time with Yannis, a psychiatrist who has so far completed two art-therapy programs involving special needs schoolchildren from Grecìa Salentina. Thanks to him, the municipality of Ilion (Athens) and that of Corigliano d'Otranto are now twinned. In Athens and Grecìa Salentina, I also met Alessandro, an Italian national of Greek descent, a screenwriter who has directed documentaries in Calabria and is planning one in Salento. Likewise, I traveled to Thessaloniki to interview Dimitris, a lawyer specializing in human rights who was involved in a project with the University of Macedonia,[17] which resulted in the 1997 publication of a book entitled *Greek-speaking Contemporary Poetry in Southern Italy* that is written in both MG and Italian. In Athens I also met Michalis, who helped finance the publication of a book in Griko (Lambropoulou 1997; Tondi 2008).

Linguistic Kinship

Figure 28. The leaflet of the trip to Grecìa Salentina

When I met Niko in Ioannina in 2009, he proudly showed me the brochure of a recent trip his cultural association had organized, called 'We are Crazy about Grecìa Salentina' (see Figure 28). The trip allowed for a few stops in the best-known towns and villages of the area, such as Sternatia and Calimera, but it also included Otranto, Gallipoli, and Taranto. I had met Niko in Sternatia in June of that year, when he organized a cultural exchange and invited the theatrical company of Ioannina to perform in MG in the village square. After the performance, we all went to eat at the local taverna, Mocambo, a focal point of Griko/Greek encounters; run by the late Vito, it was a gathering place for Greek tourists and visitors with whom Niko met regularly. Over dinner, Niko told me again about his fascination with Griko: "I like discovering words and expressions in Griko, I like searching for their origins." His friend and a fellow association member, who was sitting next to him, promptly remarked about the similarities in

---

17   The INTERREG II program Italy-Greece (training in the language of Grecìa Salentina) 2000 involved instead the participation of three Greek universities: the University of Patras, the University of Ioannina, and the Ionian University, in addition to the University of Salento.

pronunciation between certain sounds in both Griko and Cretan—the sound /k/ is pronounced /tʃ/ in both—and how it reminded him of his own mother. Here, the very sounds of the language became the focus of attention; they connected this Greek aficionado of Griko with his own memories and a sense of nostalgia about his past, as he went on recalling his mother throughout the conversation. The sounds of Griko provoke different comments, at times more vague; for instance, I have repeatedly heard my Greek friends commenting that Griko is 'such a sweet language; it is music to my ears.' At times, simply hearing words that are no longer used in MG elicits emotional reactions among Greek aficionados of Griko. One such example is the Griko verb *polemò* (to work), which retains this meaning in some local variants of Greek[18]—although nowadays it is largely used in MG to indicate 'to fight' or 'to battle.' The very hybridity of Griko—meaning the presence of borrowings or adaptations from Salentine or Italian—may acquire an attractive aura; the alternation of words with Greek origins and words with Latin origins represents "the known among the unknown—this is Griko," as Vangelis, member of the band Encardia, put it to express his fascination with the language.

During my encounters with members of the association Amici della Grecìa Salentina, from Ioannina, what struck me repeatedly was the absolute command they showed in dealing with philological matters. Most would reference linguistic details and the presence of archaisms in Griko—elements from the Doric Greek of classical times; for instance, the retention in Griko of the infinitive after verbs of volition, seeing, and hearing, whereas the infinitive is no longer present in MG:[19]

English	Griko	Modern Greek
I cannot eat	*'E' sozzo fai*	*Den boró na fao*

The following archaisms are the ones most often cited:

English	Griko	Modern Greek
now	*arte*	*tora*
yes	*umme* (<συν μέν)	*Nai*
no	*denghe* (<ουδένγε)	*Oxi*

The members of the Ioannina association are particularly fascinated by the language's archaic flavor, and this can lead at times to misunderstandings when Griko speakers who attend MG classes insert Modern Greek words 'to facilitate

---

[18] For instance on Naxos, as Charles Stewart informed me in one of our conversations.
[19] It persists in the Pontic dialect (Manolessou 2005:117).

communication' and are chastised for doing so, being told something to the effect that MG corrupts the very nature of Griko. Griko very often sparks etymological discussions among Greek aficionados of Griko, who venture etymological explanations, acting as verbal archeologists.[20] For instance, they often refer to *spirì* (little)—used in the variants of Zollino and Martignano and deriving from *spòros* (seed)—and *armàzo* (MG: *pandrèvomai*, which means 'to get married' and derives from *armègo*, 'to milk'). Their constant attempts to trace etymology shows how the centrality of philology is in fact by no means restricted to the academic world, as Greece is a country where people often engage in passionate disputes over etymology (Herzfeld 1997:352; see also Calotychos 2008).

Greek aficionados' overall metalinguistic comments about Griko appear simultaneously as metacomments about the Greek 'language question.' They ultimately show the legacy of the role that language played in the process of nation-building—alongside religion and Greek consciousness—and the role attributed to Greek in the *expression* of a national identity. The average age of Greek tourists who participate in *ekdromés* to Grecìa Salentina is between fifty and seventy—most were therefore taught *katharévousa*; their emotional attachment to Griko and the very way in which they experience it shows the legacy of Greek "political philology" (Herzfeld 1997:74–88). Greek aficionados of Griko embody this legacy, and it informs the ways in which they engage with the language. Indeed, language was considered to be something tangible in the history of Hellenism; since it could be traced back to the form it had acquired in antiquity, the origin of the nation could, it was reasoned, likewise be found in the remote past. *I glossa ine patrída*—"the language is the nation"—as Fotiní put it. Their reference to Griko as a 'living monument of Hellenism' further indicates the internalization and embodiment of this language ideology.

Griko is obviously not ancient Greek; this is clear to the ears of my Greek interlocutors, and to aficionados of Griko. Moreover, Griko and MG are not mutually intelligible—at least not easily. Many among the Greek aficionados of Griko state that they understand Griko fairly or very well, but cannot speak it (some of them are learning it). However, Greek speakers can pick up its archaic features, and if they make an effort to overcome pronunciation differences, may retrieve the meaning of simple sentences.[21] Those with even a rudimentary knowledge of Italian clearly have an easier time of it. However, they tend to choose the archaizing forms of Griko selectively as evidence of the link to the past, of that longed for continuity of Hellenism from antiquity to the present day. In these

---

[20] For the notion of 'verbal archeology' see Herzfeld 1986. This points to the archaeological nature of folklore studies, he argues (1986:100).

[21] This is not a bidirectional process, as Griko speakers do not understand Modern Greek, although they are clearly able to 'pick up' on those words that are identical. I will return to this point.

instances we see at play the legacy not only of the discipline of philology but also of archaeology and their complicity, since the latter provides background knowledge for the philological study of antiquity (Calotychos 2008; Herzfeld 1986). Not incidentally, my Greek friends and aficionados consider Griko as an 'archaeological' artifact, like the Akropolis of Southern Italy, as some argue. Indeed, as Eleana Yalouri (2008) has noted, monumentality is a quality that transcends material, physical, or visible structured space. Interestingly, the Greek word for monument, *mnimío*, derives etymologically from the word for memory, *mními*. The 'monumentality' of Griko is, however, something alive; this is why the reference to Griko as a 'living monument of Hellenism' acquires further significance as a living memory of historical continuity, as a living reminder of antiquity, as it were.

As the following vignette shows, it is particularly when discussing the topic of the history of Grecìa Salentina that my Greek aficionados of Griko evidenced the pervasiveness of the notion of historical continuity, as well as the ability to incorporate apparently contradictory data into a coherent timeline.

Intimate Historicities

I knew how to get to Fotiní's place; by coincidence, she lives in the same *polikatikía* as my friends Vaso and Panayotis—actually on the same floor. When I entered, the layout of the flat seemed different, possibly because Fotiní's place was almost literally overrun with books. She is a tiny lady with sparkling eyes, delicate and self-confident, a retired teacher of Ancient Greek and a writer. It was the middle of a windy October afternoon; it was the right time and I was in the right mood for the hot cup of tea that Fotiní immediately offered me. We started talking about her first book about Salento, *I Elláda tou Saléntou* (Salentine Greece[22]), which had just been published; it was an impressive historical, philological, and artistic exploration of the topic, the result of over a decade's research. We had met in Grecìa Salentina, in the village of Zollino that was my home until my early twenties, while she was there looking for a local editor to translate it into Italian. Fotiní stressed how her book was the first to deal with topics other than the origins of Griko—a subject that had long attracted scholarly interest in Greece. She has meanwhile published two additional books, the third being a diary of her trips to Grecìa Salentina over the years, during which she diligently made notes of her impressions and conversations with the

---

[22] Fotiní translates *Grecìa* into *Ellada*, seeming to ignore the accent put on *Grecìa*, which serves to distinguish it from Greece as a nation-state.

various *cultori del griko*, local intellectuals such as Prof. Sicuro from Martano, whom you met in Chapter 3.

Fotiní started the conversation by referring to the Messapians—the autochthonous population of Salento—and wished for more studies to be conducted on the Messapian language in order to prove that they were 'Greeks.' "Once this is established, the origins of Griko speakers will be resolved once and for all," she argued, since if the Messapians were Cretans, Griko speakers would come from a Greek population that had settled before the eighth century BCE, when the colonization of Magna Graecia began; they would be the heirs of the Minoan civilization, which flourished from 2700 to 1450 BCE. Fotiní was not the only one among my Greek friends and aficionados of Griko to exhibit such knowledge of and confidence about the topic. They repeatedly referred to Herodotus, who attested that the Messapians descended from Cretans who had been driven ashore there on their voyage homewards from Sicily, to which they had traveled to avenge the death of Minos. They were equally well informed about the Magna Graecia theory and quoted linguists as evidence for the argument of a continuous link between Griko and Ancient Greek; and they often offered comments about the perceived closeness to Homer's language. Indeed, I was often told, 'You have kept this language for four thousand years! You need to be proud of that!' What struck me time and time again was their practice of linking Griko to the most distant past possible. This shows the powerful role that the very length of the history plays for Modern Greeks at large (Stewart 2008, 2012)—and how historical awareness and reference play an exceptionally developed role in the expression of Greek personal style and national identity. Through its social significance, history becomes a treasure to be safeguarded at all costs (see also Yalouri 2001).

Fotiní soon got into the details of the debate about the Magna Graecia versus the Byzantine hypothesis of the origins of Griko (see Chapter 1); she pointed out that she had reported all such references in her own book, including those of Greek linguists such as Katsidaki, Karatzà, Kapsomenos, and Karanastasis, who argued for the Magna Graecia thesis and opposed the Byzantine thesis about the origins of Griko and Calabrian Greek supported by Italian linguists. She continued, "Rohlfs and Greek scholars believe you come from the Ancient Greeks, and this is what I think too. You have things which we lost in MG and that you are maintaining instead"—"*O Rohlfs kai oi Éllines oli pistevoun oti iste apó tous archéous Éllines kai egó nomízo auto, échete prágmata pou sta Elliniká chathikán kai échoun meínei se sas.*" Among the archaic features that Griko managed to keep or maintain and that MG 'lost,' she gave me a few examples of the use of the infinitive, such as "*pi, fai.*" As for the origins of Griko, she confidently stated, "I disagree with Italian linguists who have not understood it yet; it is clear that the basis of Griko is ancient Greek." Fotiní then provided me with examples of the practice of adding the Greek ending to verbs from Salentine or Italian, such as *pensare* (to think), which in Griko becomes *pens-èo*: "This is why I believe you come from the Ancient Greeks," she concluded.

Once again we see the centrality of philology as a discursive practice inherited from the past that makes sense of the present. When I mentioned the Byzantine hypothesis of the origins of Griko, her reply was equally reassuring: "The basis of Griko is ancient Greek. Of course, during and after the Byzantine period, more people arrived; it is simply a layered language," she clarified. Fotiní is genuinely sure about the impossibility that there could be another explanation for the current linguistic reality, and confidently bases her arguments on 'linguistic proof'; for example, she repeatedly cited Rohlfs and Karanastasis to this end. Yet her very choice of verbs such as 'believe,' 'think,' 'agree' (*pisteo, nomizo, sinfonò*) seem to indicate again how the linguistic data are 'interpreted' according to the underlying language ideology. In the name of proof, what Fotiní expressed is the state of her feelings and opinions about language origin and use. The debate about the origins of Griko in this way becomes a metalinguistic practice through which Fotiní expresses her own language ideologies, those culturally mediated lenses that are also generated and generate a cultural relationship with the past, with a specific historicity: in this case, that long past to which Hellenism is linked.

Greek aficionados of Griko more broadly tend in fact to be 'enthusiastic consumers'—to borrow the words of historian Dimitris Plantzos (2008:11)—of a culturally inscribed language ideology and ideology of historical continuity, and also influential mediators and reproducers thereof. They reproduce and project onto Griko this specific historicity, this cultural relationship with the past. They do so through what Michael Silverstein and Greg Urban define 'metadiscursive entextualization'—where a 'text' is intended as a metadiscursive construct through which participants in a culture create an image of a durable and shared culture (1996:2–11). In the case at hand, through the insertion of 'texts' of cultural Hellenism into a chosen self-reflexive discursive practice, Greek aficionados of Griko indicate the preferred modality of reading them, 'reproducing' a seemingly shareable and transmittable culture.

We have seen, however, that when and whence the first Greek settlers arrived in the area has never been established with certainty (see Chapter 1). Grecìa Salentina lacks that coherent, homogeneous, and linear timeline constructed for Greek history; the lack of any conclusive historical or linguistic data, in this case, seems to offer my Greek friends and aficionados of Griko the opportunity to render Grecìa Salentina a space for the collective imagination of the Greek spirit. By dating the origins of Griko speakers as far back as possible, my Greek friends and aficionados of Griko act as "historical constructivists" (Faubion 1993:xix) of the history of Griko and its speakers; by reproducing the practice of historical constructivism, which rendered Greek history a cultural behavior, they simultaneously reinforce their own legacy onto the past.

These intimate historicities, this shared cultural perception of the past and relationship with it, engenders among my Greek friends and aficionados of Griko a set of comparisons through which the Hellenism of Southern Italy is actively pursued and common cultural traits are highlighted.

In Search of Commonalities

The first time I met Fotiní, two of her friends—two teachers—had joined her on her trip to Grecìa Salentina. We all met at the headquarters of the Italo-Hellenic [Cultural] Association in Zollino to talk to Pompeo, who was the president of the association at the time. As we were waiting for him by the entrance to the Maniglio library on the ground floor of Palazzo Raho—the early-twentieth century building that hosts the association—Fotiní and her friends started commenting on the beauty of La Chiesa di San Pietro e Paolo, the church opposite the library that is dominated by its bell tower; they then went on to recount their experience of the place and the people in very complimentary ways. Fotiní emphatically said, "It's like being in Greece. For the English it is something different, for us it is something common; it feels it very common to me, I love it, as if I were somewhere else in Greece. And the people are hospitable, warm, beautiful. They feel like brothers." One of Fotiní's friends echoed her remarks.

The search for commonalities, as well as the expectation to find similar traits in Grecìa Salentina, were indeed the driving force for many of the cultural visits. From my Greek friends' accounts, there kept emerging strong references to 'resemblance' and at times 'sameness,' and those accounts also incorporated affinities between the landscapes: for Yiorgos, the place "resembles the area of Mani a lot: it is a piece of Greece in a wild place"—"*ena kommáti Ellinikó se ena ágrio topo*"; for Yannis, "the land, the olive trees, the types of agriculture are identical in the Peloponnese and in Crete. You feel you are in a common place." The affinities between traditional music, dances, and architecture on the two shores are likewise emphasized and at times inflated. "Your songs in Griko resemble Greek poetry," the mayor of the municipality of Ilion (Athens) told me, while Michális noticed with excitement that, "Your traditional songs for the New Year (*strine*) are just like our *kalanda!*" By the same token, people link the origin of pizzica and tarantella to Dionysian celebrations with a peculiar certainty, and they compare the polyphonic singing of the Salentine music to Greek singing.

At times this mode of identification goes so far as to resemble what Herzfeld labeled 'cultural intimacy', "the recognition of those aspects of a cultural identity that are considered a source of external embarrassment but that nevertheless provide insiders with their assurance of common sociality" (Herzfeld 1997:3). "There is a blood bond between us. I say it because your mentality is clearly Greek. The characteristic of our race [sic] is that we are always against each other, ever since the war between Sparta and Athens," says Ilias. Vasilia echoes him, "I noticed that here everyone talked about himself. That's how we are. We have the same qualities and the same shortcomings." Michalis adds,

> Greeks are not descendants of ancient Greeks; our ancestors were Bulgarian, Slav, Turkish, etc.; certainly these populations were here, but the point is: Did they change us, or did we change them? Or did we become blended [*anakateftíkame*]? In Italy you had the Normans, the Gauls, and others, you did not have the Turks; so we had completely different influences, but we speak *one language* and even today we can understand each other (emphasis in original).

The process of highlighting similarities leads my Greek interlocuters not only to justify the inconsistencies of the case of Griko but also to offer them the possibility for self-negotiation: "We may have accepted some influences, but our basic philosophy and behavior as a people, our language, our culture, and tradition have remained the same," as Yannis from Athens put it in one of our conversations. To share these 'intimate' comments in front of Griko speakers or people from Grecìa Salentina therefore shows how the latter are considered insiders and incorporated into this common sociality. What we ultimately see at play is a semiotic process called iconization—a concept introduced by Susan Gal and Judith T. Irvine to describe the essentializing process through which a linguistic system is viewed as an image of the essence of a social group (Gal and Irvine 1995, 2000). They argue that iconization

> involves a transformation of the sign relationship between linguistic features, or varieties and the social images with which they are linked. Linguistic features that index social groups or activities appear to be iconic representations of them ... This process entails the attribution of cause and immediate necessity to a connection (between linguistic features and social groups) that may be only historical, contingent or conventional.[23]

> Irvine and Gal 1995:973

---

[23] In their 1995 article, they refer to this process as 'iconicity.' They adopt the term 'iconization' from 1998 onwards. Irvine subsequently specified that, "technically it should probably be called

Through the semiotic process of iconization, the 'deep' linguistic kinship between Griko and Greek is projected iconically onto their speakers, their people; its characteristics—through the convenient erasure of any inconsistencies—are seen as a reflection of the essential characteristics of its users. In this way, Grecìa Salentina is viewed as 'a sacred land,' 'a cradle of culture' (*choma ieró; kitída politismoú*), and its people are largely described as 'beautiful, good, expressive, friendly, cheerful, hospitable, and warm' (*oréi, kaloí, ekfrastikoí, katadektikoí, gelastoí, filóksenoi kai zestoí*).[24]

This becomes yet more evident when the Hellenism of Southern Italy is elevated even over the Hellenism of Modern Greece, and when the metadiscursive adulation resembles idealization. "There people still sit at the doorsteps of their houses and talk; they still live that way. In Greece, we have stopped doing that," Panaiotis said. "This is Hellenism. If only we Greeks had kept this Hellenism"—"*Autó einai o Ellinismós. Makari na kratágame auto ton Ellinismó emeís oi Éllines,*" Kostas concluded. These comments were part of broader reflexive critiques of the modern lifestyle, which 'corrupts' and 'pollutes' the ideal image of Hellenism. Ilias explained it as follows: "Greece was a peasant society. Then the conditions changed and people changed with them. Over there [Grecìa Salentina] people still hang on to their traditions; we are losing them here." To use the words of Kostas from the Encardia musical group, "Greeks are nostalgic for Salentine Hellenism." The image of people sitting in front of their houses therefore becomes a 'sign' that Hellenism has been preserved regardless of the imprint of modern times.

Drawing from Johannes Fabian (1983), it would seem that in these instances Greek aficionados of Griko treat today's Griko speakers as temporally distanced groups. Fabian developed the notion of the 'denial of coevalness' to refer to the "persistent and systematic tendency to place the referent(s) of anthropology in a Time other than the present of the producer of anthropological discourse" (Fabian 1983:31). Greek aficionados of Griko equally tend to eclipse the contemporaneity of their Griko interlocutors and

---

rhematization, a process through which the interpretant takes a sign to be iconic" (2004:108n6). It is interesting to note that in studies attesting to iconization, this process tends to lead to the stigmatization of the language and consequently of its speakers (see Messing 2009; Andronis 2004). The case at hand instead offers a distinctive case of iconization that leads to a romantic idealization.

24   I personally became the target of 'iconization' on various occasions; for instance, I was always complimented on my Greek, only to be told that speaking it well is normal as "the language is in me." On another occasion, I was welcomed at Odeg by a secretary, who knew that I originally come from Grecìa Salentina, and who told me, "You do not look Italian! You look Greek, actually even a bit better." Or when I was living on Ikaria, I was approached by a man at a summer celebration (*panigíri*) who told me, "You have the face of an ancient Greek woman." In talking, it came out where I come from and he ecstatically said, "You see? That explains it."

friends, in so doing creating an allochronic discourse about them.[25] They define Griko as a language 'frozen in time' or 'as if it was put in a freezer,' as Nikolas expresses it. This perceived or real characteristic of the language is iconically projected onto its speakers; the recurrent sentence, "You have been Greek since ancient times" (*Íste Éllines apó tin archeótita*) captures this. Griko and Greko speakers, however, do not become 'other' but exactly what they are romantically expected to be: the living proof of the continuity with the past, the "living monument of Hellenism."

Griko is this way turned into a form of 'survival,' in accordance with what Herzfeld (1986:102–105) has defined as the Greek version of survivalism; this was theorized by the father of Greek folklore studies, Nikolaos Politis, who selectively drew on Tylor's theory of survivals, reading it not "as a theory of societal progressions which encompassed the fossils of a primitive stage but as a static doctrine of cultural continuity" (Herzfeld 1986:103). Politis could not consider survivals as relics of a primitive past, as this would go against the Hellenist argument of the superiority of Ancient Greeks; survivals were not considered atavistic traits that needed removal, but were 'upgraded' to represent a "partial but unbroken continuation of an earlier life" (Politis 1909:6, cited in Herzfeld 1986:104).

Exploring Greek popular views on Griko brought to light specific ways in which the cultural ideology of Hellenism has been internalized: Greece's gaze on Griko, as it were, is shaped by and filtered through a historically produced lens. This lens refracts the relation that Greeks by and large have with their own past and national identity. What I am arguing is that the romanticized character of the metadiscourse of Greek aficionados of Griko emerges out of dynamics inherent in their own romantic imagination. As in a mirror game of reflections, this could be defined as a two-step iconization process where the picture drawn by Greek aficionados of Griko appears as a self-portrait, an image of the historically produced and iconized 'Greek self'; this is then projected onto Griko and Griko speakers, rendering Griko an iconic representation within an iconic representation. What I am arguing is that the view from *apénandi* ultimately reveals Modern Greeks' own language ideology and ideology of history/historical continuity. Through it, Grecìa Salentina and Griko speakers become a "spatial projection of their cultural imaginary" (Calotychos 2008:158): an imagined community (Anderson 1983).

---

[25] Papagaroufali (2013) equally reports comments offered by Greek high school teachers and students who visited a Greek-speaking town and school in Calabria. They compared the place and the way locals behaved to what Greece and Greeks 'used to be like' thirty years earlier; they likewise commented positively on locals' warmth and hospitality. This seems to indicate how the 'view from *apènandi*' transcends age differences.

Cultural Synthesis and Erasure

The case of Griko seems also to offer my Greek aficionados of Griko the possibility for 'synthesis' to work at its very best, allowing for continuity not only to be preserved, but reinforced. Even the tension over the Byzantine period, which proved most difficult to incorporate into the narrative of historical continuity, is released when dealing with 'Griko history.' Herzfeld (1987) developed the notion of 'disemia' to refer both to the polarity between the two models of Greek identity, the 'Hellenic' and 'Romaic,' deriving from the Classical and Byzantine-Ottoman models, respectively, and to the battle between the official cultural form and more intimate social knowledge. For the history of Griko, the Byzantine period therefore does not represent the anxiety over self-definition between these two available repertoires of identity.

> You have here all these beautiful Byzantine crypts. Byzantium played a huge role in Greek history and in the history of Europe. And what was Byzantium? Italian. Yes. Byzantine dictators were 'Romii,' they were Italians. During the Byzantine period Greeks called themselves Romii, did you know that?

Michalis gives 'Romii' a 'modern' sense of ethnicity, which fluctuates between Greek and Italian or conflates them. "You know that it was through Byzantine scholars that Italian humanism developed? They transcribed everything coming from Greece. This is important," he concluded. His words effectively situate Byzantium as a medieval phase of Hellenic history by retracing the pathway of historiography. For my Greek aficionados of Griko, the praxis of synthesis—historical, linguistic, and cultural more broadly—was indeed also a way to overcome the apparent 'contradictions' and 'anomalies' of Griko. If religion represented the biggest stumbling block, as it were—as Griko-speakers are Catholic—Kostas, the president of the Corinth Apollonian Academy finds a reassuring narrative: "The Greek-Orthodox church existed there until recently if you think about it, until not many centuries ago. I heard that the last Orthodox priest was killed in 1750." As we have seen, Orthodoxy together with common descent is a pivotal defining character of Hellenism; the lack of this trait in the case of Griko is an 'anomaly,' which cannot be ignored but which can be 'explained away,' as Kostas does.

In reality the schism between the Orthodox Eastern and Latin Western Churches occurred in 1054, although Griko speakers kept worshipping in Greek and following the Byzantine rite until the end of the seventeenth century; yet since the schism, they were Catholics, responding to Rome (see Chapter 1). Certainly locals retain no memory of Byzantine rites and feel no anxiety about their religiosity. In Calabria, Stavroula Pipyrou (2016) argues, proselytizing on the part of the Patriarch of Constantinople has a long history and a few locals have converted to Orthodoxy (see also Petropoulou 1997:243). In the Calabrian case, equally interesting is Catholics' adhesion to the Byzantine rite rather than to Orthodoxy—which they define as the expression of a spiritual need rather than a religious statement, as it were (Squillaci, M. Olimpia, personal communication). Yet Kostas mentioned that he had put forward a proposal to build an Orthodox church in Salento "not to reintroduce the Orthodox liturgy," he clarified, "but so that people can find there not only your Byzantine crypts and churches, but also an Orthodox *naó* (church). It did not happen though," he concluded with disappointment. When I pointed out to Kostas that Griko speakers do not feel any sense of belonging to Orthodoxy, he noted that, "It might be that they cannot say it freely." The fact that he dismissed my point reflects his own anxiety over the religious conundrum, and his attempt to square the inconsistencies of the Griko case. It ultimately suggests a sort of 'misrecognition' (Bourdieu 1977) of the Griko-speaking community, a sort of denial of its lack of 'Greek consciousness.' This is a semiotic process technically defined as erasure, which entails ignoring details that are inconsistent with a given ideology, or downgrading differences to make them either irrelevant or ideologically justified (Gal and Irvine 1995). Selective erasure—downgrading differences—and highlighting similarities to reach identification ultimately leads my Greek friends and aficionados of Griko to a 'romantic iconization' of Grecìa Salentina and its people.

Kinship as Language

Kostas and I had agreed to meet by the train station in Corinth, about an hour from Athens. I understood immediately it was him when, upon exiting the station, I saw a man waving at me excitedly from across the street. At the time he was the president of the Corinth Apollonian Academy, a cultural association that was established in 1990 to manage contacts with "Greeks around the world." We walked to a nice little bar, a *kafeneío*, from where we could smell the sea—in fact we commented on it almost simultaneously. We spent a full three hours drinking *frappé* (frozen coffee) as one can do only in Greece without being told off or looked askance at by the barista/waiter. Kostas was rather chatty and enjoyed exploring the details of each topic he recounted, very careful not to miss any important information. When our coffee time was definitively over, he offered to drive me to his office. During that conversation, he mentioned in passing a funny story that also involved Antonio Anchora from Corigliano. Strangely, he mentioned it without recounting any of its details. "I had to show it to you before even telling you, because I laugh when I say it," he said. Indeed, when we arrived at his office, Kostas started laughing before recounting the actual story, pointing to his computer: "Once I found a picture of Antonio Anchora, and I put it on my computer as a screen saver and wrote on it "PER SEMPRE FFRATELLI [sic]"—*Forever Brothers*—in capital letters, but I made a mistake and wrote *fratelli* with a double 'f.' I left it that way," he said, continuing to laugh while he showed me other pictures of Grecìa Salentina and the people he had met, and with whom he was in contact. "I see Antonio as my own brother"—"*ton theoró oti einai aderfós mou,*" Kostas concluded.

On both shores, I heard narratives that were often permeated with such references to kinship: "Our languages are like sisters, but not all the children are alike, right?" remarked Niko to me once. "You are our relatives, our people. That's why we understand each other. The language is the family. That's why we are brothers too in a way," Kostas had stressed. We heard Fotiní making a similar remark. Here, we observe how smooth the transition is from linguistic kinship— "our languages are like sisters"—to kinship as the language of communication— "You are our relatives/brothers." The linguistic kinship between Greek and Griko, which emerges from the language ideology that considers Griko to be a "living monument of Hellenism," is again selectively highlighted and iconically projected onto the speakers, becoming proof of historically deep social relations. The discursive and metadiscursive use of kinship shows how pervasive the notion of kinship itself is. This also emerges in the people's own writings; e.g., the accounts of the trips to Grecìa Salentina published in the association's journals. To be sure, Nikos from Ioannina clearly told me, "Many Greeks make this mistake; they go across and call them 'our brothers' (*adérfia mas*). And I have to clarify that you are Italians first, then you are Catholics, and then that you have a spark inside of you which comes from your Greek roots (*Ellinikés rízes*)." Kostas was equally eager to point out that, "There is no politics involved, no parties, no colors, there is just the pathos for Greece, the magnificence of Greece and of the people whose roots are Greek." The mere survival of Griko (and Calabrian Greek) in remote areas of Southern Italy without any institutionalized support from the Greek State (or maybe because of it) indeed tends to fascinate the Greek population at large, despite and beyond the inapplicability of the categories of 'lost homeland' and 'diaspora' to the Griko- and Calabrian Greek-speaking communities of Southern Italy. The view from *apénandi* is moreover filtered through the view toward the other shore, to the East, to that *apénandi*; it seems to embody the nostalgia for the lands that once belonged to the Byzantine Empire, and for the people who were left behind, those 'forgotten brothers' who likewise speak varieties of Greek. Kinship therefore remains the language through which relations are conceptualized and experienced by Greek aficionados of Griko; it is a familiar language, as it were. Crucially, kinship as cultural domain and the concept of heritage are strictly linked (Graburn 2001); in this way, kinship becomes the very language through which the Hellenic cultural heritage and Hellenism as cultural ideology are reclaimed as idioms of global belonging, transcending international boundaries.

Aficionados of Griko as Ideology Brokers

The sense of commitment toward Griko that Greek aficionados of the language have shown over the years has led them to act on behalf of Griko speakers through two main modalities: by pursuing the involvement of the mass media to give visibility to the cause of Griko, and by involving Greek politicians and the State generally. They have contributed to this awareness-raising process by producing CDs of Salentine music, by hosting music events, by publishing accounts of their trips to Grecìa Salentina in the associations' journals, and/or by airing interviews with Griko speakers. For instance, Kostas proudly remarked on the contribution of his cultural association, which had produced a CD of Salentine music in the 1990s, with pictures and information in Greek about the area of Grecìa Salentina. He stressed that one of their biggest achievements was to involve the mass media in order to sensitize the Greek public to the topic of Griko: "We played our role and journalists played theirs, you know? They described the area with very nice words. We used the media, newspapers, TV, in order to give resonance to this place." Equally proudly, Kostas then referred to then-President of the Hellenic Republic Stefanopoulos's 2002 visit to Grecìa Salentina, which occurred also thanks to the involvement of the Corinth Apollonian Academy:

> I had gone to talk to him, I brought him books and a dictionary and I told him that we needed a favor. And he asked me, 'What do you do over there? Do you live there?' I replied, 'No, but we love the place so much that we would move if there was need.' So he asked me what help they needed. And I thought to myself 'That's it. We got the State (*piásame to kratos*)!' When the president went to the Greek-speaking villages, he just went crazy (*treláthike*) and then asked me, 'What was that? How beautifull I did not know that there was so much Greece there.' He became emotional (*sigginíthike*).

Likewise Kostantinos, an active member of the Organization for the Internationalization of the Greek Language (ODEG), proudly mentioned the journal *Greek, International Language* that they publish and distribute in seventy-four countries, pointing out that various issues displayed articles dedicated to Grecìa Salentina and Calabria. He also told me that ODEG was preparing a presentation for the office of *Apódimos Ellinismós* in order for the Greek-speaking communities of Southern Italy to get its support.[26] "We are trying to give prominence to this topic (*anadíksume aftó to thema*) because if the members of the parliament decide that this is interesting, they can give directives to the Ministry of Education."

Following Blommaert (1999:9), aficionados of Griko could therefore be defined as "ideology brokers", that is "the category of actors, who for reasons we set up to investigate, can claim authority in the field of debate (politicians and policy-makers, interest groups, academicians, policy implementers, the organized polity and individual citizens)." By organizing trips to Grecìa Salentina, as well as cultural activities, they 'introduce' Greek people to the topic of Griko, sharing their own knowledge, as it were. These *ekdromés* effectively helped to spread knowledge about the Griko- and Greko-speaking communities of Southern Italy among 'Greeks' at large. Cultural associations therefore are an interesting 'ideological site' (Silverstein 1998), which shows the rootedness of the state ideology in civil society and the very role that civil society plays "as a tool of the social imagination, as a cultural construct and ideological trope" (Comaroff 1999:8).

Importantly, knowledge about the case of Griko renders Greek aficionados of Griko authoritative, and this strengthens their role as 'mediators/ brokers' between Grecìa Salentina and Greece. Kostantinos stressed that, "the Ministry would not want to show an official interest in this case; this is where the associations come in." Kostas made a similar remark, saying, "For political reasons Greece did not want to say that there is a Greek minority there. This may be the role we [associations] played, as we do not have the stamp of the State (*sfragída tou krátous*)." One successful example of their role as 'ideology brokers' is provided by the teaching of MG in Grecìa Salentina; indeed, it could be argued that, by acting on behalf of Griko activists, Greek aficionados of Griko mediated the intervention of the Greek State, effectively 'bridging the gap' (see Chapter 3).

This is not to say that cultural associations on the Italian shore do not play their own role. For the Calabrian case, Pipyrou (2011, 2012) argues that self-awareness, victimization, and more recently, consumption, are categories of representation and articulation of difference utilized by the Calabrian Greek community over the past fifty years. At the same time, these are rhetorical tropes handled by the associations and adjusted according to the audience,

---

[26] This was scheduled to happen in May 2009; it was canceled because of the European elections, Kostantinos told me.

be it Greek tourists or members of the Greek government. These observations can also largely be applied to the case of Griko; self-awareness became the means for the articulation of local claims (Chapter 3); consumption has indeed become dominant in the dynamics of the current revival (Chapter 4); the victimization trope is instead not rhetorically deployed, as cultural associations in Grecìa Salentina do not portray Griko speakers as 'victims.' According to Pipyrou, writing about the Calabrian Greek case: "(a) the conditions of living in Grecanici villages, and (b) the social status of and the discrimination against Grecanici migrants to Reggio Calabria" (Pipyrou 2011:80) determine the politics of victimization. This highlights how the processes of language shift in the two scenarios were immersed in similar yet different dynamics. In the Calabrian case, natural disasters indeed exacerbated "the image of poverty, ruin and abandonment" (Pipyrou 2011:80), and had led Greko speakers to migrate to Reggio Calabria, where they were excluded because of their language—and the poverty it was associated with—and were confronted with a hostile social environment. Although it would be a mistake to treat Griko- and Greko-speaking communities as discrete and bounded entities culturally differentiated from the surrounding area that has not retained the language, we have seen how Griko speakers equally suffered stigmatization for being bilingual ('people with two tongues,' see Chapter 2); this is, however, not rhetorically deployed by Griko activists. Moreover, Griko-speaking villages had historically and geographically been integrated into the Salentine surroundings, and they had undergone a significant socioeconomic restructuring that began in the aftermath of World War II, which continued throughout the 1960s and '70s; this renders the victimization trope not applicable, so to speak.

Yet Griko activists and *cultori del griko* are also responsible for creating high expectations, beyond the 'politics of victimization.' What prevails in the case at hand is the mobilization of the Greek people's attachment to their own cultural ideology of Hellenism. We have seen in Chapter 3 how the Italian state's long neglect of the communities speaking a language of Greek origins had admittedly led local Griko scholars and activists to turn their gaze to Greece for recognition. They have in the meantime successfully mastered the very 'language of Hellenism' and of common cultural heritage—a 'professional' lexicon, as Pipyrou (2016) put it for Calabria—and also capitalize on it, aware of the warm reception given it by Greek visitors. The intimate historicity of Hellenism indeed appeals to a section of Griko scholars and Griko activists who likewise act as ideology brokers locally. Following and building on the legacy of local philhellenists (see Chapter 1), they entertain regular contact with the other shore and with Greek aficionados of Griko, sharing with them the 'intimate historicity' that connects Griko to the Hellenic past and constitutes a reason for discursive pride. This cultural but also affective relationship with *that* past (see also Knight 2015) turns Greece into a 'cultural motherland' (as Luigi from Calimera remarked), while not implying or advancing any claim of ethnic belonging. Meanwhile, Greek aficionados of Griko who have taken on the task of helping their 'forgotten brothers' and interceding on their behalf filter their gaze through the historical category of *omogéneia*; this complex intermingling of partially shared and yet differently articulated claims leads at times to confusion on both ends. Kostas from Corinth offers an example of this:

> I offered Antonio Anchora to intercede for the inclusion of the Griko-speaking community at the World Council of Hellenism and he told me, 'We do not want to.' So I asked, 'Why not?', and he replied, 'Because we are not diasporic Greeks.' And I said, 'What are you then?' and he replied: 'We are Greeks who have always been here. We are Griki.'

Interactions such as this, that are based on different interpretations, articulations, and enactments of self-understanding and belonging, may lead to a temporary breakdown in communication, to a 'lost in translation' type of interaction, as it were. This is when the incommensurability of the two languagescapes emerges: here Antonio's reply shows how the sense of belonging is rooted in the place itself, confronting Kostas with the anomalies of Griko that had been semiotically erased.

Lost in Translation I

The expectation of finding brothers in Grecìa Salentina may indeed disappoint some Greek visitors. In spring 2011, I went to join some friends at a tavern in Soleto; unexpectedly, I found the tavern packed with people because a live concert of pizzica and songs in Griko was taking place. The waiter told me that my friends were waiting for me in another pizzeria, as a group of Greek tourists had just arrived and no table was available for us at the tavern. Suddenly he asked me, "You speak Greek right?" and dragged me to meet Stavroula, a lady in her fifties, who was struggling to communicate with another waiter in a mixture of Greek and English. "Would you please see if you can help her?" When Stavroula heard me greeting her and asking her what she needed, she erupted, "Finally, finally I hear some Griko! You speak beautifully!" Flattered as I was, I had to correct her and tell her that I was speaking MG. She was happy that this allowed me to direct her where to buy cigarettes, but she could not hide her disappointment. "Tell me, *koukla*, where are the Griko speakers?" Before I could try to answer the question, Stavroula was called away by her friend as their main course had arrived. They left, but not before asking me for a cigarette.

This sort of disappointment is also reported by Petropoulou (1995:152) and Pipyrou (2011:78, 2012) in Calabria; there, too, Greek visitors who are not necessarily thoroughly informed, and who are also filled with expectations fueled by local activists, are left wondering why locals do not speak 'Greek,' as they would expect their 'forgotten brothers' to do. Eleni Papagaroufali (2013) likewise notes that Greek teenagers visiting Calabria as part of a European school twinning program comment that, "The Italians' Greek was 'poor' ... it sounded like Chinese." Such evaluative comments are not isolated; my friend Vaso from Athens—my adoptive mother while there and mother of my friends Aspa and Niko—also commented, "Your mom does not speak Greek well, does she?" after talking to her over the phone. Vaso's expectation was that she would hear Greek while my mom was speaking Griko. Indeed, while Greek aficionados of Griko 'fall in love' with Griko antiquity insofar as they wish for its 'authenticity' not be 'polluted' by MG, Greek visitors may not share such views, or they may have different expectations.

The expectation of commensurability can likewise fail for Griko speakers who do not speak the language of Hellenism, creating a similar sense of confusion. Their encounter with the Greek of Greece produces yet another 'lost in translation' situation. In such instances we see the interplay of—as well as the clash between—language seen as a means of communication between people and language as a framework for representation (see Pipyrou 2012 for Greko). This at times reveals and at times masks commensurability or incommensurability among all social actors involved.

Lost in Translation II

It was about 9 p.m., but since it was a sunny day in late June, it was still light out. After the greetings and reciprocal expressions of gratitude between the assessor for cultural affairs of the municipality of Sternatia and the representatives of the regional theatrical company of Ioannina, the performance began. The audience was composed mainly of people over the age of sixty, along with a few children. Just behind me sat two ladies in their eighties, all ears, trying to follow the story's plot. Unable to do so because of what still is a language barrier, they had instead started to identify common words and repeat them aloud.

"*Ivò ikusa krasì*" (Griko)—"I heard '*krasì*,'" said one lady to the other; not incidentally the word for wine is the same in Griko and MG. After about a minute, the other replied, saying, "*Arte ipe glossa, ikuse?*"—"Now, she said 'language,' did you hear?" Not incidentally again, '*glossa*' is the same in both languages. The ping-pong continued; they also picked up on *astèri* (star), *na se filìso* (to kiss you), and *mirizo* (to smell). The scene was momentarily interrupted by the noise of a small motorbike ridden by an elderly man who stopped by us and joined the conversation to summarize and say, "It is a kind of Greek that you don't understand much. You need to listen very carefully." "Sure, we understood many words," one lady replied, and was censured for speaking during the performance by her daughter sitting two rows in front of us. "Maybe if they did not speak this fast," commented the other lady, without lowering her voice. The elderly man, rather puzzled, concluded, "But if we do not understand, why did they come to perform it? I'd better go." The ladies had reached a different conclusion: "Let's stay and listen. At least the heat is bearable out here."

Reviewing these reactions between the elderly Griko speakers from Sternatia—who are external to the politics of the current revival—what emerges is their search for commensurability. Whereas a section of Griko scholars and activists often resorts to 'linguistic kinship' as a rhetorical tool, using 'Griko as a language of representation,' what prevailed with the two ladies was the value of Griko as a communicative tool—indeed, the search for shared words between Griko and MG intrigued and even amused them. As we also saw in Chapter 3, Griko speakers came to realize the communicative potential of Griko through the lived encounters with Greek people. Significantly, however, the elderly Griko speakers commenting on the theatrical performance do not speak the language of Hellenism; their phenomenological references to Griko link them to a recent and local past, as we have repeatedly seen. The limits of intelligibility between Griko and MG, and their respective worlds, may however emerge at any moment, and their expectation of commensurability can also fail; indeed, we heard the elderly Griko speaker watching the performance comment that MG is "a different kind of Greek"—and if we cannot understand it, then what is the point of listening, as he crudely put it.

We see, therefore, a variety of claims put forward by different social actors and based on different references; it comes as no surprise that the result is a polyphony of expectations that may produce 'lost in translation' scenarios. These are, however, mitigated by the festive character of the typical Griko-Greek encounters on both shores; during them the actual interactions between Griko speakers and Greek visitors are limited, while the limits of commensurability we have just seen are balanced and overcome by the 'recreational' climate in which these encounters take place, where food, wine, music, and dance create an important bonding setting, and where common cultural traits are celebrated.

Equally dominant in these encounters is the atmosphere of staged monumentality of Griko in front of a Greek audience. Interestingly, in fact, Griko is not a monument that one goes to see, but to hear; indeed, it is a living monument because its speakers embody its very monumentality. We saw above how Stavroula was longing to hear Griko; likewise Vasilis told me, "When we go to

Grecìa Salentina we always want to hear Griko; we know that Greek visitors like to hear it, so we ask someone to speak it to us. Many of us go there to hear the language—it is an instinct." The following two vignettes address the theatricality with which Greek-Griko encounters tend to take place, and the dominant role played by music.

Greek-Griko Encounters: The Living Monument of Hellenism 'On Stage,' Athens, February 2008

I took a short field trip to Athens to attend a music event focusing on 'the music tradition of Southern Italy'; this was organized by the Greek music band Encardía, who, as hinted above, interpret the musical repertoire of Salento, but also compose new songs in Griko. Kostas is one of the founders of the band, which was established in 2003 as the result of a series of trips to Salento over the years, motivated by their interest in the local music. Once in Salento, the encounter with the Avantaggiato family from Corigliano facilitated their project. The organization of the concert derived from Encardía's desire to host the Avantaggiato family again in Greece following the success of the previous concert. The very title of the event *I Éllines sinandoún tous Éllines* (The Greeks Meet the Greeks) is indicative, since we can see

Figure 29. The poster of the event: "Greeks meet Greeks," Athens

how through the semiotic process of iconization Griko speakers here become 'Greeks' *tout court*; as Mary Bucholtz and Kira Hall (2004:380) argue, iconization represents practice through ideology.

The hall hosting the event is crowded with mostly middle-aged people. Kostas introduces the stars of the event: Giovanni and Maria, in their mideighties, and the couple's son Rocco, in his early fifties, who is handed the microphone and says in Griko:

Sekùndu ipe o Kosta imì erkumèsta a'ttò Salentu, a' ttin addhi Grècia, ìmesta i Griki ka stene so' addho mero ti' ttàlassa ce milùme Grika. 'Na pramma poddhì importànte leme imì,'en itsèro pos ènna po, ene na min allimonìsume ti' ttradiziùna, jatì o kosmo ka ichànni ti' memoria, ichànni tikanè.

As Kosta said, we come from Salento, from the other Greece,we are the Griki who live across the sea and we speak Griko. Something very impotant, we say, I don't know how to say it, is never to forget our tradition, because who loses memory, loses everything.

The loud clapping of hands interrupts Rocco twice. He continues:

Àrtena ikànnume 'na travùdi ka fonàzzete i ghetonìa. Milà ats' enan àntrepo ka diavènni ats' enan dromo [Modern Greek], dromo lete isì nde? ce itorì nan ghinèka sti' ffenèstra.

Now we will sing a song which is called neighborhood. It talks about a man who passes by a street—you say 'dromo', don't you?— and sees a woman by the window.

Griko from Corigliano d'Otranto

A few people sitting in the first row pipe up, "*Paráthiro, paráthiro* (window) is the word you are looking for," suggesting to Rocco the Greek word for window as he had borrowed *fenèstra* from the Romance variety. Again, a much moved and clearly enthusiastic audience starts clapping its hands. Kostas intervenes to translate "the two or three words which you [the audience] probably did not understand," and he then tells the audience about his frequent trips to Grecìa Salentina, and refers to the previous summer spent there as the most beautiful of his entire life. He leaves the stage to Rocco, who starts singing a song in Griko, followed by a few pizzica songs in Salentine, which Greeks tend to refer to more generically as 'tarantella.' He is accompanied by his father Giovanni playing the accordion, and by the musicians of Encardía; his mother also sings and dances, although she is visibly uncomfortable, while the old man sitting next to me ecstatically keeps repeating, "*Bravo, brava,*" alternating Greek and Italian.

Sternatia (Grecìa Salentina), October 2008

It was Monday evening and I had just attended the MG course held at the association Chora-Ma in Sternatia; you have already met some of the locals attending the course, like Gaetano, Uccio, and Cosimino. At the end of the class, we are told by the Greek teacher, Eleni, that there is a surprise for us. Suddenly the main door opens and about eighty people enter. They are Greek people from Athens, from the municipality of Ilion. The 'elderly center' they belong to had organized a trip to Grecìa Salentina.

Figure 30. The entrance of the association Chora-Ma, Sternatia

Giorgio—a Griko teacher from Sternatia and member of Chora-Ma you have already met—had been informed of their arrival and had organized the reception. He greets the audience—who in the meantime had sat down—and in perfect MG summarizes the history of Sternatia (*i chora*) and the area of Grecìa generally. He stresses that regardless of the open debate about the origin of Griko, Greek people have constantly been present in the area over the centuries. It is now Eleni's turn. She introduces herself, explaining that she is one of the five Greek philologists sent by the Greek Ministry of Education to teach MG in local primary schools and cultural associations. Talking about her class in Sternatia, she points out that some of the attendants could speak MG fairly well (she was clearly generous in saying this, I add). She stressed that everyone showed enormous interest not only in the language, but in Greek culture in general. At that point, every single person in the audience started clapping joyously.

After this introduction, the 'show' begins. Firstly Mimmo greets the audience in Griko. This is followed by a poem in Griko recited by Gaetano; then Uccio tells them some anecdotes in Griko, stressing before starting that he was going to speak "In our Greek, right?"—"*Is Grika-ma, nde?*" The attempt by the audience to follow the flow of the story is evident; some Greek tourists even intervene and ask directly for the meaning of some words. The 'show' becomes suddenly more interactive when Giorgio starts playing some songs in Griko. The escalation of enthusiasm goes on and reaches its climax when Giorgio starts playing *Àndramu pai* (My Husband Goes), a song written by Franco Corlianò from Calimera, which became famous in Greece thanks to its performance by Maria Farandùri. Everyone in the room is now singing the refrain of the song in unison!

What emerges from both vignettes is a 'staged performance' of Griko and its monumentality: Griko speakers were literally on stage on both occasions, performing the language through poems, songs, and anecdotes, whereas real interactions between Greek visitors and Griko speakers were very limited.[27] As we have seen, Rocco's attempts to create commensurability between the two languages—inserting MG words and contextualizing Griko, an effort in which the audience participated—were promptly followed by his musical performance. Likewise, after Uccio's anecdote and Gaetano's poem in Griko, Giorgio took the stage to perform a Griko song that was very well-known in Greece. Greeks at large in fact tend to know about Griko and the place through songs—the historical music band from Calimera, Ghetonìa, is for instance more popular in Greece than in Italy—and music groups or individual singers or musicians from Grecìa Salentina are indeed often invited to play in Greece. Importantly, both vignettes demonstrate how songs in Griko, but also Salentine music more generally, are a dominant feature of these encounters. The potential breakdown in Griko-Greek communication is avoided through these performances, as music becomes the very language of communication. In these instances 'the music speaks Griko,' as it were, reaching and entertaining the Greek audience. Indeed, as we heard Rocco say in Chapter 4, "the music has wheels and travels," carrying Griko alongside. While discussing encounters among Greeks and Grecanici, Pipyrou similarly notes how "through simple and clever lyrics Greeks and Grecanici found a performative space where they could communicate" (Pipyrou 2011:84). Likewise, as we have seen, pizzica songs further animate these encounters: Greek visitors are particularly attracted by this music and its dance, as it represents the 'exotic,' 'the unknown among the known'—to paraphrase Vangelis, cited earlier. There is, however, also space for Greek music and dances: a typical Griko-Greek encounter does not end without an alternation of traditional Greek and Griko music and dances, which cultivate further bonding.

These recreational moments through music and language performances dissipate the potential frustration on both sides: in both scenarios described above the Greek visitors left by-and-large enthusiastic. The Greeks had 'heard' Griko, had gotten a flavor of its speakers, and largely found their expectations

---

[27] See MacCannell (1976) on his notion of 'staged authenticity' in tourism, and his application of the work of the sociologist Erving Goffman (1956). See Victor Turner (1987) on the anthropology of performance.

met. The locals were equally satisfied: they had 'performed' to their expectations by using some MG words, showing this way their interest and reassuring
the Greeks of their strong attachment to Greece. However, these Greek/Griki
encounters actually hide more than they reveal. As I hope to have demonstrated, Greek visitors have largely a ready-made romantic and idealized image
of Griko and its speakers; they have high expectations when visiting Grecìa to
find the 'living monument of Hellenism.' Local Griko scholars and activists are
very aware of the enthusiasm and involvement that Greek aficionados of Griko
and visitors show when they witness the use of Griko, and they utilize it too.
Likewise, those Griko speakers who have come in contact with Greek visitors
and aficionados of Griko are certainly flattered by the attention received after
they have been long ignored and also stigmatized; they now feel appreciated as
they have seldom felt before. Moreover, as opposed to the elderly Griko ladies we
heard commenting on the theatrical performance, and who are foreign to the
politics of the revival, Griko speakers such as Gaetano, Mimmo, and Uccio, who
'performed' for the Greek visitors, have been sensitized to Greece generally—by
also attending the MG course and by meeting Greek tourists. They therefore
take particular pride in meeting them, as they feel like the center of attention;
this is particularly important since, for them, Griko has effectively shifted from
being considered a language of backwardness to a 'language of pride'—as a meta-
effect of Greek interest. To use Pipyrou's (2011:83) words again with reference to
the Calabrian Greek case, what happens in these Griko-Greek encounters is that
they project their Griko essence mainly to Greek tourists. In other words they
'perform' this essence and tend to emphasize their sentimental link to Greece
in front of Greek visitors, as they know this will strike the right chord. Am I
suggesting that Greek-Griko encounters are a 'farce'? No, I am not. What I want
to emphasize is that these are not simple 'encounters with tourists' but loci of
self-representation (Goffman 1956), where Griko social actors conflate the front
and back stages, and blur the boundary between them, ultimately rendering
redundant the dichotomy. Indeed, control over the audience's perception takes
place in the back as much as in the front space. In both spaces, equally crucial is
self-perception alongside managing the impression of the other; in both spaces
actors may drop their pretenses, their 'masks,' as it were. 'Performing Griko'
ultimately becomes an embodied cultural communication—a cultural performance as much as a performance of culture.

Conclusion
Chronotopes of Re-presentation

WHEN I embarked on this journey though Griko I was often told that there was no point in learning a language that only the elderly used and mastered—'a language of the past.' Indeed, I was often confronted with what seemed at the time a rather resigned attitude. It is not surprising that, having long dealt with the chronicle of Griko's death foretold, locals have internalized the scholarly predicament of Griko as a 'dying language.' This ethnography has confirmed that Reversing Language Shift (à la Fishman 1991)—reintroducing Griko as a language of daily communication—is not a project locals have faith in; more to the point, it is not what they now expect or strive for, and this is probably the least contested aspect of this story. One could interpret this resigned attitude as inevitable in the face of a reality that includes only a limited pool of speakers and of people engaged with or learning the language. In this book I have shown, however, how this eternal precarity of Griko—whether perceived or real—has also fueled the moral imperative to preserve it, leading some locals to strive to keep Griko 'alive,' as it were. Or rather, I have shown the multiple ways in which these locals *live with Griko*, highlighting the activities they promote, the cultural rules they follow, and the ideological references they evoke. By debating, performing, singing, and composing in—or translating into—Griko, they express their multiple understandings, feelings, and ideas about the role of this language in both the past and the future.

Through this process Griko keeps forming part of the textures of these locals' lived experiences, acquiring a meta-meaning that has not just replaced but overtaken its value and function as a language of communication. The use of Griko for performative and artistic purposes has indeed increased while its use as a vehicle to convey information has progressively faded; ultimately, the more Griko seems to be 'dying,' the more it is being performatively 'resurrected' in a dialectical process. But Griko is not simply used for performative and artistic purposes; I contend that it is precisely through the conscious and intentional use of Griko that linguistic identities are performed—however limited, partial, and circumstantial such use may be. Instead of treating this phenomenon as a failure, I consider it a cultural performance in itself, a reenactment of the value infused in Griko and in its cultural distinctiveness. This led me to argue that the revival of Griko is ideological in nature, as it is based on a broader reevaluation of the past and its cultural manifestations, in a reflexive negotiation of being-in-time. Griko has ultimately become a post-linguistic resource and a metalanguage for talking about the past in order to position oneself in the present.

The past and its multiple accounts have been ever present in this book. Throughout it we have continually encountered examples of the cultural temporality of language, of the multiple relations that locals entertain with Griko through its past, and with the past through it. By engaging in this temporal dialogue through these performances they evoke, redeem, and reenact the past, expressing in the process their moral alignments and projections. Yet, Griko meant, continues to mean, and is meant to mean different things to people of different ages, backgrounds, and ideological orientations. To elderly Griko speakers, and to the majority of those who remember Griko as a language of communication, the relevant historical touchstone remains a recent experiential past embedded in the subalternity of the Italian South. Here is at play the semiotic process of indexicality, which creates meaning through relation; Griko therefore points to that historicity, and to locality becoming indexical of them. Meanwhile, Greek aficionados of Griko, as well as some *cultori del griko* and activists, advance claims to the Hellenic and/or Byzantine past, influenced by the modern cultural ideology of Hellenism. They evoke the similarity between Griko and MG—that is, the iconic relationship between them—and interpret it as inevitable. Indeed, in semiotic terms, iconization describes the process of creating meaning through resemblance.

Yet, as Herzfeld points out, the very notion of resemblance needs to be problematized for being potentially misleading, and this is reflected in the modern popular misuse and abuse of the term 'icon' itself. An iconic relationship, however persuasive, is never totally organic; it is rather created to cultivate a shared sense of thingness potentially carrying political implications (Herzfeld 2005: 93, 94). Or to use the words of Umberto Eco, cultural resemblance becomes conventional "step by step, the more its addressee becomes acquainted with it" (1976:204–205). I have in fact shown how local dynamics have been increasingly interacting with the modern-Greek cultural ideology of Hellenism and historical continuity; this has been embedded into the construction of the Greek nation-state, and is now being recursively and retroactively applied to Griko and its speakers. Indeed, the perceived resemblance between Griko and MG and/or other 'Greek dialects'—what I have referred to as romantic iconization—is increasingly evoked, and is used to invest Griko with a more than local symbolic significance. Griko thereby transcends locality and is projected as a symbol of global Hellenism.

Griko ultimately exists in a non-homogeneous, non-synchronous present, since its very subjects do not share the same phenomenological points of reference to it. "Not all people live in the same Now," as Ernst Bloch (1977:22) points out. Griko has entered what we might call a symbolization process, through which multiple temporalities collapse and new meanings emerge and compete. An arbitrary sign functions as a symbol by creating meaning through convention, yet a symbol becomes a social force that broadens the space of what it actually 'stands for'. It is exactly the vagueness and openness of any symbol that makes it possible to indicate what is always beyond one's reach (Eco 1984:130). Such a surplus of meaning emerges as people start to impute to Griko plural meanings and a variety of claims. Griko remains therefore open to evaluation and interpretation: According to which historicity is evoked and by whom, Griko functions as a symbol of a redeemed and revalued local past, or as a symbol of the distant and glorious Hellenic past.

The complex dynamics through which all these semiotic terms of description simultaneously operate contributes to the continuous shifting of the chronotopes of the re-presentation of Griko. The cultural temporality of language presupposes in fact a semiotic relationality of time and space, since they are not separable from one another in our living perception (Bakhtin 1981:243). According to Bakhtin, "it is common moreover for one of these chronotopes to envelope or dominate the others ... Chronotopes are mutually inclusive, they co-exist, they may be interwoven with, replace or oppose one another, contradict one another" (1981:252). The multiple chronotopes associated with Griko indeed co-exist in dynamic and dialogical tension, while locals keep negotiating the meanings and values they attach to the language by reacting to and interacting with the changing historical, socio-cultural, and economic environment—but also by proactively shaping it themselves.

The Land of the Re-bitten

As I have shown over the course of this book, Griko and the community at large have been engaged with these dynamics across a spectrum of micro- and macro-level processes, from the personal and interpersonal to the institutional and international. Through the current revival and its recent legal recognition as a minority language, though, Griko and its community have ultimately entered what Hacking labeled "the matrix within which an idea, a concept, or kind is formed" (1999:10), in this case the very social setting within which the category or kind of 'linguistic minority' is socially constructed. Yet, the essentializing approach to minority languages that prevails in policy-making spheres, and that is further circulated through international bodies such as Unesco, treats languages as 'natural', static, and bounded cultural entities; such an approach implicitly reproduces the musty nineteenth-century paradigm of an unquestioned link between language and people, temporally conflating modern notions of ethnicity, identity, and belonging, and potentially also reproducing its pitfalls. As a result, Griko and its speakers are becoming obliged to communicate themselves through predefined categories of representation within which it does not seem to find an easy fit; meanwhile, those classified may begin to affect the category of classification by conforming, hyper-conforming, or contesting it (Hacking 1995:59).

Salento remains today a "concentric juncture of times and spaces" (Pizza 2015:179–180). Following Giovanna Parmigiani's (2019) application of Berardino Palumbo's concept (2006:46, for the case of Sicily), Salento is a "hyper-place," an "unstable social and political space that produces and reproduces further spaces of aggregation and contrasts." Salento has been bitten again, one could argue. Indeed, with *La Terra del Rimorso*, de Martino (1961) referred not only to the land of 'remorse' but also the land of the 're-bitten' (*ri-morso*), to the temporal recurrence of a crisis, of a critical and unresolved episode of the past. My reformulation of this concept unravels how this land has been 're-bitten' by the very processes of legitimation and recognition that locals long fought to achieve. These have generated divergent interests and claims linked to the management of Griko and its cultural heritage more broadly, producing contradictions, contestations, and clashes *within* the community in addition to those arising around it. Griko, pizzica, and the phenomenon of tarantism have equally been immersed in global processes of *patrimonializzazione* (patrimonialization), or rather *merci-patrimonializzazione*—a term through which Palumbo refers to "the construction of local cultural specificities in terms of patrimonial goods" (2013:136, my translation). These are produced and consumed by multiple social actors—local, national, and transnational—who create further spaces of 'collective imagination.' Yet, in the process, fears of losing control over Griko and its management are also revealed at the local level.

Locals are caught once again in the web of the tarantula, and keep contesting the legacy of the past, present, and future in terms of authenticity, authority over practices, access to resources and channels of re-presentation. The ethnographic present that I have recorded is ultimately to be interpreted as the result of a complex interplay between local claims and the global framework of re-presentation that these claims are immersed in, which sees a host of social actors competing for the authority to *present* and *re-present* Griko and its heritage in time and space. What I witnessed and have captured in this book is this transition, and the resultant destabilization: a temporal collapse through which multiple chronotopes of re-presentation converge and transform themselves, thereby re-storying the past-present-future of Griko and this land between the seas.

> *"Kàngesce o kosmo, kiaterèddhamu."*
> *"Umme, tata. Kangèsce o kosmo.*
> *Kàngesce mapàle," ipe i Rosalìa, "kundu panta."*

> "The world changed, my child."
> "Yes, Dad. The world changed.
> It changed again," replied Rosalia, "as always."

Bibliography

Anderson, B. R. 1991. *Imagined Communities: Reflections on the Origin and Spread of Nationalism.* London.

Andronis, M. A. 2003. "Iconization, Fractal Recursivity, and Erasure: Linguistic Ideologies and Standardization in Quichua-Speaking Ecuador." *Texas Linguistic Forum* 47:263–269.

Apolito, P. 2000. "Tarantismo, identità locale, postmodernità." In *Quarant'anni dopo de Martino: Atti del convegno internazionale di studi sul tarantismo*, ed. Gino L. Di Mitri, 137–146. Nardò.

Appadurai, A. 1996. *Modernity at Large: Cultural Dimensions of Globalization.* Minneapolis.

Aprile, G. 1972. *Calimera e i suoi traùdia.* Galatina.

Aprile, P. 2010. *Terroni.* Milan.

———. 2011. *Giù al Sud.* Milan.

Aprile, R. 1994. *Grecìa Salentina: Origini e storia.* Calimera.

Avineri, N. 2012. *Heritage Language Socialization Practices in Secular Yiddish Educational Contexts: The Creation of a Metalinguistic Community.* Ph.D. diss., University of California, Los Angeles.

———. 2014. "Yiddish Endangerment as Phenomenological Reality and Discursive Strategy: Crossing into the Past and Crossing out the Present." *Language & Communication* 38:18–32.

Banti, G., and F. Giannattasio. 2004. "Poetry." In *A Companion to Linguistic Anthropology*, ed. A. Duranti, 290–320. Oxford.

Bakhtin, M. M., and G. S. Morson. 1986. *Bakhtin: Essays and Dialogues on his Work.* Chicago.

Bakhtin, M. M. 1981. *Dialogic Imagination: Four Essays.* Trans. J. Wright and M. Holquist. Austin.

Barth, F. 1995. "Other Knowledge and Other Ways of Knowing." *Journal of Anthropological Research* 51:65–68.

Battisti, C. 1959. *Sostrati e parastrati nell'Italia preistorica.* Florence.

Bauman, R., and C. L. Briggs. 2000. "Language Philosophy as Language Ideology: John Locke and Johann Gottfried Herder." In *Regimes of Language: Ideologies, Polities, and Identities*, ed. P. V. Kroskrity, 139–204. Oxford.

Berruto, G. 1993. "Le varietà del repertorio." In *Introduzione all'Italiano Contemporaneo: Le Variazioni e gli Usi,* ed. A. A. Sobrero. Bari.

———. 2005. *Fondamenti di sociolinguistica.* Rome-Bari.

Besnier, N. 1990. "Language and Affect." *Annual review of Anthropology* 19:419–415.

Bloch, E. 1977. "Nonsynchronism and the Obligation to Its Dialectics." Translated by M. Ritter. *New German Critique* 11:22–38.

Blom, J.-P., and J. J. Gumperz. 1972. "Social Meaning in Linguistic Structures: Code-switching in Norway." In *Directions in Sociolinguistics,* ed. J. J. Gumperz and D. Hymes, 407–434. London.

Blommaert, J. 1999. *Language Ideological Debates.* New York.

———. 2004. "Grassroots Historiography and the Problem of Voice: Tshibumba's Histoire du Zaïre." *Journal of Linguistic Anthropology,* 14(1):6–23.

Boissevain, J. 1992. "Introduction." In *Revitalizing European rituals,* ed. J. Boissevain, 1–9. London.

Bonamore, D. 2004. *Lingue minoritarie, lingue nazionali, lingue ufficiali nella Legge 482/1999.* Milan.

Bourdieu, P. 1991. *Language and Symbolic Power.* Cambridge.

———. 1977a. "The Economics of Linguistic Exchanges." *Social Science Information* 16(6):645–668.

———. 1977b. *Outline of a Theory of Practice.* Trans. R. Nice. Cambridge.

Bourdieu, P., and R. Nice. 1984. *Distinction: Social Critique of the Judgement of Taste.* London.

Brenzinger, M. 2003. *International Expert Meeting on UNESCO Programme Safeguarding of Endangered Languages,* 10–12. Paris.

Brown, M. F. 1998. "Can Culture Be Copyrighted?" *Current Anthropology* 39(2):193–222.

Browning, R. 1958. *L'origine des dialects Néo-grecs de l'Italie méridionale.* Paris.

———. 1983. *Modern Greek.* 2nd ed. Ed. S. Caratzas. Cambridge.

Bucholtz, M., and K. Hall. 2004. "Language and Identity." In *A Companion to Linguistic Anthropology,* ed. A. Duranti, 369–394. Oxford.

Butler, J. 2015. *Notes toward a Performative Theory of Assembly.* London.

Calotychos, V. 2003. *Modern Greece: A Cultural Poetics.* Oxford.

———. 2008. "The Dead Hand of Philology." In *A Singular Antiquity: Archaeology and Hellenic Identity in Twentieth-Century Greece,* ed. D. Plantzos and D. Damaskos, 237. Athens.

Cameron, D. 1995. *Verbal Hygiene.* New York.

———. 2007. "Language Endangerment and Verbal Hygiene: History, Morality and Politics." In *Discourses of Endangerment,* ed. A. Duchene and M. Heller, 268–285. London.

Caroli, E. 2008. "Entre renaissance culturelle et persistance de la question méridionale." *Journal of Urban Research* 4: https://doi.org/10.4000/articulo.759.

———. 2009. "La tarentule est vivante, elle n'est pas morte. Musique, tradition, antropologie et tourisme dans le Salento (Pouilles, Italie)." *Cahiers d'études africaines,* 193–194:13, 257–284.

———. 2010. "Localismi e nuovi sviluppi locali." In *Conferenza annuale della sezione Sociologia del Territorio AIS (Associazione Italiana di Sociologia).* Alessandria. Accessed from http://www.sociologiadelterritorio.it/archivio/ricerca/r5.pdf, 2013.

Cassano, F. 1996. *Il pensiero meridiano.* Bari.

Cassoni, M. 2000. *Il tramonto del rito greco in Terra d'Otranto.* Nardò.

Cavanaugh, J. R. 2004. "Remembering and Forgetting: Ideologies of Language Loss in a Northern Italian Town." *Journal of Linguistic Anthropology* 14(1):11, 24–38.

———. 2009. *Living Memory: The Social Aesthetics of Language in a Northern Italian Town.* Hoboken, NJ.

Chiriatti, L. 1995. *Morso d'amore. Viaggio nel tarantismo salentino.* Lecce.

Clifford, J. 1986. "On Ethnographic Allegory." In *Writing Culture: The Poetics and Politics of Ethnography,* ed. J. Clifford and G. E. Marcus, 98–121. Berkeley.

Clogg, R. 1979. *A Short History of Modern Greece.* Cambridge.

———. 2002. *A Concise History of Greece.* Cambridge.

Cohen, S. 1979. *Folk Devils and Moral Panics: The Creation of the Mods and Rockers.* London.

Collins, J. 1998. "Our Ideology and Theirs." In *Language Ideologies: Practice and Theory,* ed. B. B. Schieffelin, K. A. Woolard, and P. V. Kroskrity, 256–270. New York.

Coluzzi, P. 2007. *Minority Language Planning and Micronationalism in Italy: An Analysis of the Situation of Friulian, Cimbrian and Western Lombard with Reference to Spanish Minority Languages.* Oxford.

Comaroff, J., and J. L. Comaroff. 2000. *Civil Society and the Political Imagination in Africa: Critical Perspectives.* Chicago.

Coupland, N., H. Bishop, and P. Garret. 2003. "Home Truths: Globalisation and the Iconising of Welsh in a Welsh-American Newspaper." *Journal of Multilingual and Multicultural Development* 24(3):153–177.

Cowan, J. K., M. Dembour, and R. A. Wilson. 2001. *Culture and Rights.* Cambridge.

De Giorgi, P. 1999. *Tarantismo e rinascita. I riti musicali e coreutici della pizzica-pizzica e della tarantella.* Lecce.

De Martino, E. 1941. *Naturalismo e storicismo nell'etnologia.* Bari.

———. 1948. *Il mondo magico. Prolegomeni a una storia del magismo.* Torino.

———. 1949. "Intorno a una storia del mondo popolare subalterno." *Società* 5:248, 411–435.

———. 1976. *La terra del rimorso. Contributo a una storia religiosa del sud.* Milan.

De Mauro, T. 1970. *Storia Linguistica dell'Italia Unita.* Bari.

———, and M. Lodi. 1979. *Lingua e dialetti.* Rome.

Di Lecce, G. 1994. *La danza della piccola taranta: cronache da Galatina 1908-1993, a memoria d'uomo.* Roma.

———. 2001. *Tretarante: taranta/pizzica/scherma. Le tarantelle-pizziche del Salento.* Nardò.

Dorian, N. 1981. *Language Death: The Life Cycle of a Scottish Gaelic Dialect.* Philadelphia.

———. 1982. "Language Loss and Maintenance in Language Contact Situations." In *The Loss of Language Skills,* ed. R. D. Lambert and B. F. Freed, 203–222. Rowley, MA.

———. 1994. "Purism vs. Compromise in Language Revitalization and Language." *Language in Society* 23(4):479-494.

———. 1999. "The Study of Language Obsolescence: Stages, Surprises, Challenges." *Languages and Linguistics* 3:99–122.

Douglas, M. 1966. *Purity and Danger.* London. Reprinted 1991.

Duchêne, A., and M. Heller, eds. 2007. *Discourses of Endangerment: Ideology and Interest in the Defense of Languages.* London.

Eco, Umberto. 1976. *A Theory of Semiotics.* Bloomington.

———. 1984. *Semiotics and the Philosophy of Language.* Bloomington

Errington, J. 1998. "Indonesian('s) Development: On the State of a Language of State." In *Language Ideologies: Practice and Theory,* ed. B. B. Schieffelin, K. A. Woolard, and P. V. Kroskrity, 271–284. New York.

Fabian, J. 1983. *Time and the Other: How Anthropology Makes its Object.* New York.

Fanciullo, F. 2001. "On the Origins of Modern Greek in Southern Italy." In *Proceedings of the First International Conference of Modern Greek Dialects and Linguistic Theory,* ed. A. Ralli, B. J. Joseph, and M. Janse, 67–77. Patras.

Farnetti, T., and C. Stewart. 2012. "An Introduction to 'Crisis of Presence and Religious Reintegration.'" *HAU: Journal of Ethngraphic Theory* 2(2):431-433.

Faubion, J. 1993. *Modern Greek Lessons: A Primer in Historical Constructivism.* Princeton.

Ferguson, C. A. 1959. "Diglossia." In *The Bilingualism Reader,* ed. L. Wie, 58–73. New York. Reprinted 2000.

Fishman, J. A. 1965. "Who Speaks What Language to Whom and When?" *La Linguistique* 1:67–88.

Foucault, M. 1989. "The Subject and Power." *Critical Inquiry* 8(4):777–795.

Frazee, C. 2002. "Catholics." In *Minorities in Greece: Aspects of a Plural Society,* ed. R. Clogg, 24–43. London.

Gal, S. 1978. "Peasant Men Can't Get Wives: Language Change and Sex Roles in a Bilingual Community." *Language in Society* 7:1–16.

———. 1979. *Language Shift: Social Determinants of Linguistic Change in Bilingual Austria.* New York.

———. 1989. "Lexical Innovation and Loss: The Use and Value of Restricted Hungarian." In *Investigating Obsolescence: Studies in Language Contraction and Death,* ed. N. Dorian, 313–332. Cambridge.

Gal, S., and J. Irvine. 1995. "The Boundaries of Languages and Disciplines: How Ideologies Construct Difference." *Social Research* 62(4):967–1001.

———. 2000. "Language Ideology and Linguistic Differentiation." In *Regimes of Language,* ed. P. V. Kroskrity, 35–84. Oxford.

Garrett, P. B. 2004. "Language Contact and Contact Languages." In *A Companion to Linguistic Anthropology,* ed. A. Duranti, 46–72. Oxford.

Gefou-Madianou, D. 1993. "Mirroring Ourselves through Western Texts." In *The Politics of Ethnographic Reading and Writing,* ed. H. Driessen, 160–181. Saarbrücken.

Giannachi, F. 2012. "La Poesia greco salentina. In margine ad una nuova antologia curata da Brizio Montinaro." *Quaderni Urbinati di Cultura Classica New Series* 100:211–220.

———. 2017. "Learning Greek in the Land of Otranto: Some Remarks on Sergio Stiso of Zollino and His School." In *Teachers, Students, and Schools of Greek in the Renaissance,* ed. F. Ciccorella and L. Silvano, 213–223. Leiden.

Goffman, E. 1959. *The Presentation of the Self in Everyday Life.* Edinburgh.

Goodale, M. 2005. "Empires of Law: Discipline and Resistance within the Transnational System." *Social and Legal Studies* 14(4):553–583.

Grimaldi, M. 2010. "Dialetto e italiano in rete. Chat ed Instant Messaging nel Salento." In *Lingua e Linguaggio dei media,* ed. M. Aprile and D. De Fazio, 250–280. Rome.

Grimaldi M., and B. Sisinni. 2006. "Il dialetto sopravvive in rete ... e in rap." *Italienisch Zeitschrift für Italienische Sprache undLiteratur* 56:84–94.

Gruppo di Lecce. 1979. "Il caso Grecìa." In *I dialetti e le lingue delle minoranze di fronte all'italiano,* ed. F. Albano Leoni, 343–403. Roma.

Hacking, I. 1995. "The Looping Effects of Human Kinds." In *Causal cognition: A Multidisciplinary Approach,* ed. D. Sperber, D. Premack, and A. J. Premack, 351–383. Oxford.

———. 1999. *The Social Construction of What?* London.

Hartley, L. P. 1953. *The Go-Between.* London.

Herzfeld, M. 1982. *Ours Once More: Folklore, Ideology and the Making of Modern Greece.* New York.

———. 1983. *The Social Production of Indifference: Exploring the Symbolic Roots of Western Bureaucracy.* Chicago.

———. 1987. *Anthropology through the Looking-Glass: Critical Ethnography in the Margins of Europe.* Cambridge.

———. 1992. "La pratique des stéreéotypes." *L'Homme* 32(1): 67–77.

———. 1997. "Political Philology: Everyday Consequences of Grandiose Grammars." *Anthropological Linguistics* 39(3):351–375.

———. 2003. "Localism and the Logic of Nationalistic Folklore: Cretan Reflections." *Comparative Studies in Society and History* 281–310.

———. 2004. *The Body Impolitic. Artisan and Artifice in the Global Hierarchy of Value.* Chicago.

———. 2005. *Cultural Intimacy: Social Poetics in the Nation-State.* 2nd edition. London.

Hill, J. 1993. "Structure and Practice in Language Shift." In *Progression and Regression in Language,* ed. K. Hyltenstam and A. Viberg, 68–93. Cambridge.

———. 1998. "'Today There Is No Respect': Nostalgia, 'Respect' and Oppositional Discourse in Mexicano (Nahuatl) Language Ideology." In *Language Ideologies: Practice and Theory,* ed. B. B. Schieffelin, K. A. Woolard, and P. V. Kroskrity, 68–86. New York.

———. 2002. "'Expert Rhetorics' in Advocacy for Endangered Languages: Who is Listening and What Do They Hear?" *Journal of Linguistic Anthropology* 12(2):119–133.

Hill, J. H., and K. C. Hill. 1986. *Speaking Mexicano: Dynamics of a Syncretic Language in Central Mexico.* Tucson.

Hirsch, E., and C. Stewart. 2005. "Introduction: Ethnographies of Historicity." *History and Anthropology* 16(3):261–274.

Horrocks, G. 1997. *Greek: A History of the Language and its Speakers.* New York.

Imbriani, E. 2015. "Il dio che danza non c'entra." *Palaver* 2:33–46.

Ineschi, F. 1983. *Identità grìca in terra d'Otranto. Analisi del conflitto socio-culturale di una minoranza etnico-linguistica.* Lecce.

Irvine, J. T. 2004. "Say When: Temporalities in Language Ideologies." *Journal of Linguistic Anthropology* 14(1):99–109.

Irvine, J. T., and S. Gal. 1995. "The Boundaries of Languages and Disciplines. How Ideologies Construct Difference." In *Social Research* 62(4):974.

Jakobson, R. 1960. "Closing Statement: Linguistics and Poetics." In *Style in Language,* ed. Thomas A. Sebeok, 350–377. Cambridge, MA.

Jaffe, A. 1999. *Ideologies in Action: Language Politics in Corsica.* Berlin.

————. 2007. "Discourses of Endangerment: Contexts and Consequences of Essentializing Discourses." In *Discourses of Endangerment,* ed. A. Duchene and M. Heller, 57–75. London.

Kapsomenos, S. G. 1977. "Le isole di lingua greca nell'Italia meridionale dal punto di vista strico-linguistico." *Magna Graecia* 12(9–10).

Karanastasis, A. 1992. "Origine e sviluppo dei dialetti italogreci." In *Studi linguistici e filologici offerti a Girolamo Caracausi,* 177–193. Palermo.

Knight, D., and C. Stewart. 2016. "Ethnographies of Austerity: Temporality, Crisis and Affect in Southern Europe." *History and Anthropology* 27(1):1–18.

Knight, D. 2015. *History, Time, and Economic Crisis in Central Greece.* New York.

Kristeva, J. 1980. *Desire in Language: A Semiotic Approach to Literature and Art.* Ed. L. S. Roudiez. Trans. T. Gora, A. Jardine, and Leon S. Roudiez. Oxford.

Kroskrity, P. V. 2009. "Language Renewal as Sites of Language Ideological Struggle: The Need for 'Ideological Clarification.'" In *Indigenous Language Revitalization: Encouragement, Guidance and Lessons Learned,* ed. J. Reyhner and L. Lockard, 71–83. Flagstaff.

————. 2010. "Language Ideologies—Evolving Perspectives." In *Society and Language Use,* ed. J. Jaspers, J. Östman, and J. Verschueren, 192–205. Amsterdam.

Kulick, D. 1992. *Language Shift and Cultural Reproduction: Socialization, Self and Syncretism in a Papua New Guinean Village.* Cambridge.

Labov, W. 1966. *The Social Stratification of English in New York.* Washington, DC.

Lanternari, V. 1977. *Crisi e ricerca d'identita. Folklore e dinamica culturale.* Naples.

————. 1995. "Tarantismo: Dal medico neopositivista all'antropologo, all' etnopsichiatria di oggi." *Storia, antropologia, e scienze del linguaggio* 3:67-92.

Lapassade, G. 1994. *Intervista sul tarantismo.* Maglie.

————. 2005. *Gente dell'ombra. Trance e possession.* Nardò.

————. 2000. "Tarantismo: Vecchie teorie, saperi nuovi." In *Quarant'anni dopo De Martino,* ed. Gino di Mitri, 119–134.

Lepschy, G. 2002. "The Languages of Italy." In *Mother Tongues and Other Reflections on the Italian Language,* ed. G. Lepschy, 35–48. Toronto.

Liakos, A. 2008. "Hellenism and the Making of Modern Greece: Time, Language, Space." In *Hellenisms, Culture, Identity and Ethnicity from Antiquity to Modernity,* ed. K. Zacharia, 201–236. Aldershot.

Livanios, D. 2008. "The Quest for Hellenism: Religion, Nationalism, and Collective Identities in Greece, 1453–1913." In *Hellenisms, Culture, Identity and Ethnicity from Antiquity to Modernity,* ed. K. Zacharia, 237–269. Aldershot.

Lüdtke, K. 2009. *Dances with Spiders: Crisis, Celebrity and Celebration in Southern Italy.* Oxford.

McDonald, M. 1989. *We Are Not French.* London.

MacCannell, D. 1973. "Staged Authenticity: Arrangements of Social Space in Tourist Settings." *American Journal of Sociology* 79(3):589–603.

Malinowski, B. 1923. "The Problem of Meaning in Primitive Languages." In *The Meaning of Meaning*, ed. C. K. Ogden and I. A. Richards, 296–336. London. Reprinted 1949.

Manolessou, I. 2005. "The Greek Dialects of Southern Italy: An Overview." *Cambridge Papers in Modern Greek,* 103–125.

Marcus, G. E. 1995. "Ethnography in/of the World System: The Emergency of Multi-sited Ethnography." *Annual Review of Anthropology* 24:95–117.

May, S. 2001. *Language and Minority Rights: Ethnicity, Nationalism and the Politics of Language.* Harlow.

Meek, B. A. 2007. "Respecting the Language of Elders: Ideological Shift and Linguistic Discontinuity in a Northern Athapascan Community." *Journal of Linguistic Anthropology* 17(1):23–43.

Merianou, A. 1980. *Taxidevontas sta Ellinofona xoria tis Kato Italias.* Athens.

———. 1989. *Laografika ton Ellinon tis Kato Italias.* Athens.

Mertz, E. 1989. "Sociolinguistic Creativity: Cape Breton Gaelic's Linguistic 'Tip.'" In *Investigating Obsolescence: Studies in Language Contraction and Death,* ed. N. Dorian, 103–116. Cambridge.

Mertz E., and J. Yovel. 2000. "Metalinguistic Awareness." In *The Handbook of Pragmatics,* ed. J. Verschueren, J.-O. Östman, and J. Blommaert, Amsterdam.

Messing J. 2007. "Multiple Ideologies and Competing Discourses: Language Shift in Tlaxcala, Mexico." *Language in Society* 36:555–577.

Mina, G., and S. Torsello. 2005. *La tela infinita.* Nardò.

Montinaro, B. 1994. *Canti di pianto e d'amore dall'antico Salento.* Milan.

Most, G. 2008. "Philhellenism, Cosmopolitanism, Nationalism." In *Hellenisms: Culture, Identity, and Ethnicity from Antiquity to Modernity,* ed. K. Zacharia. Aldershot.

Moore, R. 1988. "Lexicalization versus Lexical Loss in Wasco-Wishram Language Obsolescence." *International Journal of American Linguistics* 54(4):453–468.

Morosi, G. 1870. *Studi sui dialetti della terra d'Otranto.* Lecce. Reprinted 1970.

Nicholas, N. 2006. "Negotiating a Greco-Corsican Identity." *Journal of Modern Greek Studies* 24:91–133.

Nucita, A. 1997. *Il Griko 20 anni dopo. Nella scuola elementare di Castrignano de' Greci.* Casarano.

Nucita, A., and A. Cotardo. 1985. *Dieci anni dopo. Lingua cultura e folklore nella Grecìa Salentina.* Corigliano d'Otranto.

Ochs, E. 2004. "Narrative Lessons." In *A Companion to Linguistic Anthropology,* ed. A. Duranti, 269–289. Oxford.

Ochs, E., R. C. Smith, and C. E. Taylor. 1996. "Detective Stories at Dinnertime: Problem Solving through Co-narration." In *Disorderly Discourse, Narrative, Conflict and Inequality*, ed. C. L. Briggs, 238–257. Oxford.

Ochs, E., and B. B. Schieffelin. 1989. "Language Has a Heart." *Text* 9(1):7–25.

Odermatt, P. 1996. "A Case of Neglect? The Politics of (Re)presentation: A Sardinian Case." In *Coping with Tourists: European Reactions to Mass Tourism*, ed. J. Boissevain, 98–99. Oxford.

O'Reilly, C. 2001. *Language, Ethnicity and the State*. Vol. 1. *Minority Languages in the European Union*. New York.

Palma, D. 2013. *L'autentica storia di Otranto nella guerra contro i turchi*. Lecce.

———. 2018. "E glossa-ma sìmmeri." In *Mala Agapi: Nuove musiche d'amore e disamore nell'antica lingua greca del Salento*, ed. L. Garrisi. Otranto.

Palumbo, B. 2001 "Campo intellettuale, potere e identità tra contesti locali, 'Il pensiero meridiano' e 'identità meridionale'." *La Ricerca Folklorica*, 43, 117–134.

———. 2006. "Iperluogo." *Antropologia Museale*. 14:45–47.

Papagaroufali, E. 2005. "Town Twinning in Greece: Reconstructing Local Histories Through Translocal Sensory-Affective Performances." *History and Anthropology* 16(3):335–347.

———. 2013. *Soft Diplomacy: Transnational Twinnings and Pacifist Practices in Contemporary Greece*. Athens.

Parlangeli, O. 1952. "Il linguaggio delle donne della 'Grecìa' salentina (Italia)." *Orbis* 1:46–64.

———. 1953. *Rapporti fra il greco e il romanzo nel Salento*. Louvain.

———. 1960. *Storia linguistica e storia politica nell'Italia meridionale*. Florence.

Parmigiani, G. 2018. "Femminicidio and the Emergence of a 'Community of Sense' in Contemporary Italy." *Modern Italy* 23(1):19–34

———. 2019. *Feminism, Violence and Representation in Modern Italy: "We are Witnesses, not Victims"* Bloomington.

Pedregal, A. M. 1996. "Tourism and Self-consciousness in a South Spanish Coastal Community." In *Coping with Tourists: European Reactions to Mass Tourism*, ed. J. Boissevain, 56–83. Oxford.

Peirce, C. S. 1910. "Logic as Semiotic: The Theory of Signs." In *Semiotics, an Introductory Anthology*, ed. R. Innis, 1–23. Bloomington. Repr. 1985.

Pellegrino, M. 2013. *"Dying" Language or "Living Monument"?: Language Ideologies, Practices and Policies in the Case of Griko*. PhD diss., University College London.

———. 2015. "La lingua greco-salentina: fra passato e futuro." In *Raccontare la Grecìa: Una ricerca antropologica nel Salento griko*. Martano.

———. 2016a. "Performing Griko Beyond Death." *Palaver* 5(1):137–162.

———— 2016b. "I toponimi griki e le ideologie linguistiche riguardanti il griko." In *Topos logos, La vita dei luoghi*, ed. C. Carluccio, Cirino and M. Pellegrino, 13–28. Martano.

————. 2018. "I glossa pu simèni. La lingua che 'ri-suona'." In *Mala Agapi: Nuove musiche d'amore e disamore nell'antica lingua greca del Salento*, ed. L. Garrisi, 71–100. Otranto.

————. 2019. "'O jeno me diu glosse: il bilinguismo griko-salentino come risorsa." In *La diglossia nell'area ellenofona del Salento. Atti della mattinata di studi*. Zollino.

Pellegrino, P. 2004. *Il ritorno di Dioniso. Il dio dell'ebrezza nella storia della civiltà occidentale*. Galatina.

Pennycook, A. 2004. "Performativity and Language Studies." *Critical Inquiry in Language Studies* 1(1):1–19, 216.

Petropoulou, Ch. 1995. "Γλώσσα και διάλεκτος στην ελληνόφωνη περιοχή της Καλαβρίας: όψεις γλωσσικές και πολιτισμικές." *Γλώσσα* 35:32–51, 152.

————. 1997. *Μνήμη, συγγένεια, ταυτότητα σε ενα ελληνόφωνω χοριό της Κάτω Ιταλίας*. PhD diss., Aristotle University of Thessaloniki.

Phillipson, R., M. Rannut, and T. Skutnabb-Kangas. 1995. *Linguistic Human Rights: Overcoming Linguistic Discrimination*. Berlin.

Pipyrou, S. 2010. *Power, Governance and Representation: An Anthropological Analysis of Kinship, the Ndrangheta and Dance within the Greek Linguistic Minority of Reggio Calabria, South Italy*. PhD diss., Durham University. http://etheses. dur.ac.uk/465/.

————. 2011. "Commensurable Language and Incommensurable Claims among the Greek Linguistic Minority of Southern Italy." *Journal of Modern Italian Studies* 17(1):70–91.

————. 2016. *The Grecanici of Southern Italy: Governance, Violence and Minority Politics*. Philadelphia.

Pizza, G. 1999. "Tarantismi oggi: un panorama critico sulle letterature contemporanee del tarantismo (1994–1999)." *AM. Rivista della società italiana di antropologia medica* 7–8:253–273.

————. 2004. "Tarantism and the Politics of Tradition in Contemporary Salento." In *Memory, Politics and Religion: The Past Meets the Present in Europe*, ed. F. Pine, D. Kaneff, and H. Haukanes, 201–203, 219, 261. Münster.

————. 2005. "Ancora nella 'terra del rimorso' per smascherare la retorica sul sud." http://www.vincenzosantoro.it/salentopizzicamusiche.asp?ID=282.

————. 2015. *Il Tarantismo Oggi*. Alessano.

Plantzos, D. 2008. "Archaeology and Hellenic Identity, 1896–2004: The Frustrated Vision." In *A Singular Antiquity: Archaeology and Hellenic Identity in Twentieth-Century Greece,* ed. D. Plantzos and D. Damaskos, 11–30. Athens.

Prelorenzos, I. 1978. *Dorikoi antilaloi stin kato Italia: ellinofonoi tou Salento kai tis Kalavrias.* Athens.

Profili, O. 1985. "La Romanisation d'un Parler Grec de l'Italie du Sud par les Parlers Romans Environants." In *Actes du XVIIe Congres International de Linguistique et de Philologie romanes,* 129–139. Aix-en-Provence.

Rampton, B. 1995. *Crossing: Language and Ethnicity among Adolescents.* London.

———. 2009. "Crossing, Ethnicity and Code-Switching." In *The New Sociolinguistics Reader,* ed. N. Coupland and A. Jaworski, 287–298. Basingstoke, UK.

Razfar, A. 2012. "Narrating Beliefs: A Language Ideologies Approach to Teacher Beliefs." *Anthropology & Education Quarterly* 43(1):61–81.

Ricento, T. 2006. "Americanization, Language Ideologies and the Construction of European Identities." In *Language Ideologies, Policies and Practices: Languages and the Future of Europe,* ed. C. Mar-Molinero and P. Stevenson, 44–57. New York.

Romano, A., F. Manco, and C. Saracino. 2002. "Un giorno a Martano: riflessioni sulla situazione linguistica della Grecìa Salentina." *Studi Linguistici Salentini* 26:63–109.

Romano, A. 2016. "Isole linguistiche del Sud–Italia tra conservazione e rivitalizzazione: analisi di alcuni dati linguistici relativi alle parlate alloglotte greche." In *Lingue delle isole e isole linguistiche,* ed. S. Medori, 227–247. Atti del Convegno internazionale (Corte, 2014). Alessandria.

———. 2018. "Vitalità dell'alloglossia nelle comunità greca e albanese di Puglia." In *Le isole linguistiche dell'Adriatico,* ed. Šimičić, L, Škevin, I., Vuletić, 227–258. Atti della Giornata di studio, Università di Zara (Croazia, 14 sett. 2016). Arricia.

Rohlfs, G. 1980. *Calabria e Salento. Saggi di storia linguistica.* Ravenna.

Rouget, G. 1980. *Musica e trance. I rapporti tra la musica e i fenomeni di possessione.* Torino. Reprinted 1986.

———. G. 2000. "Tarantismo, 'musica giusta' e iniziazione". In *Quarant'anni dopo de Martino: Atti del convegno internazionale di studi sul tarantismo,* ed. Gino L. Di Mitri, 43–52. Nardò.

Sanguin, D. 1992. "Les minorités ethnolinguistiques de la Republique Italienne." In *Les minorités ethnolinguistiques en Europe,* ed. D. Sanguin. Paris.

Sant Cassia, P. 2002. "Exoticizing Discoveries and Extraordinary Experiences: 'Traditional' Music, Modernity, and Nostalgia in Malta and Other Mediterranean." *Ethnomusicology* 44(2):281–301.

Santoro, V., and S. Torsello, eds. 2002. *Il ritmo meridiano. La pizzica e le identità danzanti del Salento.* Lecce.

Sasse, H. J. 1989. "Language Decay and Contact-Induced Change: Similarities and Differences." In *Language Death: Factual and Theoretical Explorations with Reference to East Africa,* ed. M. Brenzinger, 59–80. Berlin.

Saunders, G. 1995. "The Crisis of Presence in Italian Pentecostal Conversion." *American Ethnologist* 22(2):324–340.

Schneider, J., ed. 1998. *Italy's "Southern Question": Orientalism in One Country.* Oxford.

Scholz, A. 2004. *Subcultura e lingua giovanile in Italia: hip-hop e dintorni.* Rome.

Shandler, J. 2004. "Postvernacular Yiddish: Language as a Performance Art." *The Drama Review* 48(1):19–43.

———. 2006. *Adventures in Yiddishland: Postvernacular Language and Culture.* Berkeley.

Silverstein, M. 1992. "The Indeterminacy of Contextualization: When is Enough Enough?" In *The Contextualization of Language,* ed. P. Auer and A. DiLuzio. Amsterdam.

———. 1998. "The Uses and Utility of Ideology: A Commentary." In *Language Ideologies: Practice and Theory,* ed. B. B. Schieffelin, K. A. Woolard, and P. V. Kroskrity. New York.

Silverstein, M., and G. Urban. 1996. *Natural Histories of Discourse.* Chicago.

Sobrero A., and A. Miglietta. 1974. *Dialetti diversi. Proposte per lo studio delle parlate alloglotte in Italia.* Lecce.

———. 2010. "Per un monitoraggio sociolinguistico e socioculturale della minoranza grica: indagine a Sternatia (LE)." In *Atti delle seconde giornate dei diritti linguistici (Teramo, 21-22 maggio 2008).* Rome.

Spano, B. D. 1965. *La grecità bizantina e i suoi riflessi geografici nell'Italia meridionale e insulare.* Pisa.

Stewart, C. 1978. *Gli Italo-Greci d'Italia Meridionale.* BA thesis, Brandeis University.

———. 1989. "Hegemony or Rationality? The Position of the Supernatural in Modern Greece." *Journal of Modern Greek Studies* 7(1):77–104.

———. 1994. "Syncretism as a Dimension of Nationalist Discourse in Modern Greece." In *Syncretism/Anti-syncretism: The Politics of Religious Synthesis,* ed. C. Stewart and R. Shaw, 127–144. London.

———. 2003. "Dreams of Treasure: Temporality, Historicization and the Unconscious." *Anthropological Theory* 3:481–500.

———. 2006. "Forget Homi! Creolization, Omogéneia and the Greek Diaspora." *Diaspora: A Journal of Transnational Studies* 15(1):61–88.

——. 2008. "Dreams of Treasure: Temporality, Historicization, and the Unconscious." In *Hellenisms: Culture, Identity, and Ethnicity from Antiquity to Modernity,* ed. K. Zacharia, 273–295. Aldershot.

——. 2012. *Dreaming and Historical Consciousness in Island Greece.* Cambridge, MA.

——. 2013. "Dreaming and Historical Consciousness." *Historically Speaking* 14(1):28–30.

——. 2016. "Historicity and Anthropology." *Annual Review of Anthropology* 45(15):79–94.

——. 2017. "Uncanny History. Temporal Thought in the Post-Ottoman World." *Social Analysis* 61(1):129–149.

Stomeo, P. 1958. *Vito Domenico Palumbo e la Grecìa Salentina.* Galatina.

Strathern, M. 1987. "The Limits of Auto-Anthropology." In *Anthropology at Home,* ed. A. Jackson, 59–67. London.

Telmon, T. 1993. "Varietà Regionali." In *Introduzione all'Italiano Contemporaneo: Le Variazioni e gli Usi,* ed. A. Sobrero. Bari.

Tondi, D. 1935. *Glossa.* Bari.

Tosi, A. 2004. "The Language Situation in Italy." *Current Issues in Language Planning* 5(3):247–335.

Triandafyllidou, A., and M. Veikou. 2002. "The Hierarchy of Greekness: Ethnic and National Identity Consideration in Greek Immigration Policy." *Ethnicities* 2(2):189–208.

Tsitselikis, K. 2006. "Citizenship in Greece: Present Challenges for Future Changes." In *Multiple Citizenship as a Challenge To European Nation-States,* ed. Kalekin-Fishman and P. Pitkänen, 145–170. Rotterdam.

Tsitsipis, L. D. 1991. "Terminal-fluent Speaker Interaction and the Contextualization of Deviant Speech." *Journal of Pragmatics* 15:153–173.

——. 1995. "The Coding of Linguistic Ideology in Arvanítika (Albanian) Language Shift: Congruent and Contradictory Discourse." *Anthropological Linguistics* 37(4):541–577.

——. 1998. *A Linguistic Anthropology of Praxis and Language Shift: Arvanítika (Albanian) and Greek in Contact.* Oxford.

Tsopanakis, A. 1968. "I dialetti greci dell' Italia meridionale rispetto a quelli neogreci." *L'Italia dialettale* 31(8): 1–23.

Tziovas, D, ed. 2009. *Greek Diaspora and Migration since 1700.* Farnham, UK.

Van Dyck, K. 2008. "The Language Question and the Diaspora." In *The Making of Modern Greece: Nationalism, Romanticism, and the Uses of the Past (1797-1896),* ed. R. Beaton and D. Ricks, 189–198. Aldershot.

Venturas, L. 2009. "'Deterritorialising' the Nation: The Greek State and 'Ecumenical Hellenism.'" In *Greek Diaspora and Migration Since 1700. Society, Politics, and Culture*, ed. D. Tziovas, 125–140. Farnham, UK.

Vogli, E. 2009. "A Greece for Greeks by Descent? Nineteenth-Century Policy on Integrating the Diaspora." In *Greek Diaspora and Migration Since 1700. Society, Politics, and Culture*, ed. D. Tziovas, 99–110. Farnham, UK.

Voutira, E. 1991. "Pontic Greeks Today: Migrants or Refugees?" *Journal of Refugee Studies* 4(4):313, 400–420.

———. 2001. *The 'Right to Return' and the Meaning of 'Home': A Post-Soviet Greek Diaspora Becoming European?* Berlin.

———. 2006. "Post-Soviet Diaspora Politics: The Case of the Soviet Greeks." *Journal of Modern Greek Studies* 24:379–414.

Vranopoulos, E. 1999. *Οδοιπορικό ζηη μεγάλη Ελλάδα*. Athens.

Woolard, K. 1989. *Double Talk: Bilingualism and the Politics of Ethnicity in Catalonia*. Stanford.

———. 1998. "Introduction: Language Ideologies as a Field of Inquiry." In *Language Ideologies: Practice and Theory*, ed. K. A. Woolard, B. B. Schieffelin, and P. V. Kroskrity, 3–47. New York.

———. 1999. "Simultaneity and Bivalency as Strategies in Bilingualism." *Journal of Linguistic Anthropology* 8(1):3–29.

Wright, S. 2004. *Language Policy and Language Planning: From Nationalism to Globalization*. New York.

Yalouri, E. 2001. *The Acropolis: Global Fame, Local Claim*. Oxford.

Index